W9-AVK-427

What We Won

What We Won

AMERICA'S SECRET WAR
IN AFGHANISTAN, 1979–89

BRUCE RIEDEL

BROOKINGS INSTITUTION PRESS
Washington, D.C.

The Brookings Institution is a private nonprofit organization devoted to research,
education, and publication on important issues of domestic and foreign policy.
Its principal purpose is to bring the highest quality independent research and
analysis to bear on current and emerging policy problems. Interpretations or
conclusions in Brookings publications should be understood to be solely those
of the authors.

Library of Congress Cataloging-in-Publication data
Riedel, Bruce O.
    What we won : America's secret war in Afghanistan, 1979–89 / Bruce Riedel.
    pages   cm
    Includes bibliographical references and index.
    ISBN 978-0-8157-2584-8 (hardcover : acid-free paper)—ISBN 978-0-8157-
2595-4 (paperback : acid-free paper) 1. United States—Foreign relations—
Afghanistan. 2. Afghanistan—Foreign relations—United States. 3. Espionage,
American—Afghanistan—History—20th century. 4. United States. Central
Intelligence Agency—History—20th century. 5. National security—United
States—History—20th century. 6. United States—Military policy. 7. Afghani-
stan—History—Soviet occupation, 1979–1989. 8. United States—Foreign rela-
tions—Soviet Union. 9. Soviet Union—Foreign relations—United States.
I. Title.
    E183.8.A3R54 2014
    327.730581—dc23   2014011190

9 8 7 6 5 4 3

Printed on acid-free paper

Typeset in Sabon

Composition by Cynthia Stock
Silver Spring, Maryland

In loving memory of
MILTON AND RUTH SIGNE RIEDEL

CONTENTS

INTRODUCTION AND
ACKNOWLEDGMENTS

THE WAR IN Afghanistan that took place between 1979 and 1989 was a pivotal event in modern history. The defeat there of the Soviet 40th Red Army proved to be the final battle of the cold war, a struggle between the United States and its allies on one hand and Russia and its allies on the other that lasted from 1945 to 1990. For those four decades, the cold war dominated global politics. It was a conflict between democracy and communism that shaped the history of millions of people across the globe, and the modern U.S. national security state—including institutions like the National Security Council and the Central Intelligence Agency—was fashioned to fight it.

The Soviet army left Afghanistan in February 1989; the Berlin Wall fell in November of the same year; East and West Germany were reunited a year later; and the Soviet Union ceased to exist in December 1991. The near-constant threat of global nuclear war between the two superpowers that had dominated world politics for four decades vanished almost overnight. Victory for the U.S. side in the cold war seemed complete. The Soviet defeat in Afghanistan was followed so quickly by the collapse of the Soviet state that one former U.S. ambassador observed that the "defeat led to the rapid collapse of a five-hundred-year-old system [and] the last great European empire came to an end." 1

The Afghan war also marked the beginning of a new era, the era of global jihad. The Afghan war was not the first in which Muslims defeated a Western power (the Algerian war for independence from France preceded it), but it was an Islamic triumph over a superpower. What is now known as the global jihad movement began as an unintended (by the

United States) consequence of the Afghan war. This new threat—global jihad and especially al Qaeda—has seen another restructuring of the U.S. national security state. Once again new institutions have been created to ensure national security, including the Director of National Intelligence, the Department of Homeland Security, and the National Counterterrorism Center. Armed drones and global surveillance systems have become instruments of U.S. policy.

At the core of the Afghan war in the 1980s—what might be called the first part of the conflict, because it did not end with the defeat of the Soviets in 1989—was an intelligence war between the United States and its allies and the Soviets and their ally, the Afghan communist party. The Central Intelligence Agency was given the mission—first by President Jimmy Carter and then by his successor, President Ronald Reagan—of turning Afghanistan into a "Russian Vietnam." In 1989, when the Soviets crossed the border to go home after the most successful covert intelligence operation in U.S. history, the CIA's chief in Islamabad famously cabled headquarters this simple message: "WE WON."

Both presidents had a clear definition of "victory." Carter wanted Afghanistan to become a Soviet quagmire, a drain on its resources that would discourage further aggression in South Asia and isolate the Soviet Union diplomatically. Reagan initially had the same definition, but he upped the ante in his second term when the goal became defeating the Soviet army and driving it out of Afghanistan for good. All of those goals were achieved by early 1989. The defeat in Afghanistan helped precipitate the collapse of the Union of Soviet Socialist Republics, although, of course, its collapse had many causes besides the defeat. Nonetheless, it can never be known whether the USSR would have survived if its army had not lost the Afghan war. Those issues lie beyond the scope of this work; they are for other experts to debate.

It is very clear that many Russians remain angry at the results of the war. In his 2005 state-of-the-nation address, Russian president Vladimir Putin called the demise of the USSR the "greatest geopolitical catastrophe of the century." Putin served as a KGB intelligence officer in East Germany from 1985 to 1990, while the war in Afghanistan was going on, and he undoubtedly followed the progress of the clandestine war closely.

The U.S. secret war in Afghanistan was initiated by Jimmy Carter and accelerated by Ronald Reagan. It was done legally, under congressional oversight. Indeed, Congress was very involved in the management of the war, as Hollywood would later recall dramatically in the movie *Charlie Wilson's War*. The war enjoyed broad bipartisan support and the support of the media, which heralded the success of the mujahedin while for the most part keeping the role of the CIA a secret.

[margin note: WAR TACTICS]

It was a complex intelligence operation. One central task was to collect information on Soviet and Afghan communist capabilities and intentions and then assess that information to produce final estimates of the enemy's strengths, weaknesses, and plans. In retrospect it can be said, on the basis of declassified intelligence, that for the most part capabilities were accurately assessed but intentions, as always, were harder to divine. The success rate there is more nuanced. The covert action itself—supplying arms and money to the Afghan insurgency by way of Pakistan—was the heart of the operation. Both the collection and analysis of information and the covert action involved a secret alliance of many other countries and intelligence services. Of course, their objectives and priorities were not exactly the same as those of the United States; that is the nature of alliance warfare. All wanted a Soviet Vietnam for their own reasons. The management of this secret intelligence alliance is a central focus of this book.

[margin note: complex issues of intelligence work]

[margin note: Focus of this book]

For the United States, the secret war in Afghanistan was relatively inexpensive in terms of both blood and money. Two U.S. ambassadors, Adolph "Spike" Dubs in Afghanistan and Arnie Raphel in Pakistan, died in violent incidents related to the war, making the ultimate sacrifice for their country. Raphel's military deputy died with him, in a mysterious plane crash that also killed President Zia ul-Haq. No other Americans lost their lives. The material cost of the war peaked at about $700 million a year. That's a lot of money for an intelligence operation—the entire budget for Britain's intelligence community in 1987 was less than the CIA's budget for the war in Afghanistan alone. The total cost for the 1979–89 period was about $3 billion. But in terms of U.S. wars, the cost was insignificant. The Vietnam War cost the United States well over $300 billion, and the Iraq War cost well over $1 trillion. From a taxpayer's perspective, there may be no other federal program in history that produced so much historic change in world politics at such a small price.

[margin note: cost of war. who died]

The Afghan people paid a much higher price. They did the fighting. At least 1 million Afghans died, and many millions more were made *who got what* [margin note]

homeless. It is a tragedy that the Afghans got little or nothing from the victory in 1989. Their sacrifices helped to liberate Eastern Europe and changed the world, but they got only several more decades of bloody civil wars. Pakistan also paid a high price. It hosted millions of Afghan refugees, a humanitarian action that nonetheless led to the destabilization of the country's borderlands and to what came to be known as the "Kalashnikov culture" of lawlessness and violence in those areas.

It is sometimes suggested that the CIA war in Afghanistan created the global jihad and even al Qaeda. That is just bad history. As this book demonstrates, the Arabs who came to Pakistan to join the war against the Soviet Union came because they were determined to fight the Soviets. They cared very little that their ally was the CIA. It was the Soviet invasion of Afghanistan that created the firestorm of anger across the Islamic world that brought thousands of young men to fight in Afghanistan and become radicalized. One such volunteer for the jihad gave their anger an ideology and a narrative. Abdullah Azzam was the father of the modern global jihad, and his story is critical to understanding the history of the war. Azzam, who died just as the war was coming to an end, was also Osama bin Laden's first partner in jihad.

FATHER of JihAd [margin note] *178* [margin note]

The war's single most important figure, however, is a Pakistani. General Zia ul-Haq was the most significant strategist and risk taker in the epic battle with the Soviet army, and his decisions were more important than Carter's or Reagan's. Indeed, both presidents' friendship with Zia is central to the history of the war and to what came later: both overlooked Zia's pursuit of a nuclear weapons arsenal and his support for terrorists in India to ensure his support in the war against the Soviets. In many ways, the Afghan war was Zia's war. Zia died mysteriously just as the war's finale was about to unfold.

189 [margin note] *o ZiA* [margin note]

This book is primarily about the U.S. role in the covert war in Afghanistan. It seeks to answer one simple question: why did this intelligence operation succeed so brilliantly? Many books have been written about intelligence failures, from Pearl Harbor to 9/11. Much less has been written about how and why intelligence operations succeed. The answer is complex; it involves the weaknesses and mistakes of the adversaries as well as their good judgment and strengths. Any book on a secret intelligence operation faces unique challenges with respect to finding sources. No classified material is included in this book. I have tried to use the best sources available to tell the story, drawing on many declassified intelligence documents and memoirs and interviews with those who were actively engaged in the operation and the war. This book, which also draws heavily on what other authors have already written, is primarily a work of synthesis and analysis. But it also provides new insights on several key issues. The Soviets' support for terrorism by the Zulfiqar organization inside Pakistan gets more attention here than in previous books, drawing on an inside account by Raja Anwar, a one-time member of the group. The extension of the war across the Durand Line played a key part in shaping both Zia's and Reagan's world view of the conflict.

In this book, the crucial role of Pakistan and Zia ul-Haq gets the attention it deserves. It was not Charlie Wilson's war, or Jimmy Carter's, or Ronald Reagan's. It was Zia's. The book also provides new insights on the role that the Arabs, the Saudis in particular, played in the war. The Saudi intervention was not just official; in fact, the unofficial intervention—in terms of both funds and volunteers—was more crucial to both the war and what came next, the global jihad. The book also puts President Carter back into the war's narrative. During a few weeks in January 1980, he and his team made the really crucial decisions about the strategy that the United States would pursue to win the Afghan war and the cold war. Finally, the book also puts the decision to escalate the war in the mid-1980s in its proper perspective. It was Zia who decided to escalate the war, first with British equipment and cross-border raids into the USSR and then with the famous Stinger missile. The United States abetted those decisions, but Zia made them.

This book is organized into two main parts. Part 1, "The Players," is about the combatants, those who actually fought on the battlefield. One of the features of the war was that no Americans fought on the battlefield; the CIA did not send its officers into Afghanistan to fight or even to train Afghans to fight. Robert Gates, who served in the Carter White House and the Reagan CIA, has said that the CIA was the "quartermaster" of the war, arranging the supplies but not running the strategy or tactics. That was smart policy in many ways, not least because no CIA officers' lives were lost. The United States was always trying to keep its part in the war a secret or at least to maintain plausible deniability about its role. Boots on the ground, even just a few, would have compromised that deniability.

Because the instigators of the war were the Afghan communists, the book begins with them. The fractured and incredibly violent Afghan communist party started the war by a coup d'état in April 1978, beginning what the communists called the Saur (April) Revolution. Few of the Afghan communists are still alive today, so I start with a portrait of one that I know personally, Abdul Rashid Dostum, who is not only still alive but still a key figure in Afghan politics. Thanks to the collapse of the USSR, researchers have extensive access to Soviet documents from the war that reveal a great deal about the communists and their relationship with Moscow. However, because the Soviet archives have been only partially opened and revealed to the outside world and the current Russian government has tried to close even some of the records that were open, the picture is still incomplete.

The Soviets, the Afghans' main enemy, are the subject of chapter 2. They suffered many casualties in what proved to be a losing effort. Here again, the once-closed Soviet archives convey a rich but incomplete sense of Moscow's decisionmaking. A former British ambassador to Moscow during part of the war has written an insightful analysis of the Soviet role in the war that was invaluable to me in writing the chapter. Some key declassified CIA studies about the Soviet invasion and occupation, including in-depth post mortems, also were very useful.

Those who did the bulk of the fighting and dying—the Afghan mujahedin, or holy warriors—have left the fewest records. They were not a conventional army or bureaucracy. They never formed a cohesive, organized force; they remained deeply divided by ethnicity, ideology, and tribe. I have focused on two key mujahedin leaders, Ahmad Shah Massoud and Jalaluddin Haqqani, to tell the mujahedin's story. Each has been the subject of recent biographical accounts, one unpublished and the other just published. Their campaigns in the Panjsher Valley and along the Pakistani border were the two most critical in the war.

Pakistan's state archives have not been opened, and the two most important decisionmakers in Pakistan's conduct of the war died in 1988. Fortunately, two books are available by Mohammad Yousaf, the chief of the Directorate for Inter-Services Intelligence (ISI) branch that ran the war. General Zia has not yet been the subject of a detailed biography, but his ISI chief, General Akhtar, has been, thanks to Yousaf. These two insider accounts are openly hostile to the CIA and United States, which the author blames for all that went wrong in the war. He was not much loved by the CIA officers who worked with him, but no one disputes the accuracy of the accounts presented in his books.[6]

The archives of the House of Saud, the last absolute monarchy in the world, have not been opened. The architect of the Saudis' part in the clandestine war, Prince Turki, has been gracious enough to speak to me about it and has also been interviewed by other scholars. Prince Bandar, who was then the Saudi ambassador to the United States, has also been generous, over many years, in giving me his views of the war and the intelligence business. There is an increasingly rich and detailed literature about the Arab volunteers, including Osama bin Laden. Much of this literature has not been assessed in the context of the Afghan war itself.

Part 2, "The U.S. War," looks at the U.S. role in the war. Here the record is more complete. President Carter and his key advisers did not write about the war or their decisionmaking in their memoirs, which came out while the war was still in progress and the CIA's role was still top secret. But President Carter did generously grant me an interview to discuss his role publicly for the first time, and he gave me access to the private diary that he kept while in office. I have interviewed other members of his team, including his national security adviser, Zbigniew Brzezinski. Their story of how U.S. strategy was developed to wear down the Soviets in Afghanistan has not been aired so fully before.

President Reagan's illness precluded his writing a memoir, and his spy chief, Bill Casey, died in office. Fortunately Casey's deputy, Bob Gates, has written a thorough history of the secret war. Gates also graciously granted me an interview. Numerous declassified documents are available, most at the National Security Archive. Interviews with many of the key decisionmakers in the CIA added more detail. A superb account, *The Main Enemy*, by Milton Bearden, Casey's man in Islamabad, and James Risen, provides a rich source for understanding the involvement of the Reagan administration during Reagan's second term.

Surprisingly, the Afghan war has not been studied as widely as its huge impact would seem to warrant. Bob Woodward, the *Washington Post*'s legendary reporter, wrote *Veil*, an early account of the CIA in the 1980s, but Afghanistan is a side issue in his book. Steve Coll, another excellent journalist and writer, put the war in the post-9/11 context in *Ghost Wars*, but he focused for the most part on the growth of al Qaeda and less on the war itself. George Crile's magnificent book *Charlie Wilson's War*, and the movie that was made from it, is an excellent account, but it is told from the perspective of one Texas congressman and tends to distort his importance.

It is crucial to understand the lessons of past covert operations to better plan for the future. This book tries to offer some lessons from what was arguably the most successful covert operation ever in U.S. history. Accordingly, part 2 concludes with an analysis of why the United States and its allies won the war in Afghanistan in the 1980s. It presents some observations on what came next in Afghanistan and what is likely yet to come. It also examines the lessons that this intelligence operation has to offer for future operations.

Covert operations will continue to be a major instrument of U.S. foreign policy for the foreseeable future. The CIA already has fought two more major covert wars in Afghanistan since the end of the 1980s. In 2001 CIA operatives led the campaign to topple the Taliban's Islamic Emirate of Afghanistan and destroy al Qaeda's base in Afghanistan. Since 2002 the CIA has led the campaign to track down and defeat al Qaeda's base in Pakistan, most memorably in finding bin Laden's safe house in Abbottabad in 2011. Each has lessons for future operations as well.

Many individuals in addition to those already named were helpful as I researched this work, including Strobe Talbott, Michael O'Hanlon, Martin Indyk, Fiona Hill, Paul Pillar, John Scarlett, Steve Hochman, Bradley Porter, John Helgerson, and Zvi Rafiah. Other individuals also assisted, in Afghanistan, Austria, Belgium, Britain, Canada, Denmark, Finland, France, Germany, Holland, Iceland, India, Israel, Italy, Norway, Oman, Pakistan, Qatar, Russia, Saudi Arabia, Spain, Sweden, Uzbekistan, the United Arab Emirates, and the United States. I also want to thank the National Security Archive in Washington, the Carter Center in Georgia, and the Ronald Reagan Library in California for their help. In addition, I thank Howard Cox for his support of the research activities for and publication of this book. The Brookings library and the Brookings Institution Press, especially my editor, Eileen Hughes, deserve special thanks. Finally my students at Georgetown and Johns Hopkins Universities, especially those on active duty in the U.S. military, have been a tremendous source of insight and provocative thinking. My darling wife, Elizabeth, has been my companion in this effort, listening to endless discussions of Pakistani and Saudi politics and the history of the cold war. Her energy and enthusiasm have helped me more than she knows.

I was a CIA officer in the 1980s, serving part of the time in the Near East Division in posts in the Middle East. I know Stansfield Turner, Robert Gates, Charles Cogan, Tom Twetten, Milt Bearden, and Frank Anderson, the key decisionmakers at CIA headquarters in Langley, Virginia, during the war, and I regard them as friends and admire their patriotism and good sense. Some have been generous in discussing the war and the CIA in the 1980s with me. This book was reviewed prior to publication by the CIA to ensure that there was no inadvertent disclosure of classified information. The judgments and arguments in this book are my own responsibility. All statements of fact, opinion, or analysis are those of the author and do not reflect the official position or views of the CIA or any other U.S. government agency. Nothing in the contents should be construed as asserting or implying U.S. government authentication of information or agency endorsement of the author's views.

PART 1

THE PLAYERS

CHAPTER ONE

THE AFGHAN COMMUNISTS

SHIBIRGHAN, THE CAPITAL of Jowzjan Province, is a remote and barren place, even by Afghan standards. To the north, Jowzjan borders on the Amu Darya River and Turkmenistan, a former part of the Union of Soviet Socialist Republics. Shibirghan is a city of about 150,000 on a flat, dry plain that extends past the river into Central Asia. Most of the city's population is made up of ethnic Uzbeks, with a minority of Turkmen; the province as a whole is 40 percent Uzbek and 30 percent Turkmen. Natural gas has been exploited in the province since the 1970s, initially by a Soviet energy project. Shibirghan is on the Afghan ring road, the country's main highway, which connects the country's main cities. Shibirghan lies between the largest city in the north, Mazar-e Sharif, to the east and the largest city in the west, Herat.

Since the 1980s Shibirghan has been the stronghold of Abdul Rashid Dostum, an Uzbek Afghan warlord who has played a complex role in the wars that have wracked Afghanistan since 1978. In 1998 Dostum was my host during a visit to Shibirghan. I had met him before, in my Pentagon office, where he had related his life's journey to me. A physically strong and imposing man, he has an Asian appearance, a hint of his Mongol roots. That day he was dressed to look like a modern political leader, in a suit and tie. The notorious warlord was hosting a meeting of the Northern Alliance, the coalition of Afghan parties that opposed the Taliban, in his hometown. In addition to Dostum, Afghan president Burhanuddin Rabbani, Hazara Shia leader Karim Khalili, and Mohammad Abdullah, a deputy of the legendary Ahmad Shah Massoud, were in attendance. The U.S. party was led by Bill Richardson, the U.S. ambassador to the United

Nations, and Karl "Rick" Inderfurth, assistant secretary of state. At the start of the meeting, all the Afghans and Americans held each other's hands in a symbol of unity for the cameras.

In the photo my face is grim. I was bleeding slowly from a bad leg wound that I'd received just an hour earlier, when we got off the small plane that the UN had provided to fly us from Kabul to Shibirghan. Dostum had arranged an elaborate welcome for us. At the airport an honor guard greeted us, and we boarded a convoy of vehicles to drive into the city. Hundreds of children and adults lined the road to welcome the U.S. delegation to Jowzjan, waving flags and banners in English that proudly carried the names of their schools, businesses, and trade unions. Many of the children were in their school uniforms. Most striking was that almost half were girls without head scarves, a rare sight in 1998 in Afghanistan, where very few girls went to school. The event had the look of a communist state celebration of May Day or the Russian Revolution—and it looked that way because Dostum was once a prize pupil of the Soviet Union's intelligence service, the KGB.

Once we arrived in the city center, we moved rapidly into the main stadium. There we were to watch a game of buzkashi, a much more violent variant of polo played by Uzbeks and other Afghans. As we entered the stadium, I slipped and cut my leg badly. Watching the game, I realized that I was in distress and asked for help. Dostum himself summoned a doctor, who arrived carrying a satchel with a large saw on top that was used for amputating limbs. I demurred. Fortunately, NBC News anchor Andrea Mitchell had come along to do a story on the talks, and her camera team included a former British Royal Marine commando who had been trained as a medic. He stitched me up quickly, using a can of 7UP as disinfectant. Ten hours later, doctors at the U.S. Embassy in Islamabad, Pakistan, gave me more thorough medical treatment. Andrea described the whole scene very well in her autobiography, *Talking Back to Presidents, Dictators, and Assorted Scoundrels.*[2]

Dostum certainly falls into the scoundrel department. He is a useful subject to study for those seeking to understand the violent politics of Afghanistan over the last half-century—especially the intrigues of Afghanistan's communists, who seized power in 1978 and invited the Soviet Union to send an army into their country, setting the stage for the covert involvement of the United States. Participants on both sides in the war in Afghanistan in the 1980s claimed to be more than warlords and militias. The Afghan communist government claimed to represent a new modern socialist world order. The Afghan resistance, the mujahedin, claimed to be holy warriors—jihadists—and freedom fighters defending their country from foreign invasion. The mujahedin narrative was much more honest than that of the communists.

At the commander level, however, there was not much difference between the two sides. Most commanders were warlords and behaved like warlords. The best of them, like Ahmad Shah Massoud, the commander of mujahedin forces in the Panjsher Valley, rose above the others in caring for the welfare of his supporters and the people of his fighting zone. The worst—like Gulbuddin Hekmatyar, the strongest mujahedin leader in the Pashtun community, and Dostum himself—exemplified the more typical commander on both sides: ruthless, corrupt, volatile, and violent. Dostum switched sides many times during his blood-soaked career. He has been backed over the years by the Soviet Union, Iran, Turkey, Uzbekistan, Russia, and the United States. He even temporarily aligned himself with the Taliban and Pakistan. After 35 years Dostum is still a major player, so taking a more in-depth look at my host in Shibirghan is a good introduction to the Afghan war.

Dostum began his political life as a communist. Born in 1955 into a peasant family in a village near Shibirghan, he joined the communist party, the People's Democratic Party of Afghanistan (PDPA), as a teenager, and in 1973 he became a paratrooper in the Afghan army.[5] The Afghan communist party was badly divided from its birth in 1965. The two factions of the party, the Parcham (the Banner) and the Khalq (the People), were literally at each other's throat throughout the party's history. The Parcham drew its support from urban Afghans and from the country's diverse ethnic groups. The Khalq was more oriented toward rural areas and drew its support almost exclusively from the Pashtuns, Afghanistan's largest ethnic group. The Soviets tried endlessly to convince the two to work together, with only the most limited success. The PDPA's deep factional conflict would bedevil it and the Soviets until the collapse of the communist state in 1992, a collapse in which Dostum was a central player.

On April 27, 1978, the PDPA's supporters in the Afghan army staged a coup d'état in Kabul and overthrew the government of President

Mohammad Daoud Khan, who had staged his own coup five years earlier, ousting King Zahir and creating the first Afghan republic. The Saur (April) Revolution would precipitate an Afghan conflict that continues to this day. Dostum was then commander of an armored unit in the army and a member of the Parcham faction. The April coup was led by the Khalq faction and its leader, Nur Muhammad Taraki, who became president of the new People's Democratic Republic of Afghanistan. The Khalq quickly purged many Parchamists from the party and the country, ignoring advice from Moscow to try to build a broad-based government, including noncommunists. The Khalqis were violent ideologues who saw enemies on every side, and they quickly acquired them.

Dostum fled the country to Pakistan, where he lived in exile in Peshawar. As a communist, Dostum did not fit in well in Pakistan, which was rapidly emerging as the main patron of the resistance to the communist takeover and the principal sponsor of the mujahedin. Dostum stayed in exile until December 1979, when the Soviet 40th Red Army invaded Afghanistan and killed Taraki's successor, Hafizullah Amin, and installed Babrak Karmal in his place. Dostum then returned to Afghanistan to become a local militia commander defending the natural gas fields, the only domestic source of energy in the country, in his home province of Jowzjan. Dostum was a natural soldier and a good leader whose troops admired his charisma and tough military approach. He specialized in frontal assaults on the enemy, and he quickly acquired a reputation for brutal and extreme violence. In 1982 Dostum was promoted to command a battalion of the militia run by the communist government's secret police, the State Information Service, known as the KHAD (Khedamati Ittlaati-e Dawlat). The KHAD was the KGB's Afghan protégé; it also got some assistance from the East German intelligence service. At its height it had about 30,000 employees and another 100,000 informants. Its founder was Mohammad Najibullah Ahmadzai, a Pashtun known for his ruthlessness in a regime that extolled extremism. In 1986 Najibullah would become Afghanistan's fourth and last communist dictator. He was nicknamed Najib (the bull) for his cruelty.

Under Najibullah's leadership Dostum thrived as a commander of the KHAD militia in Jowzjan, and soon his Jowzjani militia was the most successful communist fighting force in the country. Dostum's Jowzjanis formed a disciplined force that often defeated mujahedin commanders in the northern part of the country and even persuaded some to defect to the communist cause. Within a year Dostum's force was upgraded to a division of 10,000 men, called the 53rd Division or the Jowzjani Division. The Jowzjani Division became one of only a few Afghan communist units that the 40th Red Army felt that it could rely on to fight well. For his performance, Dostum was given the Hero of Afghanistan award, the highest honor bestowed by the People's Democratic Republic of Afghanistan.[4] In 1988, with the 40th Red Army withdrawing from Afghanistan, the Jowzjani militia was given responsibility for leading the communist military campaign in north-central Afghanistan along the southern border of the Soviet Union. After its defeat in Afghanistan, Moscow wanted Dostum controlling the Amu Darya. By then his control of his home province and the surrounding area was complete.

In 1989 Dostum was promoted again, becoming commander of the 7th Afghan Army Corps, with even more responsibility for the north. Najibullah was by now president of Afghanistan, and the KHAD effectively ran the communist state, which was under siege by the mujahedin. Estimates of the size of Dostum's command in the north range from around 20,000 to 45,000.[5] His forces included 3 infantry divisions, an armored brigade, 60 MiG aircraft, 60 helicopters, and 200 Soviet-made tanks. He ruled a state within a state. He sent elite units of his force to buttress Najibullah's garrisons in other parts of the country, including at the key battle of Jalalabad in 1989, which halted the mujahedin advance on Kabul.[6]

Early in 1992 Dostum read the handwriting on the wall. The USSR had ceased to exist, and its aid to Najibullah was coming to an end. In December 1991, Dostum turned to the newly independent country of Uzbekistan and its dictator, President Islam Karimov, for aid.[7] In 1992 Dostum "defected" to the side of the mujahedin and joined in the battle to take Kabul and oust Najibullah. Afghanistan's civil war entered a new phase: the communists were finished, and a new power struggle arose, between the warlords. Dostum would be a central player, shifting alliances constantly from his power base in Jowzjan. He solicited aid from many regional players, including Iran and Uzbekistan in particular but also Russia and Turkey. In 1998 it was Iran that backed him most actively. A senior delegation from the Iranian intelligence service, MOIS, arrived right after my delegation left to check on what Dostum had been up to with the Americans.[8] He went into exile twice in the late 1990s, on both occasions spending much of his time in Turkey. In 2001 he again became an Iranian protégé, fighting the Taliban from exile. The United States became his new patron when he joined the CIA campaign to oust the Taliban in the last months of 2001, after the 9/11 attacks. Dostum famously led Uzbek cavalry charges supported by U.S. B-52 bombers to defeat the Taliban.[9]

Dostum remains a power broker today, although his health has deteriorated from the effects of a hard life and heavy drinking. He still commands Jowzjan and can deliver 1 million votes, mostly Uzbeks, in a national election. He was a key supporter of President Hamid Karzai's reelection in 2009. Dostum is a warlord par excellence and a classic product of Afghan politics, which is both local and volatile. He has been accused of numerous war crimes against prisoners and sadistic treatment of his own supporters when they crossed him. In a country with many brutal warlords, his brutality is legendary. Yet in his state-within-a-state in the 1980s and 1990s, Dostum ensured more gender equality than almost any other Afghan leader. In the second decade of the twenty-first century, he is one of the few prominent communists from the 1980s to still play a role on the Afghan stage. In the deadly politics of Afghanistan, Dostum is a proven survivor.

From the Great Game to the Great Saur Revolution

Afghanistan has been invaded by foreign armies since the beginning of history. Its location—in the middle of Asia, with Iran, Russia, China, and the Indian subcontinent as neighbors—has placed it at the center of world politics for centuries, often to the detriment of its people. Persians, Greeks, Arabs, Mongols, and Moghuls have marched through Afghanistan, and Alexander the Great conquered the country on his way to India (the modern city of Kandahar is named for him). For much of the last two centuries it was either at the fault line between Russia and the British Empire or, after the end of the Raj, at the fault line between Russia and the United States. The Russians and British referred to their rivalry in Afghanistan as the Great Game. Moscow, London, and Calcutta (the capital of the British empire in India until 1911) were convinced that Russia and Britain were colliding great powers in Afghanistan and Persia and that the winner of the collision would tip the global balance of power. The British were convinced that the tsar intended to seize the Ottoman capital at Constantinople (today's Istanbul) and then drive south through Afghanistan to give the Russian Empire access to the warm-water ports on the Mediterranean Sea and Indian Ocean. Much of London's paranoia about Russian ambitions in Afghanistan was excessive, but it was real enough to lead Britain to go to war three times to keep Afghanistan from being absorbed by Russia.

The First Anglo-Afghan War (1838–42) was fought between the Afghans and a British Indian army organized by the British East India Company, which ruled India until 1858. However, the company never provided competent leadership or adequate support for the Afghan war because almost as soon as it began, London and Calcutta became engaged in the First Opium War with China, a much more lucrative and significant venture for British diplomats, military officers, and business-men. Much as the United States did in Afghanistan in 2002 when it pre-pared to invade Iraq, the British took their eye off the ball in Afghanistan in the nineteenth century to focus on forcing China to open its doors to the opium trade. Many of the army's best units were diverted from Afghanistan to the China front, and the result was a disaster for Britain. The army that took Kabul was forced to retreat from the city in the dead of winter, and it was annihilated on its way back to Peshawar. The story has been brilliantly retold by my friend William Dalrymple in *Return of a King: The Battle for Afghanistan.*[10]

The Second Anglo-Afghan War began with the visit of a Russian del-egation to Kabul in 1878, during the midst of a larger crisis between the Russian Empire and the Ottoman Empire. London was convinced that the Russians were intent on taking control of both Constantinople and Kabul. Again, the British took Kabul for a time and then withdrew. The major result of the second war was the demarcation in the 1890s of the border between Afghanistan and the British Empire in India. The foreign secretary of British India, Mortimer Durand, drew the line in 1893 and secured grudging Afghan agreement to it. It split the Pashtun community into two parts, and it also cut Afghanistan off from the sea and created a tiny finger of Afghan territory, the Wakhan Corridor, that separated the Russian Empire from India and opened a link from Afghanistan to China. By the terms of the Treaty of Gandamak, the government of India (the Raj) gained control of Afghan foreign policy. The Afghans agreed not to establish diplomatic relations with Moscow, thus, for a time, eliminating London's rival from the game.[11]

Afghanistan stayed neutral during the First World War, although it flirted with joining the German-Austrian-Turkish alliance against Britain and Russia. In 1919 the Afghans, sensing that Britain was weakened by the war effort and nationalist unrest in India, started the Third Anglo-Afghan War, with a border incursion in the Khyber Pass. It was a relatively short conflict marked by the use of British air power, which brought about a stalemate between the two armies. The parties agreed to a cease-fire in June. The Treaty of Rawalpindi ended the war and gave Afghanistan its independence on August 19, 1919. The Afghans built a victory monument in Kabul portraying the British lion in chains. They had wanted London to cede Waziristan as part of the deal, but the Raj conceded no territory.[12] The Durand Line was reaffirmed as the border, but Afghanistan was given total independence in conducting its foreign policy, and it promptly became the first country in the world to recognize the new communist government in Moscow. Russia's new leader, Vladimir Lenin, sent a Soviet delegation to Kabul in September 1919 to open diplomatic channels, and the Soviets equipped and trained an Afghan air force. The countries signed a treaty of friendship in 1921. Soviet involvement in Afghan affairs had begun.

The three Anglo-Afghan wars shaped modern Afghanistan both literally and figuratively. The Durand Line settled the country's longest border, to the east and south, and settlement of the borders with the Russian Empire and Iran followed. The wars also provided Afghans with a national narrative of resistance to imperialism and the West. Few third-world countries could portray themselves as having resisted European imperialism as well as Afghanistan had.

Afghanistan's modern political history can be said to have begun on November 8, 1933, with the assassination of King Nadir Shah by a Hazara student radical. The king was succeeded by his 19-year-old son, Muhammad Zahir, who would rule the country for the next 40 years. For most of his four decades on the throne, Zahir, who was educated in France and Afghanistan, was content to leave effective power in the hands of two of his uncles, both of whom acted at prime minister. Hashim was prime minister until 1946, followed by Mahmoud until 1953. Zahir's cousin Mohammad Daoud Khan then acted as prime minister until 1963.

Diplomatic contacts with the United States began in 1922, when an Afghan ambassador came to Washington to present his credentials to President Warren Harding, but a permanent U.S. envoy was not posted to Kabul until 1942, after the bombing of Pearl Harbor by the Japanese. Until Japan attacked, Washington was isolationist and uninterested in Afghanistan. Twenty years earlier, Cornelius Van H. Engert had been the first U.S. diplomat ever to visit Kabul. Engert, who later became the first U.S. ambassador to Afghanistan, published a 225-page study of the country in 1924 and lobbied Washington with little success for a modest aid program to Afghanistan.[13] At the beginning of World War II, Afghanistan again flirted with supporting Germany. However, once the Germans invaded the Soviet Union in 1941, Moscow and London invaded Iran and surrounded Afghanistan, putting an end to any flirtation with the Nazis. When the Soviets and British demanded that all German agents and diplomats be expelled from Afghanistan, Prime Minister Hashim reluctantly gave in and sent the Germans home. Afghanistan spent the first three decades of the cold war as a buffer between the two hostile superpowers. The king and his ministers very adeptly maneuvered between them to secure economic and military assistance from both. The United States helped fund a large agricultural production project in the Helmand River Valley between 1946 and 1953, modeled in part on similar projects in the U.S. Southwest. But the United States would not sell arms or provide military assistance to Afghanistan because of the emerging U.S. alliance with Pakistan. When the Afghans asked for military aid from President Harry Truman in 1948, Secretary of State George Marshall dismissed the request by asking "Who's the enemy?"[14]

When the Raj was partitioned in 1947, the Islamic state of Pakistan inherited the Durand Line and a border with Afghanistan. The Afghan government had never accepted the legitimacy of the Durand Line, which it correctly argued had been imposed on the Afghans by force of arms by an imperialist power. Afghanistan pressed the British either to return to Afghan sovereignty the disputed Pashtun- and Baluchi-inhabited portions of what was to become Pakistan or to let the inhabitants form their own state, to be called Pashtunistan. The Afghan claim would have cost Pakistan almost half its territory and provided Afghanistan with access to the sea by absorbing all of Baluchistan into either Afghanistan or Pashtunistan. Instead, after local votes and tribal councils were held, the British announced that the disputed areas had chosen to become part of Pakistan.

Kabul rejected the British decision and was the only member of the United Nations to vote against admitting Pakistan in 1947 (Afghanistan had joined in 1946). Tensions between the two states began at Pakistan's birth and continue to the present day. The cause of Pashtunistan haunts the relationship. No Afghan government has ever recognized the Durand Line as the border of Afghanistan, and successive Afghan governments have flirted with supporting Pashtun and Baluchi irredentism or independence.

Instead of building a relationship with Kabul, Washington developed a close relationship with Pakistan, which sought U.S. support against both Afghanistan and India. Pakistan eagerly sided with the United States and the United Kingdom in the cold war in order to obtain military aid and diplomatic support. In 1954 Pakistan joined the Southeast Asia Treaty Organization (SEATO), which was intended to extend the containment of the Soviet Union into Asia, and in 1955 it joined the Central Treaty Organization (CENTO), which connected NATO and SEATO in a line of containment encircling the Soviet Union and its then-ally, Communist China.[15] The United States became Pakistan's major source of weapons in the 1950s, and Pakistan was enthusiastically welcomed into the camp of the "Free World" by the Eisenhower administration. In contrast, Kabul was told in 1954 that the United States would not provide arms to Afghanistan until it settled the Pashtunistan dispute with Pakistan.[16]

The Soviets saw and eagerly exploited the opening in Afghanistan. If the United States tilted toward Pakistan, Russia would tilt toward Afghanistan. Moscow and Kabul signed a barter agreement in 1950 to trade Afghan wool and cotton for Russian oil, and trade rapidly expanded. The Soviets opened a trade office in Kabul, and prospecting for oil and gas began in Jowzjan and other parts of northern Afghanistan. When Pakistan joined SEATO and CENTO and became the "most allied ally" of the United States, the Afghans turned to the Soviets for arms. King Zahir's cousin, Mohammad Daoud Khan, who had become prime minister in 1953, signed a $3 million arms deal with Moscow's puppet

Czechoslovakia in 1955 and a $32.5 million arms deal with the Soviet Union in 1956 to buy T-34 tanks and MiG-17 jet fighters. Soviet training for the Afghan army and air force began in earnest. By 1973 a quarter to a third of all Afghan officers had been trained in the USSR.[17] In his first trip abroad as leader of the Communist Party, Nikita Khrushchev visited Kabul in 1955 and endorsed Afghan claims to Pashtunistan.[18]

By 1979 the Soviet Union had provided a total of more than $1 billion in military aid and $1.25 billion in economic aid to Afghanistan. In contrast, U.S. assistance totaled less than a half-billion dollars; of that, only a little more than $25 million was military aid. The Soviets built the 1.7-mile-long, 11,500-foot-high Salang Pass tunnel connecting Kabul to the northern part of the country, providing an all-weather road from the Soviet border to the capital. Russian aid built the air base at Bagram, north of Kabul. U.S. aid built roads connecting Afghanistan to Pakistan and Iran and a major air field at Kandahar. Daoud's government played on the Soviet and U.S. rivalry to get as much help as possible from both, but the Soviets had the inside track because they were geographically close to Afghanistan and they did not support Pakistan. In 1957, King Zahir made a state visit to Moscow to thank Russia for its assistance.[19]

In 1959 President Eisenhower became the first U.S. president to visit Kabul, on a trip that took him to India and Pakistan too (it was also the maiden voyage of Air Force One). The trip was soon overshadowed by a crisis with Moscow that arose when an American U-2 spy plane, flying from a secret base in Peshawar, Pakistan, was shot down over Soviet territory in 1960. The incident revealed that Pakistan had become a major base for U.S. espionage against the USSR, hosting both a secret CIA air base and a major National Security Agency signals intelligence collection facility.[20] In the late 1950s the CIA also began flying missions to supply anticommunist Tibetan rebels inside Communist China from an air base in East Pakistan provided by the Pakistani army.[21]

By pursuing its policy of *bi-tarafi* ("without sides") in the cold war, Daoud's government secured 80 percent of its development budget from the two superpowers. Daoud's major investment was in education and women's rights. Schools were opened, and by the Saur Revolution more than 1 million Afghan students were in school—of a population of 15 million—and many of them were girls. In August 1959, on the fortieth anniversary of Afghan independence from British control of its foreign policy, Daoud ordered the wives and daughters of the royal family and prominent government officials to appear in public without veils, a shocking move in Afghanistan's conservative society that was denounced by many in the Islamic clergy (ulema). In addition, women were admitted to Kabul University as students and faculty and even as stewardesses on the national airline, Ariana Airways.[22]

In 1961 Daoud instigated a crisis with Pakistan over the Pashtunistan issue, sending a combined army and tribal force across the border into Pakistani territory. Pakistan's military dictator, Field Marshal Ayub Khan, shut Pakistan's consulates in Afghanistan. U.S.-supplied Pakistani F-86 Sabre jets bombed Afghan positions in Konar Province, and Ayub Khan shut the border to trade and cross-border tribal migration.[23] The closing of the border hurt Afghanistan, a landlocked country dependent on trade through Karachi, much more than it hurt Pakistan, and it went on for eighteen months. Daoud was disgraced and resigned in March 1963. President John F. Kennedy urged Khan to avoid further conflict with Kabul when he hosted him for a state dinner at Mount Vernon, George Washington's home in Alexandria, Virginia. After the Shah of Iran hosted a tripartite meeting with U.S. support in Tehran, Khan agreed to reopen the border. King Zahir ceased disseminating anti-Pakistan propaganda and traveled to Washington to meet with Kennedy in September 1963, the first visit by an Afghan head of state to the United States.[24]

In the 1960s King Zahir allowed political parties to begin to operate; while they were tolerated, they were not, strictly speaking, legal. In January 1965 the PDPA was formed, led by a Khalqi, Nur Muhammad Taraki. The party was funded by the Soviet Communist Party and followed the Soviet line. Within two years the party split into the two factions that became its hallmark, the Khalq, led by Taraki, and the Parcham, led by Babrak Karmal. There was also a smaller Maoist, pro-Chinese faction. Islamist political parties also emerged in the 1960s, led by future mujahedin leaders Ahmad Shah Massoud and Gulbuddin Hekmatyar. The communist factions emphasized recruiting new party members among the officer corps and students, especially at Kabul University.

Mohammad Daoud Khan carefully planned a comeback, securing the support of Pashtunistan nationalists, students, and reformers and the Parcham faction of the PDPA, among others. On July 17, 1973, while the king was in Europe, Daoud staged a coup and proclaimed the end of the monarchy and the creation of the Republic of Afghanistan. The Parcham joined Daoud's government, and several members were elected to parliament. The Khalq stayed out of the government, ridiculing their rival as "royal communists." King Zahir went into exile in Rome, where his bills and expenses initially were paid for by President Anwar Sadat of Egypt, the Shah of Iran, and the king of Saudi Arabia. After Sadat's assassination and the fall of the Shah, King Fahd paid the bills.[25]

Moscow welcomed the coup, of which it had advance knowledge because many of the officers who took part were Soviet trained and the PDPA was involved. Daoud visited Moscow in 1974, where he was given debt relief and a new half-billion-dollar aid program. He also promised to prevent any Western economic activity in northern Afghanistan along the Russian border, and he again revived the Pashtunistan issue, offering Pashtun and Baluchi rebels sanctuary and safe haven in Afghanistan. For its part, Pakistan backed the Islamist parties in Afghanistan, which engaged in terror attacks in Kabul.

But Daoud did not want to become a Soviet puppet, so he turned to Iran for help. The Shah of Iran, who was beginning to enjoy a surge of oil wealth after the 1973 Arab-Israeli war, promised Daoud a ten-year, $2 billion aid package. The Shah even suggested unification of Afghanistan and Iran under his imperial crown. Iran also brokered a détente with Pakistan. Daoud and Pakistan's president, Zulfikar Ali Bhutto, traded official state visits in 1976. In 1978 the Shah offered Daoud a $3 billion aid program if Daoud would recognize the Durand Line as a permanent border and in return Pakistan would cease all aid to Afghan dissidents. Daoud agreed to consider the offer.[26] The Shah was scheduled to visit Kabul in June 1978, and Daoud was scheduled to visit Washington to meet President Jimmy Carter in September.[27]

From Moscow's perspective, Afghanistan appeared to be drifting from its camp to the other side in the cold war. The Parcham and Khalq had been declared illegal in 1976 by Daoud, who feared their links to Moscow, and all Parchamists had been removed from the cabinet. Daoud visited Moscow for a second time in April 1977, but the visit went poorly. Daoud complained about Soviet efforts to unite the two factions of the PDPA, and Leonid Brezhnev, Khrushchev's successor, demanded the expulsion of Western experts working in the northern provinces on aid projects. Daoud refused and walked out of the meeting.

The Soviets became convinced that Iran and the CIA were turning Daoud and Afghanistan against them. The Soviet conspiracy theories are easy to understand. Richard Helms, the U.S. ambassador in Tehran, was the former head of the CIA; he also had attended the same Swiss prep school as the Shah and had known him well since the CIA-backed coup that put him in power in 1953.[28] In July 1977 Moscow engineered a brief reunification of the Khalq and the Parcham, assisted by the communist Tudeh Party of Iran and the Communist Party of India.[29] The stage was set for a communist coup d'état.

The Communists in Power

In retrospect, there is a tendency to minimize the Afghan communists as simply pawns of the Soviet Union. They certainly were close to Moscow, but they were never obedient pawns. The KGB never controlled them fully and never succeeded in mending the factional rift in the PDPA. The communists had their own constituency in Afghanistan, among the urban population, students, parts of the minority ethnic communities, women's rights advocates, and believers in Marxism as the wave of the future. The PDPA would remain in power longer than the Communist Party of the Soviet Union; indeed, it would outlast the USSR.

Nonetheless, the connections between the PDPA and Moscow were deep and intimate. Moreover, by 1978 Soviet-trained personnel composed a third of the country's army officers and more than half of the air force officers. Soviet-trained personnel filled a majority of professional and technical positions in the government bureaucracy; many had been indoctrinated during their training in the Soviet Union, and some were KGB assets. The coup was planned in advance, and the KGB must have been well aware of the plot. Whether the Soviets explicitly instructed the PDPA to stage the coup is disputed by historians.[30] A CIA postmortem on the Russian invasion of Afghanistan in 1980 concluded that "there was no evidence that the Soviet Union participated in the coup," but that leaves unanswered the question of how much Moscow knew of it in advance and encouraged or discouraged the plot.[31] A later study by the CIA's Center for the Study of Intelligence concluded Moscow was aware of the plot but that the coup took place earlier than Moscow expected because of fast-moving events in Kabul.[32]

The assassination of a prominent PDPA member, Mir Akbar Khyber, on April 17, 1978, set the stage for the coup. The communists, who blamed Daoud and the CIA for his death, organized a large demonstration in Kabul. Daoud responded by arresting the leaders of the two factions, Taraki and Karmal. On April 27, 1978, Khalq faction officers in Kabul mutinied and stormed the Presidential Palace with fifty tanks, supported by air strikes from the Afghan air force. By the next day, Daoud and thirty members of his family had been killed and rapidly buried in a secret mass grave. Daoud had been shot dead in a hail of bullets while trying to resist the coup.

Nur Muhammad Taraki, the leader of the Khalq faction, became president and prime minister, with Babrak Karmal as deputy prime minister and another Khalqi, Hafizullah Amin, as foreign minister. The attempt to reconcile the factions would not last long. Taraki was born in 1917, the son of a Pashtun livestock dealer. He spent much of the 1930s in Bombay, India, where he was recruited by the Communist Party of India. In the 1960s he lived in the Soviet Union as a translator, but he was probably funded by the KGB. In 1965 he became a founder of the PDPA. He served in the early 1970s as the press attaché at the Afghan embassy in Washington. He also was a novelist, depicting classic Pashtun tribal society in Marxist dialectical terms.

The new regime moved quickly to implement its agenda. The Khalq was determined to change Afghanistan at top speed. The sexes were declared equal, and a minimum age was set for marriage, 16 years for girls and 18 for boys. Dowries were restricted to encourage girls to have more choices. In a deeply religious society, especially among the Pashtuns, the new policies were an affront to religious and tribal customs. The state now seemed determined to decide the terms of marriage and interfere in family decisions. In addition, an ambitious but poorly thought-out land reform program was embarked on that appeared to be an attack on rural farmers, the vast bulk of the population. Large land holdings were seized by the state, alienating important local power brokers. Widespread arrests were carried out of anyone objecting to the new reforms and anyone suspected of disloyalty. A reign of terror ensued.

The Khalq also turned on the Parcham faction. In early July 1978, Taraki and Amin ousted most of the Parchamists from the government. Karmal was dispatched to Prague as ambassador to Czechoslovakia.

"Plots" by Parchamists were discovered and ringleaders executed. As the regime became ever more extreme, it changed the national flag from the traditional black, red, and green tricolor to an all-red flag with a gold emblem in the upper left corner and the word Khalq, the people, at the center—an obvious imitation of the Soviet flag.

Moscow had welcomed the coup and rapidly endorsed Taraki. Amin visited Moscow in May 1978, where he was treated as a fraternal communist leader. New aid projects were announced immediately. After the Soviets and Taraki signed a treaty of friendship and cooperation in December 1978, thousands of Soviet advisers and experts entered the country to help the PDPA consolidate its power. The Soviet military presence in the country grew tenfold, from 350 advisers and experts at the time of the Saur coup to more than 3,000 by the time of the invasion in December 1979; several thousand more elite paratroopers guarded Bagram air base.[33] A series of increasingly high-level Soviet military delegations visited Kabul to take stock of the situation and report back to Moscow.

Resistance to the regime began almost immediately after the coup. By the fall of 1978, Kabul and the communists had lost control of parts of the country, including remote Shia-inhabited Hazarajat in the center, the Tajik-dominated northeast around Badakhshan province, and Pashtun provinces like Nuristan and Kunar along the Pakistani border. The U.S. Embassy in Kabul, which had suspended all aid projects, estimated that by mid-1978 the communist government controlled no more than half of the country.[34] In March 1979 a major uprising occurred in Herat, the largest city in the west, and the local Afghan army forces defected en mass to the side of the insurgents. Russian advisers and their families were killed in the uprising, although how many is still a source of confusion. Some accounts claimed as many as 200 Russians died, but the number was probably much smaller. Taraki pressed for Soviet military intervention to help put down the revolt, but Moscow resisted. Taraki flew to Moscow to make his case directly to the Soviet Politburo. He was promised more and better weapons along with more advisers and experts, but no combat forces. The communist regime publicly blamed the uprising on the new Islamic Republic of Iran and the regime of Ayatollah Khomeini. There is no doubt that Khomeini was sympathetic, but the origins of the uprising were Afghan and included both Shia Muslims and Pashtuns.

After a week of shock, Kabul struck back. The Afghan air force bombed Herat with Ilyushin Il-28 bombers, and an armored force loyal to the PDPA retook the city in late March. Estimates of the dead run from 4,000 to 25,000. In 1992 a mass grave was uncovered that contained 2,000 bodies. Taraki was disgraced by the Herat debacle and became a figurehead. Hafizullah Amin, who took over the job of prime minister, became the regime strong man.

Then, in September 1979, Taraki planned his own comeback. He traveled to Havana, Cuba, and then to Moscow looking for support to oust Amin. Brezhnev encouraged Taraki to get rid of Amin, whom he considered too reckless and unwilling to work with other parts of the PDPA. Taraki returned to Kabul and moved to oust Amin, but Amin had learned from his informants that a coup was under way. On September 16 Amin struck first, ousting Taraki in a coup. The Russians were still urging intraparty unity as Amin removed Taraki's supporters from office. On October 8, 1979, on Amin's orders, Taraki was smothered to death.[35] Radio Kabul announced that Taraki had died of a "serious illness" from which he had long been suffering. Brezhnev and the Politburo were furious at Amin.

Hafizullah Amin was born near Kabul in 1921. After earning a degree from Kabul University, he came to New York in 1957 to study at the Teachers College of Columbia University in its prestigious master's program. In 1962 he returned to Columbia to get a Ph.D. He was head of the Union of Afghan Students in the United States, and he was a committed communist. In 1965 he returned to Kabul to help found the PDPA. In 1969 he won the only seat in parliament ever won by a Khalq member of the party. In the 1970s he organized the recruitment of army and air force officers for the party, thus becoming in effect the godfather of the Saur Revolution.

But Amin could not stop the deterioration of communist control in the countryside or the defection of more and more soldiers from the army. The communists had bungled their chance at power, and the revolution was in danger. The scene was set for the Soviet invasion. In mid-September the U.S. intelligence community detected unusual activity at a Soviet elite paratrooper division base, the 105th Guards Airborne Division at Fergana air base in Uzbekistan. It was the beginning of Soviet preparations to invade Afghanistan and the birth of the 40th Red Army.

CHAPTER TWO

THE MAIN ENEMY: $1-52$
THE SOVIETS

THE OPERATIONS CENTER of the Central Intelligence Agency was on the seventh floor of the original headquarters building, just a short walk from the Office of the Director of Central Intelligence (DCI). In 1979 there was a large round desk in the center of the room with four chairs reserved for three watch officers and a senior duty officer who was in charge of the center. Here the CIA watched the world, monitoring the global press as well as incoming reports from all elements of the intelligence community. Incoming traffic from U.S. intelligence facilities around the world were quickly scanned for reports requiring urgent attention. During a crisis, especially if it was a surprise, the ops center would be a whirl of activity as the watch officers spotted late-breaking news, the senior duty officer called the DCI and the White House Situation Room to alert them to new developments, and CIA officers rushed in and out to get information or comment on events as they unfolded.

One floor below was the Task Force Center. If a crisis erupted anywhere in the world, the DCI would set up a task force of experts to monitor and assess developments twenty-four hours a day. Since early November, I had all but lived in the center as part of a small team covering the Iran hostage crisis. It gave us a great bird's eye view of the crisis brewing next door in Afghanistan and the Soviet preparations for invasion. Late on Christmas Eve in 1979, the pace of activity in the ops center picked up dramatically as the Soviet Union invaded Afghanistan.

In 1979, and for many years before, during, and after the cold war, there was no higher priority for U.S. intelligence than to monitor and assess Soviet military activity to ensure that U.S. policymakers were never surprised by a Soviet military move. It was a matter of life and death to know what was going on within the world's biggest military and to anticipate its every move well in advance. The last major Soviet military operation had been in 1968, with the invasion of Czechoslovakia; before that, it was the Cuban missile crisis in 1962. In 1979 the consensus of analysts in the U.S. intelligence community—including the CIA, the Defense Intelligence Agency, the State Department's Bureau of Intelligence and Research, and the National Security Agency—was that Moscow did not want to intervene with its own troops in Afghanistan. The argument was laid out in the CIA's top-secret newspaper, the *National Intelligence Daily*, on March 23, 1979:

> The Soviets would be most reluctant to introduce large numbers of ground forces into Afghanistan to keep in power an Afghan government that had lost the support of virtually all segments of its population. Not only would the Soviets find themselves in an awkward morass in Afghanistan, but their actions could seriously damage their relations with India and to a lesser degree with Pakistan.①

Throughout 1978 and 1979, the majority view in the U.S. intelligence community was that Russia would not intervene with large numbers of ground troops in what increasingly appeared to be a Vietnam-like quagmire in Afghanistan. As can now be seen in the Soviet archives, the majority of the Politburo had the same view. When the Soviets did intervene dramatically on Christmas Eve 1979, the intelligence community could argue that it had correctly detected and reported the military preparations for the invasion in the weeks leading up to the invasion. It would later claim in a 1980 postmortem requested by the national security adviser, Zbigniew Brzezinski, that it had provided ten days' warning that Moscow was "prepared" to invade; however, a subsequent study by the CIA's own Center for the Study of Intelligence was more honest, noting that the warnings were far from explicit and that the "warnees" in the White House did not feel warned at all.② The subsequent study highlighted that a community assessment issued on September 28, 1979, concluded that Moscow would not intervene in force even if it appeared likely that the Khalq government was about to collapse.③

A review of President Carter's diary, published in 2010, shows dramatically how the president was *not* warned. In the two months leading up to the invasion, his mind was focused on Iran and the hostages. There are only two very brief mentions of the Afghan issue, and neither suggests that the danger of invasion was high on his administration's agenda. On Christmas Day 1979 his diary makes no mention of the attack under way, and not until the evening of December 27 did he decide to cut short his holiday at Camp David and rush back to the White House to deal with the crisis. By then he notes that the Soviets had flown "215 flights, moving 8,000 or 10,000 people into Kabul—an extremely serious development.[4] The Soviet Union had pulled off a strategic surprise. When asked by ABC News on New Year's Eve whether he had been surprised by the invasion, a shaken Carter said "Yes."

Carter might well have acted differently in December 1979 if he had had better warning from the intelligence community. Washington could have signaled clearly that an invasion would have serious consequences for Moscow, and it could also have rallied other nations to weigh in with the Kremlin. But the confidence of the intelligence community in its judgment that intervention was unlikely had produced complacency among its members. The sense that the intelligence community had underestimated the Soviets' aggressive intentions also had a longer-term impact on policymakers' assumptions about Soviet plans. Under Carter and even more so under Reagan, the policy community worried that Russian ambitions would grow over time, a sentiment fueled by Pakistan's conviction that Russia's ambitions were growing. It is now known, in hindsight, that that impression was wrong, but my interviews with Carter, Brzezinski, and Robert Gates, who later became director of the CIA, all underscored how important the December surprise was in their thinking about both Moscow and the CIA.

Surprise: The December Invasion

On December 24, 1979, the Soviet Union launched a massive airlift of troops into Kabul through Bagram air base in order to overthrow the Amin government and take control of the capital. The 105th Guards Airborne Division, the elite paratrooper force that led the assault, was delivered into the capital in 300 flights from bases in Soviet Central Asia. A second airborne division provided additional support. The National Security Agency detected the flight activity and issued a report on

Christmas Day entitled "Major Soviet Move into Afghanistan Possibly Imminent.⁵ That was a bit of an understatement.

On the evening of December 27, elite Soviet Spetsnaz commando forces, some from a special KGB unit, stormed the Presidential Palace outside Kabul and killed Amin. It was a bloody affair, as Amin and his bodyguards fought to the end, and according to a defector from the spy service, over 100 KGB officers were killed⁶ While U.S. intelligence officials knew about the tensions between the Soviet leadership and Amin, none had expected the Russians to kill their own protégé in such a brutal and ruthless manner. The next day, two Soviet motorized rifle divisions crossed the border and entered Afghanistan. One headed for Herat and Kandahar; the other took the Salang Tunnel route to join the airborne forces in Kabul.

The U.S. intelligence community had observed all of those forces preparing for action during the fall of 1979. In September, the airborne division was the first to be detected on high alert. It was routinely kept fully manned and equipped, but its alert status was raised after the death of Taraki. The two rifle divisions were third-rate reserve units that normally had only 10 percent of their troops on hand, but over the autumn they were observed building up to combat strength. Other support forces and air transport and combat aircraft deployed to the Central Asia front. The Soviet Indian Ocean Naval Squadron went on alert. The intelligence community reported the steady buildup of all of these elements, but it misjudged Moscow's intentions. As the CIA postmortem noted tersely in 1980, "the coup came as a surprise to U.S. intelligence.⁷ The CIA had not given the president the intelligence that he needed to make informed decisions, and that failure would haunt the CIA's Afghan project for years to come.

Today, with the benefit of both hindsight and partial access to the Kremlin's archives, experts can put together a fairly comprehensive picture of Soviet decisionmaking in 1978 and 1979. The archives have been studied by numerous scholars, and several of the Russian participants, including at least one former KGB officer, have provided their own accounts (usually with some bias) of what happened. In retrospect it is clear that the Soviets understood that they were taking a great risk in intervening in force in Afghanistan. They understood the dangers of an open-ended mission in a hostile land, but they would not allow a communist government to fail. Like Hungary in 1956 and Czechoslovakia in 1968, Afghanistan was a neighbor of Russia, and Moscow was determined not to lose it. However, the Soviets came to that conclusion slowly and reluctantly.

There were four key decisionmakers in Moscow: party boss Leonid Brezhnev, Defense Minister Dmitri Ustinov, Foreign Minister Andrei Gromyko, and KGB chairman Yuri Andropov. Brezhnev was in charge, but his health was already slipping and he was not always firmly in the saddle. Andropov was perhaps the most influential and energetic of the four, and it was the KGB that had responsibility for dealing directly with the PDPA and its machinations. The Soviets were enthusiastic about the April 1978 coup but quickly became concerned about the deterioration of the regime's control of the country. The extremism of the Khalq became a constant problem. The uprising in Herat in March 1979 galvanized Russian decisionmakers more than any other single event. Over the course of several days in mid-March, the senior leadership met in Moscow to assess the situation. On the first day of the meeting, Andropov declared, "We cannot lose Afghanistan,"[8] and the record shows that his comrades tended to agree. But by the next day, the mood was more restrained, apparently because Brezhnev, who had not been present on the first day but was consulted overnight, was more cautious. The March meeting concluded with a decision not to send in Soviet combat troops in any significant numbers and to tell the Afghan communists not to expect relief by the Red Army. Aid, experts, and advice would be provided but no troops. Nonetheless, the Ministry of Defense was instructed to develop contingency plans for an intervention and to take steps to ensure readiness in the key units that would be needed in an emergency. The 105th Guards Airborne Division was first alerted at that time.

Over the summer of 1979 the Soviet leadership watched with increasing concern as the situation deteriorated. A mutiny by an Afghan division just outside Kabul in August suggested that the regime was losing control of the army, adding significantly to Soviet worries. On August 17, 1979, General Ivan G. Pavlovsky, the deputy chief of the Soviet General Staff and commander of the Soviet ground forces, arrived in Kabul with a delegation of a dozen generals and sixty aides to conduct an urgent review of the situation. Pavlovsky did not travel outside the Soviet Union often, but he had been commander of the Warsaw Pact forces that invaded

Czechoslovakia in 1968, a fact noted by the U.S. intelligence community. His was a very professional appraisal. His team informed Moscow that the situation was dire and began more extensive planning for intervention. Pavlovsky stayed in Kabul until sometime in November.

The death of Taraki in October and Amin's takeover in Kabul was the "crucial turning point" for Soviet decisionmakers. Brezhnev was personally insulted by Amin's actions: "What a bastard, Amin, to murder the man with whom he made the revolution," Brezhnev told his comrades.[9] A defector later wrote that the pride of the KGB itself was hurt, because the agency had lost control of its protégés.[10] Over the course of the fall, the Russians decided that Amin had to be replaced. Allegations that he was in fact a CIA agent, based on his years in New York City at Columbia University, were circulated. The KGB "discovered" evidence of his connections with U.S. diplomats and intelligence officers, which it reported to the Politburo. He was accused of plotting with the CIA to create a "New Great Ottoman Empire" on Russia's southern flank.[11] Some suggested that Amin would do a "Sadat" on Russia, in reference to the Egyptian leader who had taken Egypt out of the Soviet orbit and into an alliance with the United States in the mid-1970s, creating a major setback for the Soviet Union's foreign policy in the Arab world. Andropov's KGB was authorized to develop a plan for Amin's ouster and replacement by Parcham leader Babrak Karmal, who was safely in Prague as ambassador. Several other senior Afghan communists were smuggled out of Kabul to form the cabal.

In early December Andropov reported to Brezhnev in a personal, hand-written letter that the KGB believed that the gains of the Saur Revolution were at risk and that Afghanistan was in danger of falling to "the West."[12] With Iran already becoming increasingly hostile under Khomeini, Andropov portrayed a dangerous Islamic threat developing on Russia's southern border. As the Soviet ambassador to Hungary in 1956, when Budapest was kept in the Warsaw Pact by invading Russian tanks, Andropov would have had great credibility and his words would have resonated powerfully with his boss. The KGB spymaster reported that a new team of Afghan communists, led by Babrak Karmal, was ready to be installed in Amin's place, elite commandoes had infiltrated Kabul and Bagram for the operation, and the Red Army was preparing the larger invasion force.[13] On December 12, 1979, Brezhnev and

the senior Politburo members signed a document authorizing the operation. A new army headquarters was created to manage it, the 40th Red
Army, although officially the mission was called the Limited Contingent
of Soviet Forces in Afghanistan.(14) Whatever doubts Moscow had about
the wisdom of intervention were overtaken by events.

This reversal in Soviet thinking was difficult if not impossible for U.S.
intelligence analysts to detect and report. The CIA would have needed
real-time information on the deliberations in the innermost sanctum of
the Kremlin. Even then, the new data would have had to be so persua-
sive that they convinced the bureaucracy that its collective judgment was
wrong and did so very quickly. Neither the intelligence collection system
nor the analysts succeeded. Although it was an almost impossible task, it
was one that they would nevertheless be held accountable for.

The Soviet Era in Kabul

There is little in the records available about Soviet decisionmaking in
1979 to suggest that the idea of invading Afghanistan was the first step
in a Soviet march to the Indian Ocean. Moscow's overriding goal was
to defend the communist regime, not to take further offensive action.
The Afghan communists, however, were eager supporters of the notion
of expanding Afghanistan's border to the sea. Like many Afghans, the
PDPA leadership supported the Pashtunistan cause. Taraki raised it
directly with Brezhnev, declaring that "we must not leave the Pakistani
Pashtun and Baluchi in the hands of the imperialists" and that "now it is
possible to launch a national liberation struggle amongst these tribes and
include the Pashtun and Baluchi regions in Afghanistan." Amin was also
an eager proponent of Afghan expansion. He had told the Soviet ambassador that "the territory of Afghanistan must reach to the shores of the
Gulf of Oman and the Indian Ocean. We wish to see the sea with our
own eyes; we must have an outlet to the Indian Ocean." Babrak Karmal
was similarly eager to repudiate and erase the Durand Line and move
Afghanistan's border to the valley of the Indus River.(15)

Karmal's new government began to take steps to make Pashtunistan
a reality. Relations with Baluchi separatist groups in Afghanistan that
dated back to the Daoud era were revitalized by Karmal's new intelligence service, the KHAD, created with KGB support and money.(16) The

Afghans reached out to other dissidents in Pakistan to find assets who would take action against the regime of Pakistan's military dictator, General Zia ul-Haq. Zia had overthrown the democratically elected government of Zulfikar Ali Bhutto in 1977, and a year later Zia had Zulfikar executed in jail. Some of Bhutto's supporters in the Pakistan People's Party were ripe for inducements from the KHAD to join anti-Zia operations. Among the most prominent were Zulfikar's two sons, Mir Murtaza and Shahnawaz Bhutto, who were invited to Kabul.

The KHAD itself grew rapidly under the direction of its new leader, Babrak's protégé Mohammad Najibullah. From a relatively small base of a few hundred in 1980, it had grown to include more than 16,000 men by 1982. Almost all were trained in the USSR. It also set up bands of "bandit mujahedin," who were special undercover agents who posed as mujahedin fighters but actually sought to discredit the real mujahedin by carrying out atrocities and trying to divide the regime's opposition. This was an old KGB tactic used in the Soviet Union and in the Eastern European states to weaken anticommunist opposition groups.[17]

In other ways, Karmal's regime tried to reverse some of the excesses of the Amin and Khalq era. The flag was changed back to the traditional tricolor, and implementation of the land reform program slowed. The regime tried to look more nationalist and less communist. Islam was no longer automatically regarded as an enemy of the state. Moscow and the KGB encouraged Karmal to take steps to try to win back some elements of popular support. However, resistance got stronger, not weaker. Afghans saw through the charade of occupation for what it was, and they knew that their country was now all but a Soviet client state. The Soviets occupied all the key cities and controlled the major highways; they had even murdered the sitting head of state of the country. From the first days of the Soviet occupation of Kabul, there were nightly protests and clashes with Soviet forces. Outside the cities, the mujahedin remained the dominant force in much of the country.

The Soviets tried to win some support for the communist regime by implementing a large aid program. Thousands of experts came into the country to do "nation building." Factories, housing blocks, power stations, and other facilities were built with Soviet economic assistance, and Soviet allies in Eastern Europe were encouraged to assist as well. Between 1982 and 1986, Soviet economic aid to Afghanistan totaled $7.5 billion of about $78 billion in total Soviet assistance to allies and friends, a significant but not intolerable burden for the Soviet Union.[18] In addition, the Afghan army was rebuilt. By late 1979 the Afghan army was down to less than 25,000 troops, and its ten divisions were hollow forces. By 1989 the army was 150,000 strong, counting regular forces in twelve divisions and units like Dostam's in the north. The Afghan air force, which totaled more than 400 aircraft and 100 helicopters, was considerably larger than the air force produced by the U.S. and NATO effort in Afghanistan in the twenty-first century. But the Afghan forces suffered from poor morale and often were distrusted by the 40th Red Army command.[19]

The 40th Red Army began in 1980 with an expeditionary force of approximately 80,000 men. At its peak it numbered around 110,000 men and included three motorized rifle divisions, one airborne division, four independent infantry brigades, two independent airborne brigades, two special forces brigades, and associated communications, intelligence, and other enabling units. It also had an air corps of fighters, bombers, helicopters, and transport aircraft. On the battlefield it had more than 600 tanks, 1,800 armored personnel and infantry fighting vehicles, 900 artillery pieces, and 500 fixed- and rotary-wing aircraft.[20] It would have seven commanders during its ten-year life span, apparently because the Red Army high command kept looking for a commander who could decisively defeat the insurgency.[21] For a country the size of Texas or France, marked by extremely mountainous terrain, that was a small force. The Soviets later estimated that they probably needed closer to thirty-five divisions. In Hungary in 1956 they had subdued a much smaller (and flatter) country with an invasion force of seventeen divisions. In the invasion of Czechoslovakia in 1968, the invasion force was over 500,000 strong, composed of eighteen Soviet divisions and eight divisions from the other Warsaw Pact states (Poland, East Germany, Hungary, and Bulgaria). In 1962 the Soviets sent 50,000 troops armed with tactical nuclear weapons across the Atlantic Ocean to defend Cuba from a feared U.S. invasion, a much more difficult logistical challenge than fighting the mujahedin in Afghanistan. Neither Hungary nor Czechoslovakia involved protracted combat operations. In 1968 there was almost no fighting; in 1962 the crisis was averted by diplomacy. In short, the Russians, trying to win as cheaply as possible, put a grossly inadequate amount of resources into the Afghan effort. Given the size of the Red

Army in the 1980s, it was not for lack of men and equipment; it was a political decision.[22] Moscow could have sent more troops but decided not to send them. By severely undersupplying the war effort, the Soviet Union all but ensured its own defeat.

The relatively small size of the Russian force did mean that its economic cost to the Soviet Union was relatively small as well. A CIA analysis prepared in February 1987 estimated that the cost of the war to date was roughly $50 billion. Over seven years, that amounted to about 2.5 percent of Soviet military spending per year. The CIA pointed out in comparison that the war in Vietnam between 1964 and 1976 cost the United States $330 billion. Of course, at the height of the Vietnam War, the United States had deployed a half-million soldiers to South East Asia.[23]

Soviet costs did go up as the war progressed despite the relatively small size of the 40th Army. Much of the increase was due to improvements in the quantity and quality of equipment that the Russians sent to Afghanistan. As the war went on, they used helicopters more and more extensively, both to transport troops and equipment and to attack the mujahedin. The CIA estimated that between 1980 and 1985 the Soviets lost up to 750 aircraft in Afghanistan, 85 percent of which were helicopters. For the most part, they were lost in 1984 and 1985, *before* the introduction of Stinger surface-to-air missiles by the CIA. The heavy use of helicopters and the heavy losses that they suffered even before the Stinger arrived were driving up the cost of the conflict, but the CIA estimated that even at its height only 3 percent of the entire Soviet military machine was engaged in Afghan-related operations.[24]

Given the size of the 40th Red Army and the size of Afghanistan, the Russians had to decide how best to deploy their forces. Roughly half of the Russian forces were located around Kabul and nearby Bagram air base. Sizable forces also guarded the critical supply line that ran north from Bagram to the Soviet border at Termez and through the Salang Tunnel. This supply corridor was vital to the survival of both the Soviet forces in the Kabul region and the PDPA regime. Another significant detachment kept watch over the area near the Russian border, especially Shibirghan and its natural gas fields. That left little to cover the rest of the country. Only small garrisons were available for Herat and Kandahar. In effect, the rural areas of central, western, and southern Afghanistan were left in the hands of the insurgents.[25]

Under these circumstances, the Soviets resorted to draconian tactics to fight the insurgents. Millions of mines were air dropped into Afghanistan or placed by hand. Many were relatively small antipersonnel mines intended to wound or kill civilians, and many were disguised as toys in order to trick Afghan children into picking them up. When in 1997 I traveled to Moscow to discuss the situation in Afghanistan with the post-communist government, we asked the Russian Foreign Ministry for assistance in providing maps of areas where the Red Army had planted minefields. They responded that no maps had been made during the war. When we asked them to check with the military, they replied that they had already done so. There simply were no maps. The Red Army had not kept maps of where it laid minefields in Afghanistan; it didn't care what happened to the Afghan people.

Soviet and Afghan air power was also used with little regard for civilian casualties. For example, when the city of Kandahar rebelled against the Soviet occupation in early 1980, the Russians responded by carpet bombing the city. The city was devastated. The population fell from 250,000 to only 25,000; while most of the inhabitants left, the number killed in the bombing is unknown.[26] Kandahar was not unique. Rural areas often were the worst hit. The Soviets used TU-16 heavy bombers flown from bases in the Soviet Union to bomb the Panjsher Valley repeatedly—for example, in their campaigns against Ahmad Shah Massoud's rebels.[27]

As a consequence, millions of Afghans sought refuge in Pakistan and Iran. The United Nations estimated that by the end of the Soviet occupation, 5 million of an estimated total Afghan population of about 20 million were refugees in Pakistan and Iran. One in four Afghans had been driven from their nation by the Soviet intervention, the majority in Pakistan.[28] Neither Pakistan nor Iran had the resources to take adequate care of such large numbers of destitute people, and conditions in the refugee camps were terrible. At least 2 million more Afghans became internally displaced persons, driven from their homes to live with tribesmen or relatives elsewhere.

The Soviets fought the war "on the cheap and nasty," as a Defense Intelligence Agency account described it. Bob Gates recalls that the Soviets fought a "war of terror" that did "everything in its power to alienate Afghans."[29] The Pentagon's Defense Intelligence Agency estimated that at the height of its effort in the mid-1980s, the Red Army was fighting in Afghanistan with about 6 percent of its available divisions, financed by over 2 percent of its total defense spending. It was not an impressive effort for a global superpower.[30] Instead of the necessary resources, it used terror to try to win.

At the time, however, the effort seemed impressive to most observers and to the Russians themselves. Moscow also was reassured by Russia's history in Central Asia and the Caucasus. Russian imperial armies had conquered those territories from Islamic rulers in the nineteenth century and imposed the tsar's rule on them. After the Bolshevik Revolution, much of the region had achieved temporary self-rule, but in the 1920s the Bolsheviks restored Russian control. If previous generations of Russian soldiers could dominate Muslim lands, why not the 40th Red Army in Afghanistan? But Russia's expectations were unrealistic from the beginning. Some of the documents in the archives suggest that the Kremlin hoped that it would be able to withdraw forces quickly after the initial invasion, maybe even after a few months, and that the Afghan communists would be able to handle the situation without Russian combat forces. That fantasy was quickly erased by reality. As one author wrote, "within several months of the invasion, any hope of a quick turnaround evaporated."[31]

Then Soviets hoped that they could control the country by holding the major cities and road networks and conducting occasional sweeps of the countryside to destroy insurgent bands. Kunar Province, on the Pakistani border, was swept in March, May, and September 1980, but the insurgents were not defeated. The story was the same in other rural border areas, such as Paktia, Ghazni, and Nangarhar provinces. In September 1980 a major offensive was made into the Panjsher Valley, the first of what would be many attempts to defeat the predominately Tajik guerrilla force in the area. In 1981 the Russians began relying even more heavily on their own forces for offensive operations and leaving the Afghan communists to defend the cities. Smaller Russian units equipped with helicopters for air mobility became more common. Two more major offensives were launched in the Panjsher. At the end of the year, the Soviet deputy defense minister came to see what was going wrong.

The result was even larger Soviet sweeps in 1982, with bigger task forces. Another two offensives took place in the Panjsher Valley. Other major operations tried to sweep the area around Kabul in Wardak,

Parwan, and Logar provinces. One Soviet captain described the situation this way: "Practically every operation in the war ended in the same way. Military operations began, soldiers and officers died, Afghan soldiers died, the mujahedin and the peaceful population died, and when the operation was over, our forces would leave and everything would return to what it had been before." In the end the 40th Army counted that it had conducted 416 major operations in the war, to little effect.[32]

In 1983 the Soviets tried an air war approach, using bomber strikes against civilian targets more extensively and even more helicopter-equipped sweep operations. Kandahar was pounded from the air in March and Herat in April. In the Panjsher Valley, the Russians and the local mujahedin commander, Ahmad Shah Massoud, agreed on a temporary cease-fire and truce. Moscow had hoped that the agreement would lead to a more permanent arrangement to take the valley out of the war, but it didn't last, and the truce ended in early 1984. Another major Soviet offensive in the Panjsher followed in April 1984 and yet another in September. Rebel rocket attacks on Kabul became much more frequent in the summer of 1984, bringing the war to the capital. Herat and Kandahar were the scenes of major Russian and Afghan communist offensives in the summer, but the resistance simply fled into the rural areas.

Soviet tactics gradually improved as time went on and the Russians gained experience, but the improvement did not significantly alter the course of the war. In 1985 several more major sweep operations took place in the Panjsher Valley, but by the end of the fighting season and the approach of winter, Massoud's forces remained in control of most of the region. There was local fighting across the country, but nowhere did the Russians gain a decisive advantage.[33]

1986 was a decisive year. Pakistan's leader Zia ul-Haq decided sometime in 1985 to escalate the war and told Reagan in January 1986 that he was ready to take greater risks to win the war. The Russians also decided to take more chances in a final effort to win on the ground. The arrival in 1986 and 1987 of new U.S. equipment like the Stinger, combined with a major increase in U.S. and Saudi funding for the war, put much more pressure on the Russian army. At the same time, political support for the war effort in Moscow deteriorated and the leadership gradually decided that the war was unwinnable.

Soviet Decisionmaking in the War

Soviet decisionmaking has to be regarded as a major cause of Russia's ultimate defeat in the war. Both the military and civilian staff of the Kremlin were to blame. During the war, the U.S. intelligence community had only very limited insight into Soviet decisionmaking. The United States lacked human intelligence sources inside the top Soviet echelons and often depended on informed speculation to try to decipher what Moscow was thinking and planning. Now, due to hindsight and the partial opening of the Soviet archives, experts have a better sense of what was going on.

The Red Army in 1979 was an enormous institution with a proud past. At a staggering cost in lives—officially estimated at 8.7 million by the Russian government after the fall of communism and as high as 23 million by Russian historians (military deaths only, civilian casualities were much higher)—it had defeated the German war machine in World War II.[34] From the edge of catastrophic defeat in 1941, the Red Army had fought from Stalingrad to Berlin, facing the overwhelming majority of German forces with only limited and late assistance from the Western allies in mid-1944. Even Russians who detested Stalin and the Communist Party were justifiably proud of the Red Army.[35] After 1945, however, the Red Army did not engage in another serious military operation until it invaded Afghanistan in 1979. The operations in Hungary and Czechoslovakia involved very little if any combat. There were skirmishes with the Chinese in Siberia and opportunities for Soviet experts and advisers to serve in proxy wars like those in Vietnam, Egypt, Yemen, and other fronts in the cold war, but the Red Army as an entity had been at peace for almost 35 years in 1979. Its officers had little combat experience.

Moreover, it had fought and won a conventional war of massed tanks, artillery, and air power against the Wehrmacht and had been preparing for another such war in Germany since the late 1940s. Its generals were trained to fight a conventional war, with an emphasis on tank battles. NATO, it believed, would be defeated in a lightning campaign launched by a massive tank army. In Afghanistan, however, the Red Army had to fight a classic guerilla enemy using classic guerilla tactics. Major combat operations against the insurgency began only months after the invasion, with large offensives along the border with Pakistan and in the Panjsher

Valley north of Kabul. The mujahedin did not fight conventional battles against the vastly better equipped Russians; they fought as insurgents have always fought. The mujahedin did not have a command-and-control structure that could be degraded and then defeated. They fought in terrain that they knew and understood in small formations, often based on tribal and clan loyalties. The entire war was fought in local actions. To the extent that the mujahedin had a command structure on a national scale, it was the Pakistani intelligence service, the ISI, not the Afghan commanders or the Afghan political parties.

The Pakistani sanctuary was another major problem for the Soviet military. To invade and conquer Pakistan was not an easy or a cheap option, so the safe haven that the Zia government provided the mujahedin could never be eradicated. The Soviets had no permanent solution to the challenge posed by Pakistan's support for the Afghan insurgents. Moscow and Kabul tried hard to put pressure on Pakistan and take the offensive against Zia, but there were inherent limits to how far the Soviets were prepared to go.

The command structure of the 40th Army was another challenge. As noted, it had seven commanders in ten years. Another eleven generals served as senior adviser to the Afghan army between 1975 and 1991.[36] In practice that meant a lack of continuity at the top of the chain of command. Each new commander would take some time developing his concept of operations and then implementing it, to a certain degree reinventing the wheel over and over again. In addition, the way in which the 40th Army reported to Moscow was cumbersome. Rather than reporting directly to the high command in Moscow, the army reported to the command in the Turkestan Military District in Tashkent and through it to Moscow. In practice, over time that protocol often was dispensed with, but it still made the military decisionmaking process unnecessarily complex.[37] In Afghanistan the command system included the 40th Army, the Soviet advisory team with the Afghan army, the chief of the KGB station in Kabul, and the Soviet ambassador. Coordination was not always smooth, and rivalries—institutional and personal—had an impact on the war and the Soviet relationship with the PDPA. The KGB often had the most influence, especially as Andropov became more and more important in the Politburo.

The civilian Communist Party leadership in Moscow was even more handicapped than the military. It was ossified and became even more so as the war progressed. Brezhnev died in November 1982 after years of failing health. Andropov, who could rightly be called the father of the war, succeeded Brezhnev, but his health also was poor. Andropov experimented with new tactics, such as calling a cease-fire with Ahmad Shah Massoud to try to divide the mujahedin and bringing in more heliborne special forces units to fight smarter.[38] He also was more energetic on the diplomatic front, where he tried to energize UN-brokered talks with Pakistan. But he died in January 1984 and was replaced by Konstantin Chernenko, who was seriously ill during his entire time as party boss.

Chernenko was so ill from emphysema, chronic hepatitis, and liver failure that he could barely deliver Andropov's eulogy. He died in March 1985. Mikhail Gorbachev came into office with an agenda that was much different from that of his three predecessors. He wanted to wind down the war, not continue it. In October 1985 Gorbachev, who had no significant role in the decision to intervene in 1979, told Babrak Karmal in Moscow that the Red Army was going to withdraw and that the PDPA would have to defend itself without Russian combat troops. A year later Moscow sacked Karmal and replaced him with Najibullah.[39] But it still took Gorbachev four years to get out of Afghanistan.

So for the first five years of the war, all of the three top party bosses were seriously ill during their time in office. The best chance to win the war had been squandered before large-scale foreign assistance reached the insurgents. During this part of the war, the official estimate of army fatalities was 9,420, or about 150 per month—the bulk of its casualties in the entire conflict.[40] By the time that Gorbachev came into office, the Soviet war effort was in serious trouble because of the U.S. covert operation to help the mujahedin as well as Soviet inadequacies and mistakes. How Gorbachev redirected Soviet policy is discussed later in this book. For now it is sufficient to note that the increasingly unstable leadership in the Kremlin was a major hindrance to making effective decisions and developing good strategies.

The Soviet failure to provide the resources required to conduct the war probably had much to do with the weak leadership at the top. No one wants to report bad news to the boss. That is especially true in a dictatorship, where the penalties for perceived disloyalty are severe. If there is uncertainty about a leader's health and future, the idea of reporting bad news—for example, that a war is being under-resourced and lost—would not be very attractive. Neither the KGB nor the Red Army was eager to report failure. A dysfunctional Kremlin top leadership probably did not encourage frank and candid analysis; it was easier just to keep the force structure stable and not rock the boat. As one scholar concluded from reading the Soviet archives, "negative assessments did not always make it all the way to the Politburo . . . they were intercepted by 'gatekeepers' who did not wish to anger their bosses with bad news."[41] Experts can only speculate about what a healthy and effective top leadership might have done differently in the war. A fully engaged leader might have decided to send in more troops or to go into Pakistan. Both would have been risky moves, perhaps even inviting a much larger war. Alternatively, he might have chosen to cut his losses earlier. There is no way to know.

It also is important to consider one other factor here. The war in Afghanistan was not fought in a vacuum. The Kremlin had other crises to consider as it pursued the conflict with the CIA in the Hindu Kush. The cold war was a global battle, and each front had an impact on the others. One problem—Poland—weighed especially heavily on the Kremlin in the early 1980s. The Soviet client state in Poland began experiencing serious domestic unrest in 1980. Solidarity, an organized dissident movement led by Lech Walesa, became a formidable threat to the survival of the communist regime, and Polish Pope John Paul II added another source of opposition to the Soviet order in Eastern Europe. Russian military forces were deployed to intervene in the situation more than once. Since Poland was Moscow's most important client in East Europe and controlled the roads and railroads leading to East Germany, the dissident movement was a major threat to Moscow's domination of Eastern Europe. Soviet leaders probably spent more time and energy nervously watching the events in Poland than they did monitoring any other problem in Soviet foreign policy in the early 1980s. The Polish crisis diverted attention and resources away from Afghanistan. Elite forces that might have been very useful in Kabul were kept ready for intervention in Warsaw.

Taking the Offensive in Pakistan

The Soviets not only fought defensively to keep their communist comrades in power in Afghanistan, they also fought offensively to keep Pakistan from backing the mujahedin. In that effort the PDPA and the KHAD were important allies. For the Afghan communists, fighting Pakistan was a way to repay the Kremlin for its support and possibly to advance the cause of Afghan expansion. For the Russians, intimidating Pakistan was a means to shut down the training camps across the border that produced the mujahedin, weaken a key U.S. ally, and earn favor from India, Moscow's key ally in South Asia. Indeed, Moscow drew on its alliance with India, formalized in a treaty signed on the eve of the 1971 India-Pakistan war, to try to pressure Pakistan. The Russians also used allies in the Middle East—such as the Palestine Liberation Organization (PLO), Libya, and especially Syria—to isolate Pakistan. In the end, they had little tangible success.

The major instrument available for intimidating Pakistan was a small movement, al Zulfiqar, created by the sons of Zia's predecessor, Zulfikar Ali Bhutto. Murtaza, the elder brother, was the main leader of the group, but he was a poor organizer and lacked support inside Pakistan. Murtaza was motivated by rage at his father's hanging and by hatred for Zia and the Pakistani army. He favored dividing Pakistan into four parts, giving Afghanistan the Pashtun and Baluchi territories coveted by the advocates of Pashtunistan in the PDPA, giving India the Punjab, and creating an independent Sindhi state along the Arabian Sea with a capital in Karachi. According to his biographer, Raja Anwar, who joined him in the early days of his fight against Zia and then was imprisoned by Murtaza for disloyalty, Murtaza was convinced that the Russians wanted access to the Indian Ocean and that Moscow and New Delhi would sooner or later invade Pakistan to divide the spoils.[42] Murtaza's plan to divide his country and give much of it to Pakistan's enemies naturally did not endear him to most Pakistanis.

The al Zulfiqar group was plagued by internal divisions caused by Murtaza's quixotic personality, but it did succeed in carrying out one major terrorist operation with the help of the KHAD and the intelligence service of Syria, another Soviet ally in the region. In March 1981 al Zulfiqar terrorists hijacked a Pakistan International Airlines domestic flight from Karachi to Lahore and diverted the plane to Kabul. A Pakistani diplomat was executed by the terrorists while the plane was in Afghanistan, apparently in part because they had misidentified him as a relative of a senior general. Both Murtaza and Najibullah, the head of the KHAD, assisted the terrorists in Kabul and met with them secretly at the airport. Babrak Karmal publicly welcomed the hijacking as a victory for the revolution, and the KHAD provided the terrorists with additional weapons.[43] The KGB also supported the hijacking and advised Najibullah on how best to use the operation to intimidate Pakistan.[44] The hijackers then had the plane flown to Damascus, where General Muhammad Khuli, President Hafiz Assad's top security adviser and the head of Syria's air force intelligence agency, told the hijackers to threaten to kill the Americans among the hostages. Zia finally agreed to release fifty-four members of the Pakistan People's Party, the Bhutto political arm, to get the hostages freed.[45] Khuli engineered the trade.

The hijacking was the high point for the al Zulfiqar movement. The PDPA rewarded Murtaza with better support from Kabul, and the Indian intelligence service, the Research and Analysis Wing (RAW), began to provide training for his operatives in India.[46] The group also got assistance from the PLO and Libya, including access to their training camps for terrorist operations. In early 1982 the group tried several times to assassinate Zia, using shoulder-fired surface-to-air missiles as his aircraft arrived in Rawalpindi. However, the terrorists were poorly trained in using the missiles and Zia's aircraft evaded them.[47]

Murtaza relocated his base of operations from Kabul to New Delhi in August 1982. He promised Prime Minister Indira Gandhi and her son Sanjay help in destabilizing Pakistan and asked for aid for his Sindhi independence movement.[48] RAW provided limited assistance to his group for several years. In 1984 Murtaza and his brother, Shahnawaz, relocated again, to Nice, in southern France, where Shahnawaz died in 1985. He allegedly was poisoned by his Afghan wife, who had been recruited by the KHAD to kill him. Who really killed him is still a mystery. In 1996 Murtaza also died in mysterious circumstances after returning to Pakistan, where his sister was now prime minister. Certainly the ISI was concerned by his connections to RAW, but his death may have been the work of Benazir's husband, future president Asif Zardari, who saw Murtaza as a possible rival for the leadership of the Pakistan People's Party.[49] In her memoirs, Murtaza's daughter, Fatima, blames Benazir and Zardari.[50] His death too remains something of a mystery.

Benazir Bhutto, the daughter of Zulfikar and twice the prime minister of Pakistan, carefully avoided any connection with her brothers and publicly criticized the hijacking episode. Zia used the terrorist incident to crack down harder on the Pakistan People's Party and to keep Benazir in prison.[51] In the end, Murtaza's operation not only was a futile effort to weaken Pakistani support for the mujahedin but also probably strengthened Zia's position at home and with the United States. President Reagan and Bill Casey, his director of central intelligence, came into office convinced that the Soviets were orchestrating international terrorism behind the scenes. Al Zulfiqar's actions only reinforced that conviction.

The Soviets tried other tactics to intimidate Islamabad. Soviet air force jets overflew Pakistani territory and carried out highly provocative operations along the border. The Soviet air force and the Pakistani air force engaged in several dogfights, and Soviet pilots were shot down and captured in Pakistan on more than one occasion. Zia would exchange them for cash ransoms from Moscow. None of those tactics appreciably improved results on the battlefield for the 40th Army. It simply failed to defeat the Russian's main enemy, the mujahedin.

It is useful to consider a couple of hypothetical Russian options or counterfactuals. What if the Soviets had provided adequate resources to conduct the war? What if Moscow had sent a quarter-million or even a half-million men into Afghanistan in the early 1980s to bolster the 40th Army? In 1945 the Soviet army had invaded Manchuria to defeat the Japanese with a force of more than 1.6 million men and more than 5,000 tanks and 5,000 aircraft; it certainly could have mustered an army in Afghanistan as large as the U.S. army in Vietnam.[52] The entire Manchurian invasion was supplied on a single railroad line across Siberia to Russia. Would a Soviet force of a half-million men have turned the war decisively in favor of the communists? Even more intriguing, what if Moscow had chosen to "finish" the problem by invading Pakistan? The Soviet Union had sufficient forces in the 1980s to overrun all of Pakistan if it had chosen to do so. Pakistan had only one modern armored division; Moscow had dozens. Pakistan probably did not have a workable nuclear bomb until around 1985, and even then only a couple of such devices at most; the Soviet Union had thousands of nuclear weapons. What if India had joined Russia in a war to carve up Pakistan? That was always Zia ul-Haq's greatest nightmare. Would it have won the war or started a global conflict?

None of these questions have any real answers. At most, it can be said that Moscow had the capability to pursue those options. It can also be said that pursuing them would have made the world a much more dangerous place in the final decade of the cold war.

CHAPTER THREE

THE AFGHAN MUJAHEDIN

THE AFGHAN MUJAHEDIN defeated the Soviets. The United States, Pakistan, Saudi Arabia, and others helped them considerably, but they did almost all the fighting and virtually all the dying themselves. They and the civilian population that backed them paid an awful price—at least 1 million dead and many more wounded—but they got very little of the benefit of their sacrifice. It is the tragedy of modern Afghanistan that the Afghan people helped to bring freedom to so many in other parts of the world but did not get it themselves until many years after their victory against the 40th Red Army. The mujahedin did not need to be coaxed into an insurgency. Their usually very high morale was based on the firm conviction that their country and their religion were under attack by a foreign invader, an extremist communist dictatorship. The mass of rural Afghans was ready to revolt in 1979. However, they did not fight for one cause alone: Islam fed Afghan nationalism and Afghan nationalism fed Islamism.

The mujahedin were almost entirely an army of illiterate rural peasants. They never created a national command-and-control system or a national political leadership. The government of Pakistan made a half-hearted effort to organize a political leadership for the mujahedin during the war, but it excluded groups backed by Iran and overrepresented Pashtun groups, especially ones that shared the militant Islamic views of President Zia ul-Haq. The most successful mujahedin commander, Ahmad Shah Massoud, was largely ostracized by the Pakistanis for most of the war. The CIA had very little direct contact with the mujahedin, a function that was deliberately left to Pakistan. Bob Gates remembers that the senior CIA leadership during the war "had very little direct contact" with the fighters or their leaders.[1]

The war was a classic guerilla insurgency. There were few set-piece battles, especially in the early years of the war. The Russians did mount offensive sweep operations every year, but the insurgents usually just melted away into the mountains, from which they harassed the Soviets but did not engage in big battles. Territory did not really change hands except for limited periods of time when the Russians moved into rural spaces on sweeps. When they returned to garrison, the status quo ante returned. Thus there is no way to map the war like a conventional conflict, tracking battle lines during major engagements and noting important dates. Only in the last year of the war did the mujahedin stand and fight, and even then it was only in isolated battles very near the Pakistani border. Since the mujahedin did not keep records of their losses, it is impossible to track their casualties or strength. If the ISI kept such records, they would have been incomplete at best and probably somewhat fanciful. In any case, there is no evidence of any records kept by the ISI or the CIA.

Nor did the mujahedin resort to suicide bombing. Suicide bombing was very common in Lebanon and other parts of the Middle East in the 1980s, so the tactic was well known, but the Afghans regarded it as inconsistent with their concept of warfare and did not turn to it for another generation. In the 1980s they preferred small-unit clashes, especially ambushes, like those that their grandfathers had mounted against the British; they did not use suicide bombers against enemy targets until after the U.S. intervention in 2001. The conflict was seasonal. Winter fighting was unusual; it is simply too cold and difficult to operate during the Afghan winter. So spring, summer, and early fall, when it was relatively easy to move around, defined the fighting season. Some of the mujahedin went to Pakistan to refit and regroup during the winter; others just went home.

The mujahedin were divided by ethnicity and sect. Because a real census has never been taken in Afghanistan, there are no truly accurate estimates of the size of the country's various ethnic groups; all estimates are informed guesses. The CIA's *World Factbook* estimates that Pashtuns are the largest group, accounting for about 42 percent of the population, while Tajiks and Aimaks constitute about 30 percent; Hazara, about 9 percent; Uzbeks, also about 9 percent; Turkmen, about 4 percent; and

Baluch, around 2 percent. All but the Hazara, who belong to a Shia Muslim sect, are Sunni Muslim. While some mujahedin groups included fighters from more than one ethnic group, that was not typical; most groups were composed of members of the same tribe and clan. Especially at the start, the mujahedin war was in many ways a very local affair.

The complexity of the mujahedin movement was both an asset and a liability. It was an asset because it made the Soviet task all the more difficult. There was no central command to negotiate with, no headquarters to destroy by turning the enormous firepower of the Soviets against it. The lack of central leadership allowed for flexibility and enhanced survival, but it also made the movement disorganized and open to outside manipulation. Afghanistan's two neighbors, Pakistan and Iran, each backed their favorite groups. Pakistan was a much more active interlocutor for a number of reasons. It has a longer border with Afghanistan, and as a Sunni state, it had more connections with the Afghan Sunni majority. Since the Pashtun community straddles the Durand Line, Pakistan naturally had better ties to the Afghan Pashtuns. Iran had better ties to the Shia Hazara and groups in the west, but Iran was preoccupied with its eight-year-long war with Iraq, and most of its resources were diverted to fighting on its western border. The Saudi government also supported its favorites and encouraged groups that shared the kingdom's militant Wahhabi Islam.

All the Afghan mujahedin who operated from bases in Pakistan were Sunni Muslim. Over time they consolidated into seven groups that became known as political parties, four of which were often labeled Islamist and three of which were labeled traditionalist. The distinctions are helpful but also somewhat arbitrary. Islamists wanted an Islamic government to come to power, while traditionalists were more willing to see a return of the monarchy and somewhat more secular rule. That said, all were deeply religious and wanted a Muslim, not atheist, government. The seven parties had only loose control over the fighters on the ground inside Afghanistan, and for the most part their leaders spent the war in comparative safety inside Pakistan. They were not political parties in the Western sense, although that is what they were called at the time. In reality, they corresponded to and represented the tribal, ethnic, and ideological identity of the bands of fighters that operated loosely under their oversight. Often their leaders were more warlords than politicians.

The Islamist parties included both radical and somewhat more moderate elements. The most radical was Hezb-i Islami (Party of Islam), which was strongest around Kandahar. It was led by Gulbuddin Hekmatyar. Born in 1950, Hekmatyar was a Pashtun student activist during the monarchy who became infamous for his rough methods. As early as 1972, he fled into exile in Pakistan after serving time in prison for murder. He was the ISI's favorite and got more aid than any other mujahedin leader. Jamiat-e Islami (Society of Islam) was headed by Burhanuddin Rabbani, a Tajik; its strength was in the Tajik northern territories. The third Islamist group, led by Abdul Rasul Sayyaf, called itself Ittihad-i-Islam Bara-I Azadi Afghanistan (Islamic Union for the Liberation of Afghanistan).

The fourth group was a breakaway faction of Hezb-i Islami that used the same name. Its leader was Maulana Yunis Khalis, another Pashtun, who was born in 1919 and educated at Al Azhar University in Cairo. He was the mujahedin leader most favored by the Saudis because his puritanical view of Islam was closer to that of their Wahhabi faith, and he was famous for throwing acid in the faces of unveiled women at Kabul University in his youth. The Islamist parties were stronger players in the war than either the traditionalists or the Shia groups based in Iran. They did the bulk of the fighting and got most of the outside aid.

The largest traditionalist or more moderate party was the Mahaz-i-Milli-i-Islami (National Islamic Front), headed by Sayyid Ahmad Gailani, a wealthy businessman from Kabul who claimed to be a direct descendant of the prophet Muhammad. He supported the return of King Zahir, alienating the Pakistanis who had no fondness for the royal family. Another royalist was Sebghatullah Mujadidi, who led the Jabha-i-Nijat-i-Milli (National Liberation Front). He had spent many years in exile in Denmark before the war. Finally, Maulvi Nabi Muhammadi, another Pashtun, headed Harakat-i-Inqilab-i-Islami (Islamic Revolution Movement). The three traditionalist parties attracted fewer fighters than the Islamists and got less ISI (and CIA) aid. Because they were weaker, after the Soviets left their leaders often were acceptable compromise candidates for positions in the postcommunist government.

The mujahedin had other strengths and weaknesses. The average Afghan fighter was very brave; indeed, the culture placed a high premium on the display of courage under fire. At the same time, that meant that Afghan insurgents were averse to carrying out sabotage because it seemed unmanly and dishonorable. The ISI, for example, pressed hard to encourage the mujahedin commanders to come up with a plan to sabotage the Salang Tunnel with explosive truck bombs. Despite many efforts to convince the commanders to destroy the tunnel and thus cut off supplies to half the Russian army, the mujahedin never carried out the plan. In his memoirs, Mohammad Yousaf, the ISI commander in charge of the Afghan war, writes that "it would have been a magnificent Mujahedin victory, crippling a modern army for weeks, but sadly it was not to be." He points to the character of the Afghan fighter for the failure to destroy the tunnel.[4] In keeping with the warrior traditions of the Afghan nation, the insurgents preferred to conduct ambushes and firefights. It was the strategy of a thousand cuts, as Yousaf calls it, and it was how Afghanistan had defeated the British in the First Anglo-Afghan War. It was classic guerrilla warfare, and fortunately for the insurgents, they had a number of commanders who excelled in it.

This chapter takes an in-depth look at two of the most successful mujahedin leaders—Ahmad Shah Massoud and Jalaluddin Haqqani—and the groups that they led. Their experiences were crucial to the insurgents' success in two pivotal areas, the Panjsher Valley north of Kabul and Paktia and Khost provinces south of the capital. To bring victory to the PDPA, the Soviets had to win control in those two theaters of operation and the territory that they abutted. When they lost both, the outcome of the war was settled. By the end of the war, Ahmad Shah Massoud's largely Tajik force controlled most of northeast Afghanistan. By controlling the Panjsher Valley near the exit of the Salang Tunnel, it threatened the crucial supply line for the 40th Red Army and the capital itself. Although he spent five years in Pakistan before the 1979 coup, much of it in training with the Pakistani intelligence service, Massoud received little aid from Pakistan and the United States during the war. He was largely on his own, with some valuable but limited British assistance.

In contrast, Jalaluddin Haqqani's Pashtun force fought along the Durand Line in the crucial provinces south of Kabul across the border from Pakistan's Federally Administered Tribal Area (FATA). The FATA is another British legacy. Rather than trying to rule directly in these remote mountains, the Raj allowed local tribal leaders to run their own affairs with minimal British involvement, thereby saving costs and avoiding conflict. After partition, in 1947, the Pakistani government simply continued that policy. The Haqqani family was the beneficiary of that benign neglect in the Waziristan area, and in the 1980s it formed the mujahedin group most closely aligned with Pakistan. It remains so today.

The Lion of the Panjsher

The formative experience in the life of Ahmad Shah Massoud, by his own account, was the Israeli air force attack on Egypt that began the war between Israel and its Arab neighbors in June 1967. The 14-year-old Ahmad, the son of an army colonel, was fixated on the war, and for six nights and days he listened to the BBC Persian service for news from the battlefields of the Sinai, West Bank, Golan Heights, and Jerusalem. The Six-Day War was the first military campaign that he followed in real time, and his interest in military affairs became an obsession. At school he would lecture his classmates on battles and on why Israel had won its dramatic victory over its Islamic enemies. Years later he told a biographer that the 1967 conflict not only made him determined to be a soldier but also exposed him to Islamic nationalism. Massoud no longer saw himself only as a Panjsheri or a Tajik or an Afghan, he saw himself as part of a broader Islamic struggle against the enemies of Islam. He told his interviewer that the experiences of Jordanian soldiers fighting to defend Jerusalem and Egyptians and Syrians fighting to defend their countries had profoundly moved him.[5]

For the next four years Massoud continued his studies at a French-run school in Kabul, where he became fluent in French and an admirer of Charles de Gaulle. In the fall of 1972 he entered Kabul Polytechnic University. During that time he also became a member of the Muslim Youth Movement, an Afghan Islamist group with connections to the Muslim Brotherhood. The Muslim Brotherhood, the oldest Islamist political party in Egypt, has inspired similar political parties and movements in many Muslim countries and provided them modest financial assistance and ideological direction.

Massoud's life was transformed by the Daoud coup against King Zahir in July 1973. The new government of Afghanistan was at first pro-Soviet and heavily influenced by the PDPA, and Massoud and other *ikhwanis*—or brothers, as they called themselves—had to go underground to avoid arrest by the regime. In August 1974, they attempted a coup against Daoud that failed, and Massoud had to flee into exile in Pakistan. There he began working with another major figure in Islamist politics in Afghanistan, Gulbuddin Hekmatyar. Born in 1948 to a peasant family, Gulbuddin was older than Massoud and already famous as a violent and ruthless student activist at Kabul University.[6] As a Pashtun, Gulbuddin was much more at home in Peshawar, Pakistan, than a Tajik like Massoud. Gulbuddin set up a new party, Hezb-i Islami, which Massoud joined in 1974. Together they plotted another coup attempt in 1975. By that time, Gulbuddin was already getting support from Pakistan's intelligence service, the Directorate for Inter-Services Intelligence (ISI), which was looking for assets to use against the Daoud government in the Pashtunistan quarrel.

Massoud made a clandestine return to the Panjsher Valley the spring of 1975 and launched an insurrection there in June, expecting a coup led by Gulbuddin's supporters to take place in Kabul at the same time. Nothing happened in Kabul, and Massoud was left in the lurch in the valley. Again he had to flee into Pakistan, but this time he broke with Gulbuddin and helped form another political party, Jamiat-e Islami, led by Burhanuddin Rabbani, an Islamic scholar and a fellow Tajik from Badakhshan Province in Afghanistan's far northeast. Rabbani was born in 1940. He had studied at Al Azhar University in Cairo, the most prestigious and oldest Islamic university in the world, in the 1960s. He translated the works of Sayyid Qutb, the most influential Muslim Brotherhood ideologue of all time, into Persian and Dari. He had worked in Saudi Arabia, where he developed close ties to some members of the Saudi royal family, which provided him with financial backing.[7]

For two years Massoud studied military affairs at an ISI-run training school outside of Peshawar. While the ISI favored the Pashtun Hekmatyar group, in the mid-1970s it was looking for as many Afghan protégés as possible. In Pakistan, Massoud carefully studied the guerilla warfare writings of Che Guevara, Mao Tse-tung, and Ho Chi Minh and tried to adapt their teachings to Afghanistan and especially his homeland, the Panjsher Valley.[8] When General Mohammed Zia ul-Haq overthrew the elected government of Zulfikar Ali Bhutto in 1977, the new regime became increasingly Islamic and less tolerant of Afghans like Massoud, who were not regarded as fully loyal to the ISI. Still, Massoud stayed in Pakistan working with the ISI until the Saur Revolution in 1978.

With the PDPA now clearly in charge in Kabul, rural uprisings began across Afghanistan. Mujahedin groups along the border with Pakistan immediately began to receive aid from the ISI and both Hekmatyar and Massoud. In May 1979, with a small cadre of two dozen followers, the 27-year-old Massoud slipped across the border and made his way home to the Panjsher Valley to begin his insurgency, applying the lessons that he had learned in Peshawar. Massoud proved to be a genius at guerilla warfare. Within months he had consolidated his control of the Panjsheri Tajiks and began attacking the communists. His raids alarmed Moscow, as his success threatened the key highway linking Kabul to the north and the Soviet border via the Salang Pass as well as the key air base at Bagram. A key component of the December Soviet intervention was the deployment of Soviet units to guard the highway and pass from the air base at Bagram.

The Panjsher Valley runs from the northeast of Afghanistan down to the southwest, where it opens just north of the Bagram air base. It is not far from the Salang Tunnel and the road running from Kabul to the Russian border, which was the jugular vein of the 40th Army. The tunnel itself, a masterpiece of Soviet engineering, was blasted through solid rock in 1964; at an elevation of 11,000 feet, it was the highest tunnel in the world at the time. It is two lanes wide and 2.5 kilometers long, but it has inadequate ventilation. More than one observer has called it a "death trap." An accident in the tunnel in 1982 killed 900 Russians and Afghans after vehicle upon vehicle piled up in a crash.[9]

The 40th Red Army launched six major offensives between April 1980 and September 1982 to try to defeat Massoud's forces and clear the Panjsher of the insurgency. Each offensive was progressively more sophisticated and complex, using special forces, armor, helicopter gunships, and bombers. All failed to defeat the Tajik fighters. This has been accurately described by Afghan, Pakistani, and Soviet experts as "by far the most pivotal time" in the entire war. Had the Russians won in the first two years and defeated Massoud, the insurgency might have lost critical territory, momentum, and morale. However, Massoud did not lose, and he avoided losing largely without any foreign assistance in the early months of the war.[10] He became a legend—the "Lion of the Panjsher"—and "a symbol of hope for the anti-communist resistance"[11] at home, inside Afghanistan, and around the world. A BBC television team covered the last offensive in 1982 and broadcast coverage of the battles that made Massoud a hero.

Massoud displayed great personal courage in fighting. He was active on the battlefield in the early days, as a fighter as well as a commander. He was severely wounded in 1979, yet stayed in the campaign. The Russians, who had tried to kill him more than once, came to see him as a very dangerous foe. But he was also very pragmatic. By 1983 the Panjsher Valley was under great strain, and the civilian population was suffering immensely from the fighting and bombing. So when the KGB offered a cease-fire for a year, Massoud agreed despite criticism from other mujahedin commanders and from the ISI. The cease-fire was largely observed by both sides, but it was not renewed in 1984 and the fighting began again. By the end of the Soviet occupation of Kabul in 1989, Massoud's forces controlled not just the Panjsher Valley but the better part of seven provinces in northeastern Afghanistan. It was an extraordinary accomplishment for a man who was still under 40 years of age. Throughout the war Massoud's forces got only limited assistance from the ISI and CIA, in part because of the Pakistani preference for the Pashtun parties and the more radical Islamist warlords like Hekmatyar. The cease-fire often was used as an excuse not to send more arms to the Tajiks. Geography also played a part: it was simply harder to get aid to the Panjsher than to the border provinces along the Durand Line. However, Massoud found an ally in the British secret intelligence service, MI6, which partly filled the gap in aid left by Pakistan. Prime Minister Margaret Thatcher was an enthusiastic supporter of the Afghan war and wanted the United Kingdom to do its own part on the battlefield. She also was more willing to take risks with her spies than her U.S. counterparts were. MI6 was authorized to send small teams of intelligence officers and retired commandoes into Afghanistan to train and equip Massoud's forces. It was an extraordinarily dangerous operation, and the British had absolutely no hope of rescue if captured by the Russians or the PDPA. Twice a year, a small band of seven or eight British intelligence officers would leave Pakistan to infiltrate the Pansjher Valley to deliver key pieces of equipment, such as secure radios and sniper rifles with silencers. The teams would also train Massoud's mujahedin in using small-unit tactics and building improvised explosive devices. Some of Massoud's men went to the United Kingdom for training at MI6 facilities in Scotland and Sussex. British support was small in comparison with the larger U.S. effort with Pakistan, but it was critical to the Tajik war. MI6 also provided equipment to the ISI effort, some of which failed (Blowpipe missiles) and some of which succeeded (limpet mines).[12]

Ahmad Shah Massoud's Tajik forces played a key role in the capture of Kabul in 1992, when the communist Najibullah-led regime finally collapsed. Massoud went on to be defense minister in the new successor mujahdedin government led by Rabbani. He defended the city against attacks by Gulbuddin Hekmatyar's forces in 1992–95 and then by the Afghan Taliban in 1996–98. Both of those forces enjoyed the backing of the Pakistanis and the ISI. Massoud got aid from Iran, India, and Russia, but it was much more limited than the aid that the Pakistanis gave to Hekmatyar and the Taliban. Massoud left Kabul when the Taliban closed in and retreated to his stronghold in the Panjsher Valley and Badakhshan Province, in the remote northeastern corner of the country. As the Taliban gradually consolidated control over the rest of the country, Massoud became the last bastion of resistance and the de facto leader of the anti-Taliban faction, called the Northern Alliance.

Massoud was a very private man who avoided the limelight, even though it sought him. He was supposed to appear at a meeting that Bill Richardson had with the rest of the Northern Alliance in Shibirghan but failed to show, despite having frequently said that he wanted more U.S. support. After returning from Pakistan in 1979, he did not travel outside the country until April 2001, when he made a trip to Belgium and France to ask for European support against the Taliban. He pressed European leaders in the EU parliament in Strasbourg to pressure the Pakistanis to stop helping the Taliban. He told them that "without Pakistan's support, the Taliban's military campaigns would not even last a year." He also met with CIA officers in Paris to discuss getting aid from the United States.[13]

By the time that Massoud returned, his men controlled less than 10 percent of the country. They were the last significant military force confronting the Taliban and their Arab ally, Osama bin Laden's al Qaeda terrorist group. Al Qaeda planned Massoud's death carefully. On bin Laden's orders, an al Qaeda cell in Brussels organized the attack. Belgium has a considerable community of Muslims, most from Morocco, Tunisia, or Turkey; many live in run-down neighborhoods with high unemployment that are fertile recruiting grounds for the jihad.

On September 9, 2001, two al Qaeda assassins posing as journalists entered Massoud's office and set up their camera. They asked one question, about Osama bin Laden, and when Massoud replied, they detonated the explosives hidden in the camera. Massoud was fatally wounded and died within a few minutes. The cameraman died instantly, and his companion was killed trying to run away. Later bin Laden sent one assassin's widow a letter in which he included some money and a martyr tape of her husband telling her that he loved her but that he was "already on the other side" in heaven.[14]

The assassination of Massoud ended the career of perhaps the most brilliant mujahedin commander of the war against the Soviet 40th Red Army and a major political figure in the history of modern Afghanistan. It also set the stage for the attacks on the United States on September 11, 2001. On 9/11, like many CIA officers with Afghan experience, I instantly linked the two events together. Massoud had been killed because he would have been too great a threat to al Qaeda and the Taliban if he had been alive after the 9/11 attacks. Today, September 9—Massoud Day or Martyrs' Day—is a national holiday in Afghanistan, honoring his life and death. His tomb in Saricha in the Panjsher Valley is a pilgrimage site for many Afghans.[15]

Fountainhead of Jihad: Haqqani

Jalaluddin Haqqani is still alive. He founded a dynasty of warlords that remains active and important to this day as a crucial part of the Afghan Taliban movement, a major source of support for al Qaeda, and a tool of the ISI. Admiral Mike Mullen, former chairman of the Joint Chiefs of Staff, called the Haqqani network "a veritable arm" of the ISI in 2011. Yet until recently the story of Jalaluddin Haqqani had never been comprehensively explored and researched. That omission in the history of the Afghan war was corrected in 2012 by researchers at the Combating Terrorism Center at the U.S. Military Academy at West Point, who drew on sources collected in Afghanistan and Pakistan and translated for the first time into English.[16] Their portrait of Haqqani has rewritten some of the key aspects of the war, particularly by highlighting the crucial importance of the Zhawar military base to the success of the ISI and the mujahedin.

Jalaluddin was born in 1939 in Paktia Province into the family of a relatively well-to-do landowner who did business in both Afghanistan and Pakistan and was wealthy enough to provide his sons with an advanced religious education. Unlike Massoud, who pursued a largely secular education in a French-run school in the capital, Jalaluddin studied for six years at the Dar al-Ulum Haqqaniyya madrassa in Pakistan. Located in a village about thirty miles outside Peshawar, the Haqqaniyya madrassa was founded in 1947 in the Deobandi tradition of militant Sunni Islam, which predominates in the Pashtun community today. The Deobandi school has its origins in the uprising against the British East India Company in 1857, known also as the Indian Mutiny or the First Indian War for Independence. It has long been associated with the militant Wahhabi faith of Saudi Arabia. Many other key mujahedin figures graduated from the Haqqaniyya madrassa, including Yunis Khalis, another major warlord of the 1980s. After graduating from the school in 1970, Jalaluddin made the pilgrimage to Mecca, the hajj, and became active in politics at home in Afghanistan.[17]

As it was for Massoud, the 1973 coup in Kabul by Daoud against King Zahir would be a turning point in Haqqani's life. He too began working with the ISI in Pakistan's effort to destabilize Afghanistan in retaliation for Daoud's support for Pashtunistan. Using his credentials as a religious scholar, Jalaluddin declared a jihad against the Daoud government. For all practical purposes, that jihad would continue against Daoud, then the PDPA, and then the enemies of the Taliban. Haqqani began working with both the ISI and Hekmatyar from bases in Pakistan—again, much as Massoud did. In 1974 Haqqani also was part of the attempt at a national insurrection and a coup against Daoud that failed. However, unlike Massoud, Haqqani continued to work with Hekmatyar as well as with Yunis Khalis after the failure of the coup.[18]

The Saur Revolution and the communist takeover in Kabul added urgency to the ISI's support for Pashtun insurgents like Haqqani, who organized an increasingly effective insurgency in Khost, Paktia, and Nangarhar provinces from base camps in Pakistan's tribal area. His networks were tribal based and crossed the border naturally because the tribes straddled the border. By the time of the Soviet invasion, Haqqani's network was the most effective mujahedin force in eastern Afghanistan.

With his large beard and commanding presence, Jalaluddin was a charismatic and popular leader. One American journalist witnessed him at work in 1981.

> The men gathered in a circle like players do around their coach before a game. It was Azon, the call for jihad. Jalaluddin prayed and each man bowed, then raised his hands to the sky, palms upwards, to receive the blessings of Allah. For a moment it was silent; then each man, single file, passed underneath an unwound turban held by two men over the path. A Koran lay wrapped in the cloth. They shouted, raised their rifles.[19]

The combination of Haqqani's religious scholarship, tribal affiliation, and charismatic appeal made him a powerful player in the mujahedin. He also benefited tremendously from Pakistani support; in practice, that meant that he also was a big beneficiary of U.S. support, because CIA assistance moved through the ISI. At the start of the war against the Russians, the Pakistanis were careful to keep the logistics and base camps on their side of the border. But by 1981 they were ready for bolder moves, and they selected Haqqani as the principal recipient of their help. In 1981 the Haqqani network began to build a vast military base in the Zhawar Valley, just four kilometers inside Khost Province from the Pakistani border. It was expanded regularly over the course of the decade. The facilities were in a deep canyon that made air attack difficult. The canyon opened south, facing Pakistan and the ISI's largest base, at Miram Shah, fifteen kilometers away, in nearby Waziristan.[20]

The Zhawar base was the first major training facility for the ISI, built by the mujahedin inside the borders of Afghanistan. It grew to include a hospital, machine workshop, garage, numerous reinforced caves for arms storage, VIP hotel, mosque, and a radio station broadcasting the Voice of Afghanistan in Pashto, Dari, Uzbek, and Russian. According to Pakistani sources, including the ISI officer running operations in Afghanistan, up to 60 percent of Pakistani aid to the insurgency ran through the Zhawar base and facilities nearby.[21] To protect the camp, the Pakistani army provided its own forces and also relied on a 500-man special Zhawar Regiment of Pashtun mujahedin. At Zhawar, the Pakistani army and ISI were directly on the front line with the 40th Red Army. The Defense Intelligence Agency noted that the Zhawar base was "built by Pakistani contractors, funded by the ISI, and protected under the patronage of Jalaluddin Haqqani [while] the real host in the facility was the ISI.'[22]

The Russians and PDPA attacked the Zhawar camp in three major assaults between 1985 and 1987. The last attack, in 1987, was part of the largest Soviet offensive operation of the entire war.[23] The first attack, in 1985, was carried out largely by Afghan army forces with Soviet air support. Haqqani was in Saudi Arabia when the battle began and arrived only at the end. The Afghan communists, who suffered very heavy casualties in forty-two days of combat, failed to seize the camp.[24]

The Pakistanis decided to defend the Zhawar camp in 1986 by taking a conventional warfare approach using Haqqani's mujahedin backed by Pakistani advisers. That decision was contrary to guerrilla warfare theory, which argues for abandoning ground to conventional forces, and it was a controversial one within the ISI. A combined Soviet and Afghan communist force of 12,000 soldiers attacked the base camp. Losses were severe on both sides. The mujahedin's biggest weakness was air defense. The best surface-to-air missile system in their inventory in 1986 was a British-supplied system called Blowpipe, which was operated by Pakistani soldiers because of its technical complexity. It was totally ineffective against the Soviet air attacks. The Blowpipe had been recommended by the CIA and the British even though it had been ineffective in the Falklands war, when the British used it against Argentina.[25]

During the attack Jalaluddin was badly wounded and had to be evacuated, and the base was briefly overrun by the Soviets.[26] The campaign to take the base took place over fifty-seven days, but due to continued pressure by the mujahedin, the Russians and Afghan communists held the facility for only five hours after they finally took it. Russian losses, including two dozen helicopters, were very heavy. The Soviet commander was amazed by the quality of the facility, which had its own electricity. The hospital had the latest American medical equipment, including an ultrasound machine; the caves were full of weapons and ammunition from around the world; and the VIP hotel had nice carpets. When the Soviets withdrew, the ISI and mujahedin rebuilt and expanded the camp. The caves were expanded to 400 to 500 meters in length.[27]

The 1987 ground campaign focused more on opening a Soviet supply line to the nearby city of Khost, which was encircled by Haqqani's forces, but the Soviet and Afghan communist air forces also focused on the Zhawar base. Ten thousand Russian and 8,000 Afghan army troops were involved in the operation, including elite Soviet airborne units. Haqqani mobilized his mujahedin, many Arab volunteers, and hundreds of Pakistani commandoes from the Special Services Group (SSG) of the Pakistani army. The road to Khost was briefly reopened, but the siege continued and the Zhawar base was not significantly damaged.[28]

Jalaluddin also benefited from support from another quarter, the Saudis and Saudi volunteers led by Osama bin Laden. The Saudi ambassador in Pakistan, Yousef Mottakbani, provided money and aid directly to Haqqani in addition to Saudi financial support for the ISI.[29] Bin Laden was the son of the kingdom's wealthiest builder, Mohammed bin Awad bin Laden. His company, which was worth billions, had constructed highways, airports, ports, and palaces across Saudi Arabia in addition to expanding and improving the holy mosques in Medina, Mecca, and Jerusalem. After the second battle at Zhawar, bin Laden helped in the reconstruction of the camp and several other nearby facilities. One was called the Lion's Den or al Qaeda al Askariyya, which is translated as "the military base." Later he would call his terrorist organization al Qaeda, the base.[30] Osama imported heavy construction equipment from his father's company in Saudi Arabia and supervised much of the work himself, becoming a "combat engineer," as one biographer put it.[31]

Haqqani had been the first mujahedin commander to welcome and invite foreign fighters to join his Pashtun forces in the war. Given his strong connections to Saudi Arabia, he was especially enthusiastic about getting Saudi and other Arab volunteers for his forces. The Arab fighters were always a small minority of the insurgents, and many came for only a brief period. Osama bin Laden stayed for most of the war and developed a strong connection to Haqqani. When the Soviets left Afghanistan, Jalaluddin Haqqani continued fighting the PDPA regime. He participated in the struggle that led to the collapse of the Najibullah regime in 1992. Haqqani joined with the Afghan Taliban movement in the 1990s and remains an integral part of the Taliban to this day. His sons now manage the day-to-day affairs of the network, which has become one of the deadliest and most effective enemies of U.S. forces in Afghanistan and the U.S.-supported Afghan government. It is responsible for hundreds of attacks on U.S., NATO, and Afghan National Army soldiers.

In the 1980s, the story was different. Congressman Charlie Wilson, the most effective supporter of the Afghan mujahedin in the 1980s and the subject of a major Hollywood movie about the conflict, visited Haqqani and praised him highly. The U.S. Embassy in Islamabad considered Haqqani the finest and most capable Pashtun commander in the war. The CIA regularly met with him face to face.[32] Contrary to some assertions, however, Haqqani did not visit the White House and meet with President Reagan. A mujahedin delegation did visit Washington and meet with Reagan, but it included Rabbani and Khalis, not Haqqani. The one constant in Haqqani's long career has been his connection with the ISI and Pakistan. Despite numerous changes in Pakistani politics—from Zulfikar Bhutto to Zia ul-Haq, Benazir Bhutto, Nawaz Sharif, Pervez Musharraf, Asif Ali Zardari, and now back to Nawaz Sharif—the Haqqani connection has remained strong and vibrant.

There were many other important commanders of the mujahedin insurgency in the 1980s. The insurgency was organized over time into seven political parties in Pakistan and several more in Iran. Each had its own commanders in the field. But Ahmad Shah Massoud and Jalaluddin Haqqani stand out as perhaps the two best military commanders of the war. The campaigns in the Panjsher Valley and the Zhawar Valley involved only a few of the hundreds of engagements in which the 40th Red Army fought, but they may be the two most important of the conflict.

CHAPTER FOUR

THE PAKISTANIS: ZIA'S WAR

BLACK SEPTEMBER MADE General Mohammed Zia ul-Haq a success. In the fall of 1970, the civil war that erupted in Jordan between King Hussein's small army and the Palestinian fedayeen movement, led by Yasser Arafat, provided the opportunity for Zia, an unknown Pakistani general, to make his mark and thereby become an up-and-comer in the Pakistani army back home. While Zia was a winner in Jordan, the rest of the Pakistani army, following the 1971 war with India, was on the verge of catastrophic failure at home. The contrast made Zia's career in Jordan all the more memorable. Zia would go on to become the moving force behind the war against the 40th Red Army. If any single person was responsible for the defeat of the USSR and the PDPA, it was Zia ul-Haq.

In the wake of Israel's stunning victory over four Arab armies in June 1967 in the Six-Day War, Arafat set up a state-within-the-state in Jordan. In the late 1960s, the Palestinian fedayeen ("fighters who sacrifice themselves") flooded into Jordan, threatening the survival of the Hashemite monarchy. Arafat and the Palestine Liberation Organization (PLO) had the backing of the Soviets and their allies in the Arab world, especially Syria and Iraq. In September 1970 the radical Popular Front for the Liberation of Palestine (PFLP) hijacked four commercial passenger jets. One was blown up at Cairo airport, and the other three were landed at a remote desert airstrip in Jordan. The PFLP demanded that Israel release Palestinian prisoners in Israeli jails in order to get the hostages released. The spectacular hijackings ignited a civil war between the Jordanian army and the fedayeen. The king narrowly escaped an assassination attempt by the Palestinians, and the Jordanian army retaliated with a harsh crackdown on the PLO. Amman became a war zone, and the survival of the monarchy was very much in doubt. It appeared that Jordan was about to become another Soviet client state in the Muslim world.

In 1970 Zia ul-Haq was a member of the Pakistani defense attaché's staff in Amman, having been posted there three years earlier. As such, he was to facilitate cooperation between Pakistan and Jordan on military matters and to observe and report back to his superiors at home on events in Jordan. He did much more. According to Jack O'Connell, the CIA chief in Jordan in 1970 and a longtime adviser to King Hussein, Zia helped organize the Jordanian army's offensive against the Palestinians, and he led Jordanian forces into battle. He was then given the crucial task of assessing Syria's intentions and capabilities at the pivotal moment of the war. To help the Palestinians, the Syrian government had invaded northern Jordan with several armored brigades, which quickly overran the Jordanian army's position on the border and headed toward Amman.

King Hussein sent Zia to the front to assess the danger and recommend a course of action. O'Connell reports that Zia said that the situation was very grave. He recommended deploying the small but efficient Royal Jordanian Air Force to stop the Syrians, using colorful language to impress on the king just how desperate the situation on the ground was. The king took his advice, and the tide of battle turned in favor of the Jordanians.[1] The royal family deeply appreciated Zia's help. Years later the king's brother Hassan, who was then the crown prince, described Zia to me as the king's "friend and confidant," adding that "he was a well-respected figure, a professional soldier, and . . . he not only advised on military tactics, he also earned the respect and trust of the *jundis* [soldiers].[2] The Pakistani military delegation in Amman was less pleased, since he had certainly exceeded his diplomatic authority and perhaps his orders in fighting with the Jordanians.[3]

In the fall and winter of 1970–71 Pakistan was heading toward its own civil war. In March 1971 Pakistan's second military dictator, Yahya Khan, had cracked down on dissent among the majority Bengali community in East Pakistan in a brutal massacre that took up to 3 million lives and led to the brief war with India in December 1971 that resulted in the creation of Bangladesh. Pakistan's generals were badly discredited by the catastrophe, in which 90,000 soldiers were taken prisoner by India, and to add insult to injury, the top two commanders of the victorious Indian army were a Hindu and a Jew.④ That disaster brought Pakistan's civilians back to govern the country, and Zulfikar Ali Bhutto became the country's leader. Bhutto needed generals who were popular but also loyal, and King Hussein recommended to Zulfi (Bhutto's nickname) that he promote Zia for his performance in Black September. On the king's recommendation, Zia was promoted from brigadier to major general on his return from Jordan. Without the promotion, Zia probably would have retired.⑤

Five years later, in February 1976, Zulfi appointed Zia chief of army staff, skipping over several more senior officers because he was convinced that Zia was a loyal sycophant. Zia had helped investigate a plot among army officers to mount a coup against Bhutto, and he had arranged a royal visit to Islamabad by Crown Prince Hassan, during which Zia had been obsequious and deferential to Bhutto. Bhutto was supremely confident that Zia was totally apolitical and too weak to challenge his control, going so far as to call Zia his "monkey general" at dinner parties and in front of foreign guests.⑥ The new elections that took place in 1977 were rigged, leading to widespread urban protests, and on July 5, 1977, the "monkey general" overthrew Bhutto, thereby becoming Pakistan's third military dictator. The code name for the coup was Operation Fair Play. After months of imprisonment, Bhutto was executed on charges of murder. Zia had refused pleas for mercy from around the world, including several from President Jimmy Carter.

Zia was born on August 12, 1924. His father was employed by the British army headquarters in New Delhi, and Zia joined the army in 1944. His class was the last to graduate from the Indian military academy before the end of the Raj and partition. Among his classmates was his future director general of the Directorate for Inter-Services Intelligence (ISI), Akhtar Abdur Rahman.⑦ The earlier generation of Pakistani military dictators, Ayub Khan and Yahya Khan, had been fairly secular, but Zia was an Islamist. When Zulfi visited Zia's residence in Rawalpindi before the coup, he had noticed that all the photos on the walls were of Mecca and other Islamic sites and remarked, "General, you have turned your living room into a mosque."⑧ Zia depicted himself as a pious Muslim and aligned himself with the country's Islamist political party, the Jamaat-e Islami; he also took steps to Islamize the army. He sought and received the endorsement of Islamic extremists, who enthusiastically praised his new regime.[9] Officers were encouraged to join communal prayers with their troops, and for the first time promotion boards reviewed officers' moral and religious behavior in addition to their performance of their normal military duties. The army's motto was changed from "Unity, Faith, and Discipline" to "Faith, Obedience to God, and Struggle in the Path of Allah" (Iman, Taqwa, Jihad fi Sabeelillah). Shuja Nawaz, the foremost expert on the Pakistani army today, concludes that "Islamization was the legacy he left Pakistan."[10] Zia also was ambitious. He declared at the height of the Afghan war in the 1980s that "we have earned the right to have a friendly regime in Afghanistan. We took risks as a frontline state, and we won't permit it to be like it was before, with Indian and Soviet influence there and claims on our territory. It will be a real Islamic state, part of a pan-Islamic revival that will one day win over the Muslims of the Soviet Union; you will see it."[11]

One measure of the Islamization process under Zia was the growth in Islamic schools, or madrassas, whose diplomas Zia recognized as equivalent to those from universities. The number of such schools grew enormously on Zia's watch, as did their influence throughout Pakistan. In 1971 there were 900 madrassas in the country; by 1988 there were 8,000 official religious schools and another 25,000 unregistered ones.[12] The army's role in Pakistani society also expanded. Pakistan's first military dictator, Ayub Khan, had begun a process whereby retiring army officers were given state land in rural areas to improve their retirement pensions and to encourage rural development. Zia expanded the program and also began giving favored officers prime pieces of property in Pakistan's growing urban areas. The practice would continue, and by 1999 the armed forces, as a group, owned the largest share of urban real estate in Pakistan.[13]

Above all, the ISI grew. Its director general was Zia's former classmate Akhtar Abdur Rahman—better known simply as General Akhtar—a Pashtun who knew the Afghan world well. His own subordinates described him as "a cold, reserved personality, almost inscrutable, always secretive."[14] Akhtar fought in the 1948, 1965, and 1971 wars with India; consequently, he saw India as Pakistan's "implacable enemy." He taught for several years at the Kakul Military Academy, and he was posted to England for advanced military training in the late 1960s. He was Zia's handpicked choice for director general of ISI in 1979. So close was their relationship that the two lived in adjacent bungalows at army headquarters in Rawalpindi until their deaths.[15] Akhtar hated publicity and the press, avoided being photographed, and was "inscrutable" to even his most senior lieutenants, but he was a gifted intelligence officer.[16] He developed close working ties to many of the Afghan mujahedin leaders, especially fellow Pashtuns, and organized them into political parties to give more legitimacy to their struggle. Akhtar also built strong links between ISI and the CIA and the Saudis.

At Zia's direction, Akhtar vastly expanded the size and strength of the service. According to one estimate, the ISI went from having a staff of 2,000 in 1978 to having 40,000 employees and a billion-dollar budget by 1988.[17] It came to be seen in Pakistan as omnipotent, allegedly having informants in every village, city block, and public space and tapping every telephone call. Politicians were on its payroll, and its enemies simply disappeared. Much of its growth was intended to keep Zia in power, but much of it was to wage jihad. One of Akhtar's deputies would later say that "the ISI was and still is probably the most powerful and influential organization in the country"; he also remarked that Akhtar was "regarded with envy or fear," even by his fellow officers.[18] In short, Zia bequeathed Pakistan an "incendiary mix of despotism and Islamization."[19]

The ISI's War

When the Soviets invaded Afghanistan, Zia asked General Akhtar for an appraisal of the threat posed by the invasion. Akhtar predicted that sooner or later the Russians would invade Baluchistan, seeking a warm-water port on the Arabian Sea. In his assessment, Pakistan was caught between the Russians to the west and India to the east and sooner or later they would join together to destroy Pakistan. To prevent that, he recommended that Pakistan substantially increase its aid to the mujahedin, thereby bogging Moscow down in a quagmire; if the 40th Army was neutralized by the mujahedin, it would not be able to threaten Pakistan.[20] But because it provoked the Soviets even as it tried to defeat them, it was a high-risk strategy. Zia had another worry as well. After several years out of power, Indira Gandhi was reelected prime minister of India in January 1980. It was a landslide victory; Indira's Congress Party won 351 of the 542 seats in the parliament. Like all Pakistani generals, Zia feared Indira more than other Indian politicians; after all, she had already helped break up the union of East and West Pakistan. Indira regarded Zia as just another Pakistani general, like those that she had defeated decisively in 1971.[21] With Indira back in New Delhi and the Soviets in Kabul, to Zia the situation looked dire.

Zia dispatched General Akhtar to Riyadh with an urgent message for the king of Saudi Arabia. Zia wanted Saudi assistance to strengthen the mujahedin, the anti-communist rebels in Afghanistan. Saudi support would give Pakistan backing across the Islamic world and access to funds to help the insurgents in Afghanistan and the Zia regime at home. According to Prince Turki, the head of Saudi intelligence, King Khalid agreed immediately, and the ISI and Turki's General Intelligence Directorate (GID) began cooperating to aid the mujahedin. Saudi state money began pouring into the ISI, and Saudi authorities also encouraged Saudi private citizens to give money and to join the jihad. The Saudi-Pakistani partnership would soon acquire another partner, the CIA.[22]

Partly in response, Zia also dispatched a Pakistani expeditionary force of brigade strength to Saudi Arabia to help it defend itself against its regional enemies. The 12th Khalid bin Waleed Independent Armored Brigade would be stationed in Tabuk, Saudi Arabia, near the border with Israel, for over six years, from 1982 to 1988. Reinforced, it had 20,000 men under command at its peak, and the Saudis paid all of its costs.[23] Pakistani officers and enlisted men who went to serve in the brigade got extra pay and the opportunity to make the hajj, the religious pilgrimage to Mecca, at Saudi expense. Some 40,000 Pakistani soldiers served at one time or another in the expeditionary force. While its stated goal was to defend the kingdom from outside aggression, it had the secret task of serving as a praetorian guard for the House of Saud if there was an internal challenge to the royals.[24]

The ISI war in Afghanistan had to be covert. Although Zia and Akhtar wanted to bog Moscow down in a guerrilla war, they did not want to give Russia an excuse to march south to the Arabian Sea or, even worse, to join forces with India in a two-pronged invasion of Pakistan. The pot in Afghanistan had to simmer but not boil, at least at the start; if it did boil, it was Akhtar's job to make it "boil at the right temperature," as Zia told him."[25] Accordingly, the operation was kept quiet and out of the public eye. For most of the war, the headquarters of the ISI Afghan branch had a staff of only 60 officers and 400 junior military personnel, who wore civilian clothes most of the time, even in their office in Rawalpindi.[26] This relatively small cadre managed the operational aspects of the war. It collected and assessed intelligence from all sources available to the ISI; controlled the supply of arms and equipment arriving in Pakistan for the insurgency, including by moving them from Karachi to a logistics camp outside Islamabad at Ojhri and to a smaller camp near Quetta; trained the mujahedin; selected the targets for attacks; determined which mujahedin commander got aid and how much; and handled liaison with the CIA, GID, MI6 (the British intelligence service), and the intelligence agencies of other allies. It deliberately provided only Soviet-produced weapons to the mujahedin in the first five years of the war to ensure that any equipment could plausibly be claimed to have been captured from either the Afghan communist army or the 40th Army rather than supplied by Pakistan.

The supply line provided less than 10,000 tons of materiel a year up to 1983; by 1987, the total was 65,000 tons a year. The vast majority arrived by sea at Karachi, while a small quantity came by air, mostly to Rawalpindi. Eighty percent or more was then moved to the Ojhri camp before being sent to the border, and the rest went to Baluchistan, to the ISI base near Quetta.[27] Training of the mujahedin also began on a small scale. Roughly 3,000 insurgents went through ISI training camps in the first three years of the war, but in the next four (1983–87), some 80,000 mujahedin were trained by ISI instructors.[28] The number of ISI training camps increased from two in 1983 to seven in 1987.

The role of the ISI did not stop at the border. Almost from the start of hostilities against the Russians, General Akhtar ordered ISI teams to cross the Durand Line and go into Afghanistan. He was convinced that only professional Pakistani military officers had the expertise and professionalism to ensure that the insurgents were a capable opponent of the 40th Army. Naturally, this was a high-risk venture. Captured Pakistani military personnel would be a propaganda coup for the Russians and a cause for war. So the officers went in out of uniform, carrying no identifying Pakistani military material. It was dangerous work, especially as many of the teams were small, composed of only a handful of officers working with mujahedin bands. Later larger formations of ISI forces would go in, even units of the Special Services Group (SSG), as in the third Zahwar battle. Even in the earlier days of the war, there could be up to a dozen ISI undercover teams inside Afghanistan at any one time.[29]

Since Pakistan was taking all the risks, Zia and Akhtar insisted on full Pakistani control of the war and demanded what would later be called "Reagan rules" for managing the relationship between the ISI and the CIA. The ISI would have sole and complete access to the mujahedin. Aside from photo ops for visiting VIPs such as members of Congress, Vice President Bush, CIA big wigs, and others, the Americans had no sustained contact with the mujahedin fighters. All training of the insurgents was done by Pakistani soldiers. If the CIA provided equipment that required special training (like the Stinger missiles), CIA personnel trained Pakistanis, who in turn trained the mujahedin. In short, the Americans "paid the piper but they did not call the tune."[30]

Bob Gates would later write that the "CIA could cajole and exert pressure, but President Muhammad Zia ul Haq and the ISI were the 'deciders.'"[31] They decided the pace of the war, which leaders got what weapons, and what the targets were. For the most part, the ISI's opinion of the CIA was not favorable. Bill Casey, Reagan's director of central intelligence, was the exception. He was well regarded as totally committed to the war effort—not just to turning Afghanistan into Russia's Vietnam but to defeating the Soviet Union throughout the world. The ISI complained that much of the CIA rank and file knew little or nothing about how to fight a guerrilla war or to conduct any kind of military operation. In the words of the ISI Afghan branch chief, the CIA often seemed "clumsy, unrealistic, and totally unprofessional." In addition, much of the equipment selected by the CIA for the war was regarded by the ISI as substandard or even so old and poorly maintained as to be useless and possibly dangerous. The Blowpipe surface-to-air missile system is a case in point. It was pushed by the CIA and the British on the Pakistanis even though it had failed when used by British troops in the Falklands war. Materiel purchased in Egypt—which had large quantities of Soviet materiel either imported from Russia or made in Russian-supplied factories in Egypt— was regarded as of especially poor quality. On the other hand, Chinese-provided materiel was regarded as consistently of the finest quality.[32]

The ISI was very impressed, however, with U.S. technical intelligence collection capabilities, especially satellite imagery and its analysis. The

United States provided a stream of high-quality images and analysis to the ISI, which proved to be invaluable in helping to select targets for mujahedin operations, briefing commanders and ISI advisers on what to expect at target locations, and assessing how much damage a raid or ambush had actually done.[3] The imagery also formed the basis for producing detailed maps of targets for raids and a comprehensive order-of-battle analysis of the 40th Army and the Afghan communist forces. It is always difficult for two intelligence services to work in harmony. By nature, secret services do not want to give their secrets to foreigners. When the services are divided by culture, religion, and language, relations are even more likely to be strained. During the Afghan war, the CIA and the ISI did not trust each other and often were disdainful of the other's performance; if something went wrong, it was always easy to blame the other. But in the end they worked together much better than the KGB and KHAD (its Afghan counterpart) did, and they created an intelligence alliance with the Saudis, British, Chinese, and others that won the war against the 40th Red Army.

Akhtar decided that the majority of Pakistani ISI teams inside Afghanistan would be devoted to the effort against Kabul. He was determined to bring the war into Kabul itself—to attack Russian and Afghan political and military installations inside the capital in order to create a sense of insecurity in the city. Because the countryside was a war zone, refugees had poured into Kabul to find safety, swelling its population from 750,000 in 1979 to over 2 million by 1984. In that environment, it was easy for the ISI to find Afghans who were willing to assassinate Russian and Afghan communist officers and diplomats or to plant bombs at government buildings. However, Akhtar wanted more than harassment attacks, and he pressed the mujahedin to shell the city with mortars and rockets from outside the security perimeter around the capital.

Shelling Kabul with rockets required rocket launcher systems that were capable of hitting targets downtown from several miles outside the city; the rocket launchers also needed to be portable so that small teams of insurgents could get them within firing range. The Chinese ultimately provided the system required. In 1985 the ISI asked the Chinese to mass produce single-barrel rocket launchers that were easily portable; by 1987 over a thousand had been delivered to Karachi and then to the mujahedin outside Kabul. The city came under sustained rocket attack. The general also pressed the mujahedin commanders to try to seize part of the capital and hold it for thirty-six hours, a symbolic gesture to demonstrate the deterioration of Soviet control. However, that task was too complicated for the mujahedin's nonexistent command-and-control system to undertake, and it was never attempted.[34]

Managing the mujahedin political parties in Pakistan and the commanders of the fighters was an endless headache for the ISI. They constantly feuded among themselves in Peshawar, where the leadership lived in exile, and occasionally fought against each other inside Afghanistan. The only unity of command came from the ISI. Every three or four months, the ISI arranged a meeting between Zia and the party leaders and senior commanders to discuss the political situation. At these secret conclaves, called "Great Bonanzas" by the ISI, Zia would inevitably urge greater unity on the party leaders. More frequently, Akhtar would hold smaller meetings, called simply "Bonanzas," to discuss tactical issues. It was a challenge for the ISI leadership to guide and cajole its clients to victory.

The ISI also took its war across the Amu Darya River and into Soviet Central Asia. The Pakistani intelligence service began sending small units of mujahedin north of the border into Soviet territory in 1984. At first, the missions were undertaken largely for reconnaissance and propaganda purposes, but in 1985 the ISI asked the CIA for detailed maps and imagery of the border region in order to begin a series of raids inside the USSR. The CIA declined to help, but the ISI went ahead, mounting small rocket and mortar attacks against airfields and other Soviet installations. The Pakistanis considered a major attack on the bridge over the Amu Darya River at Termez, which had been built in 1982 to improve the supply line to Kabul. Called the Friendship Bridge by the Russians, it was the most important road and rail link between the Soviet Union and Afghanistan, and severing it, even temporarily, would have been a major blow to Soviet credibility. The proposed operation was vetoed by Zia as too ambitious and too dangerous.[35] The ISI focused instead on barge and boat traffic in the river. The ISI turned for help to MI6, requesting limpet mines, which could be attached by swimmers to the side of a barge and later exploded. London agreed, making a "small but effective contribution to destroying barges on the Soviet side of the Amu River."[36]

The cross-border operations were extraordinarily provocative—"bear baiting," as the ISI later called them. The Russian archives show that on several occasions they successfully disrupted traffic on a critical rail line from Samarkand in Central Asia to the Termez border checkpoint, but they never sparked any dissidence against the Soviets among the Muslim populations of Soviet Uzbekistan or Tajikistan.[37] Eventually the Russians decided that the attacks were too much to tolerate. In April 1987 the Soviet ambassador in Islamabad warned the Pakistani foreign minister that if they continued, the Soviet army and air force would retaliate inside Pakistan. By April 1987 General Akhtar had been promoted to a new assignment as chairman of Pakistan's Joint Chiefs of Staff. Hamid Gul, his successor as director general of the ISI, ordered an end to cross-border operations.[38] The pot was boiling a bit too hot for Zia.

Zia's Diplomacy

Zia ul-Haq was not only a pivotal figure in the history of his country and the war in Afghanistan, he was also a pivotal figure in the final stage of the cold war, which had dominated global politics for almost half a century. It is surprising that there is no authoritative biography of Zia available in English. While today he is often vilified in Pakistan and elsewhere for his brutal dictatorship and links to Islamic extremism, Zia also was a strategist and diplomat of considerable skill. It was Zia who put together the coalition of countries that eventually won the war against Soviet aggression in Afghanistan. The Afghan mujahedin could never have done it alone; they were hopelessly divided and remained so even after their victory over the Soviets. While Washington and Riyadh were critical partners in the war effort, they were not on the front lines, taking the greatest risks. Only Pakistan could play that part, and Zia embraced it with passion and enthusiasm.

The decision to fight Moscow was an extraordinarily bold move. The ISI knew, for example, that General Akhtar was at the top of the KGB's hit list, with a huge bounty on his head.[39] In 1980 the Soviet Union was not only one of two global superpowers; it was also arguably the one on the rise. In 1987 Paul Kennedy, a very distinguished professor of history at Yale University, published a book whose thesis was that although the United States was still the foremost world power, its power was declining and would continue to decline. Russia, according to Kennedy, was a country beset by many "contradictions" and a growing economic problem but it was not "close to collapse." Kennedy expected the cold war to continue for several more decades, and its outcome was still undetermined; the Soviets might yet win. The book was very controversial in its analysis of the United States, but it was widely regarded as the "book of the year."[40] Only two years later, the Soviet Union lost the war in Afghanistan.

Soviet foreign policy had been fairly successful in the decade preceding the invasion of Afghanistan. Its client Vietnam had won the long war in Southeast Asia, and the Soviet-equipped North Vietnamese army had conquered Saigon, humiliating the United States. The fall of the Shah's imperial regime in Tehran was widely seen as another major U.S. setback, and many believed that it would be followed by a Soviet takeover of Iran. Russia's ally India had won a decisive victory over Pakistan in 1971 and exploded a nuclear device in 1974, and its advantage over Pakistan was growing. Soviet-backed insurgencies across Africa and Asia seemed to be steadily expanding the number of client states linked to Moscow.

In 1980 Zia's Pakistan not only faced a hostile Afghanistan to the west and a hostile India to the east, it also seemed to lack any significant allies. Both the United States and China had backed Pakistan rhetorically in 1971, but they had done little to help Pakistan in practical terms. China was hailed in Pakistan as the country's "all-weather friend" (unlike the fickle United States), but it was not prepared to go to war to defend the unity of the Pakistani state in 1971, and it was unlikely to go to war with the Soviets to defend it in 1980. Pakistan's relations with the United States were severely strained by Zia's coup, Zulfi's execution, and a mob attack on the U.S. Embassy in Islamabad in November 1979, which Zia seemed to react to slowly and ineffectively. Only Saudi Arabia seemed to be a firm ally of Pakistan, but it was shaken by an uprising in the holy city of Mecca in November 1979 that seemed to suggest that the House of Saud was losing control at home just as the Shah had lost control in Iran.

Yet despite the fact that the balance of power between Pakistan and the Soviet Union greatly favored the Soviets, Zia chose to go to war, albeit covertly. He must have calculated that the Soviets and Afghans would try to kill him, as in fact Zulfiqar, a Pakistani terrorist group, had tried to do at least twice.[41] Zia also was prepared to face down Soviet leaders when they tried to intimidate him, in person or indirectly. At the funeral of Konstantin Chernenko in Moscow in March 1985, for example, Mikhail Gorbachev met with Zia and tried to bully him with the threat of invasion. Calling Zia "a cunning politician," Gorbachev told him that "you are a military man yourself and understand very well that we know in the most precise way what is going on in Pakistan right now, where and what kind of camps are functioning that train the *dushman* [bandits], who is arming the bandits, and who is supplying them with money and all other necessities." Gorbachev told his colleagues after the funeral that Zia had left the meeting "clearly unhappy." But Zia did not bow to Russian threats.[42]

Nor was he worried by Indian threats. To the contrary, he saw the war against communism in Afghanistan as the perfect opportunity to develop a cadre of jihadists to fight India as well as the Soviet Union. From the earliest days of the Afghan war, Zia had already begun planning for the next stage in the jihad, turning east toward India and Kashmir. He turned initially to a political party with which he and the army had long-standing ties, Jamaat-e Islami. The party had been founded in 1941 by Maulana Syed Abul A'ala Maududi, an Islamist writer who advocated the creation of a Muslim state in South Asia—something along the lines of the Mughal Empire, which had ruled the subcontinent before the British—and the use of force to get it. It was an enthusiastic ally of the army in the war against East Pakistan in 1971, a war that helped forge an alliance between the party and jihadists like Zia in the army. Zia promised that some of the U.S. assistance that was earmarked for the Afghan jihad would be diverted to the Kashmir project and that the ISI would help both.[43] Accordingly, the ISI began allocating some of the weapons stored at its Ojhri camp for jihad in Kashmir.

Jamaat-e Islami found, however, that there was resistance among Kashmiris to Zia's promises of support. Having been let down by Pakistan in 1947 and 1965, many were uncertain that they could trust the ISI, so the new jihad took time to develop. A series of clandestine meetings between the ISI and Kashmiri militants from Indian-controlled Kashmir were held, many of them in Saudi Arabia, because it was easier for an Indian militant leader to travel to the kingdom, often under the cover of performing the hajj, than to go to Pakistan, which immediately aroused the scrutiny of Indian intelligence. Zia and General Akhtar were directly involved in the Kashmir project. Finally, in 1983 some Kashmiris began training in the ISI's Afghan camps.[44] Zia, Akhtar, and the ISI also reached out to other groups in Kashmir, including the Jammu and Kashmir

Liberation Front (JKLF), which had been founded in 1977 in Birmingham, England, by Kashmiris living in the United Kingdom. The JKLF was much more sympathetic to Kashmiri independence than to joining Pakistan. It also was reluctant to take ISI help at first, but Akhtar opened talks with the group in 1984, and by 1987 JKLF militants also were training at the ISI camps.

Meanwhile, in the mid-1980s Sikh nationalists sought to create a Sikh homeland in India, to be called Khalistan. In 1983 the Sikh independence movement took control of the Sikh holy city of Amritsar, using weapons provided by the ISI, and the Indian army responded with a major attack on the Sikhs. It ended in a furious military assault on the Golden Temple in Amritsar and hundreds of deaths on both sides.[45] Indira Gandhi, the iron lady of Indian politics, was assassinated by her own Sikh body guards a year later. In the fall of 1986, her son and successor, Rajiv, authorized a large military exercise, code-named Operation Brass Tacks, along the Pakistani border. He may have intended the exercise to deter further Pakistani activity with the Sikhs in Punjab, but he may not have fully understood the likely impact of the exercise in Pakistan. His army commander, General Krishnaswamy Sundarji, may have had more ambitious motives, hoping that the exercise would provoke a response that would allow India to destroy Pakistan's nascent nuclear program, just as Israel had destroyed Iraq's program in 1981. He would later write a novel making the case that India's decisionmaking on nuclear issues was muddled and ill-informed and that the army should be given a greater voice in strategic planning.[46] Whatever India's motives—and they were badly muddled—the deployment of two armored divisions, one mechanized division, and six infantry divisions along the border with lots of supporting air power in January 1987 prompted a major Pakistani response: Pakistan mobilized for war with India.

The militaries of both sides were deployed in dangerous postures. In Washington, the CIA was warning that war was possible. Zia pressed the CIA for intelligence on India's plans.[47] An Indo-Pakistani war would only play into the hands of the Soviets and undermine the Afghan war, and Washington urged restraint on both sides. Fortunately, cooler heads prevailed, and Zia and Rajiv backed away from conflict. Zia accepted an invitation to attend a cricket match in Jaipur, India, in February, and the meeting in the stands between Zia and Rajiv lowered tensions considerably. Not for the last time, cricket diplomacy offered a way to avoid potential disaster in the subcontinent.[48]

The largest supply depot for the ISI's war in Afghanistan was located just outside Rawalpindi at the Ojhri ammunition storage facility. On April 10, 1988, it was racked by a rippling series of massive explosions as 10,000 tons of arms and ammunition went up in smoke.[49] While most of the arms were for the Afghan mujahedin, the ISI had used the same site to store equipment for the Kashmiri and Sikh jihad. More than 100 people died in the disaster, including five ISI officers. In 2012 two former Indian intelligence service officers told me that it was their agency that had sabotaged the facility, to punish Pakistan for helping the rebels in the Kashmiri and Sikh revolts. New Delhi's spies believed that the explosion of the depot would cripple the ISI.[50] Although it did not work out that way, it did set the ISI campaign back considerably, and the ISI had to ask for resupplies from the CIA.

Zia also was not afraid to stand up to the United States. He refused to halt Pakistan's nuclear program, even though under the provisions of the Glenn Amendment, Washington would be forced to cut off aid to Pakistan if Pakistan continued to work on developing nuclear weapons. According to an authoritative account by a Pakistani general involved in the program, on March 11, 1983, Pakistan successfully carried out a secret "cold test" of its bomb—a test without fissionable material that proved that Pakistan had all the components necessary to explode a bomb. Two dozen more cold tests followed, but the March 1983 test told Zia that Pakistan was "a nuclear power."[51] Two presidents decided not to let the nuclear issue undermine the goal of defeating Russia, but there is no reason to believe that putting more pressure on Zia, including by cutting off U.S. aid, would have stopped his pursuit of the bomb.

Zia was a master of knowing how hard to push without forcing an enemy to go to war with him. His handling of the crucial weapons supply issue in the Afghan war exemplifies his skill. From the start of the war, the mujahedin's biggest weakness was air defense. They did not have their own air force, of course, and needed a portable surface-to-air missile system that could be carried easily into Afghanistan and used to shoot down Soviet and Afghan aircraft, especially helicopters. Initially the ISI armed the mujahedin with Soviet-made SA-7 shoulder-fired surface-to-air missiles, which had been used in the 1973 Arab-Israeli war with substantial success by Egypt and were available in large numbers. But by 1980 the SA-7 was no longer a state-of-the-art weapon, and it was not as effective a weapon as the ISI wanted for the mujahedin.

The state-of-the-art weapon was an American model, the Stinger surface-to-air missile, which was just being introduced in significant numbers into U.S. service in the early 1980s. If a Stinger missile was used in Afghanistan—or worse, captured by the Soviets—the fiction of Pakistani non-involvement in the war would come to an end. Zia also worried that it might fall into the hands of the Iranians, whose spies were widespread in Afghanistan, especially in the west. It would be obvious that the ISI had acquired the missiles from the United States, and Zia's plausible deniability would be gone. So Zia and Akhtar rejected acquiring Stingers even though the ISI commander of the war effort was lobbying for them from early 1984. Moreover, Zia apparently was also worried that a Stinger would get into the wrong hands and be used to shoot down his plane, as the Zulfiqar group already had attempted to do. Washington agreed with Zia.[52] In January 1986, however, Zia changed his mind. He asked for the Stinger to be provided to the ISI in significant numbers, more than 1,000 a year. U.S. experts would train the ISI to operate and maintain them, and ISI experts would train the mujahedin.[53]

On September 25, 1986, the Stinger was used for the first time inside Afghanistan, shooting down three Soviet helicopter gunships. The introduction of the Stinger, which was to become an important factor in the eventual defeat of the Russians, would mark a major milestone in the war. Zia's fears of discovery were well founded, however, because both the Soviets and the Iranians captured intact Stingers from mujahedin forces in early 1987.[54] The decision to acquire the Stinger was Zia's. It was his war. However, Zia died before it ended, on August 17, 1988, when the C-130 transport aircraft carrying him, Akhtar, and the U.S. ambassador to Pakistan crashed into the desert. They had traveled to a remote training facility to observe a demonstration of a new U.S. tank, which had performed poorly. After lunch, Zia and his entourage were to return to Islamabad; instead, everyone on board was killed. Much of the high command of the Pakistani army was dead.

General Mirza Aslam Beg, Pakistan's vice chief of army staff, had flown home on a separate aircraft. Shortly after arriving in the capital that afternoon, he convened a meeting of the remaining members of the army's top command. According to a reliable account, Beg blamed the crash on a conspiracy of the "threats against Pakistan from two sides." He pointed a finger at the Soviets, noting an official Soviet statement on August 13 that had warned Pakistan that Moscow would retaliate for its Afghan policy, and he pointed a finger at India, noting a speech by Prime Minister Rajiv Gandhi on August 15 in which he threatened that "if Pakistan did not stop aiding the Sikhs, then India will be forced to take action."[55]

Zia undoubtedly had an abundance of enemies. The KGB, KHAD, and RAW (Research and Analysis Wing, India's intelligence agency) all had a motive. Many Pakistanis, including senior ISI officials, have pointed the finger at the CIA, arguing that Zia's pursuit of nuclear weapons was its motive or that Washington had decided that it was time to ramp down the jihad in Afghanistan and make a deal with Gorbachev[56] The U.S. ambassador in India, John Gunther Dean, argued that the crash was the work of the Israeli secret intelligence service, Mossad, and was abruptly cashiered from the Foreign Service[57] In death as in life, Zia was a source of controversy. The crash remains a mystery today. An investigation by a joint Pakistani-U.S. air force team concluded that the crash was the work of criminal acts and sabotage, but it did not identify the perpetrator. In fact, there seemed to be no interest among either the Pakistanis or the Americans in identifying the perpetrator of the crash. The main concern of both was to ensure stability in Pakistan after the death of the dictator, who had ruled the country for over a decade. Zia had set elections for November 16, 1988, and Beg, as the new chief of army staff, decided to hold them on schedule. Robert Oakley, the new U.S. ambassador, also pushed for elections to be held on time.

Benazir Bhutto won the November election for prime minister, securing 93 of 207 seats in the parliament for her father's Pakistan People's Party. It was an astonishing turn of events. Benazir had spent five years in detention since Operation Fair Play brought Zia to power, including ten months in solitary confinement. After spending two more years in exile in England, she was allowed to return to Pakistan to bury her younger brother, who had died mysteriously in Nice. She was again imprisoned by Zia. She was certain that Zia would orchestrate the elections to stay in power and that she would have to spend more time fighting him.[58] Instead, she became prime minister at the age of 35. Zia's era was over in Pakistan, but his legacy remains today. The Pakistani commission that investigated how Osama bin Laden hid in Pakistan for a decade after 9/11 concluded in its secret report in 2013 that "the dark era of General Zia ul-Haq left Pakistan with a poisoned legacy of a criminal, violent, ideological and anti-national infrastructure of extremism."[59]

It is interesting to speculate on how history might have changed had Zia lived. Some diplomats have argued that unlike Benazir, Zia would have provided the discipline and cohesion that the mujahedin needed after the Soviet withdrawal to take Kabul in 1989; he would then have ended the war early and made Afghanistan a Pakistani puppet state.[60] Zia certainly would have been determined to fight to victory and not settle for the three years of stalemate that in fact followed. Moreover, Zia was absolutely determined to make Pakistan the dominant power in Afghanistan after the Soviets left. Instead, his suspicious death ultimately left Pakistan without the decisive victory that he craved.

THE SAUDIS:
FINANCIERS AND VOLUNTEERS

THE PALACES OF the House of Saud, the ruling family of the Kingdom of Saudi Arabia, were built to inspire awe in any visitor. The king's palace in the capital, Riyadh, is an enormous structure decorated inside in lovely green Italian marble; the palace grounds cover a square mile. The palace complex in Jeddah, the main port on the Red Sea, is on a stretch of land larger than the island of Bahrain. The palace of the crown prince includes a dining area built around a large indoor swimming pool; overhead, the ceiling is painted to look like a star-studded sky. A huge aquarium lines one side of the room, giving occupants the impression that they are under the sea. Most of the major princes of the kingdom have more than one private palace. Prince Bandar bin Sultan, a former ambassador to the United States, has one in Riyadh and another in Jeddah. His palace in Riyadh encompasses a full-scale replica of the fort in the center of the old city that was the scene of the birth of the modern Saudi kingdom at the start of the twentieth century—it's a bit like a Texan having a full-scale replica of the Alamo in the backyard. His palace on the Red Sea is designed to make a person feel as if he or she is inside the ancient Egyptian Temple of Luxor, complete with huge stone pillars and a ceiling that is forty or so feet high.

The Saudi royal palaces are never open to the public, and photographs of them are very rare. But here in these modern equivalents of Versailles or Schönbrunn, the war in Afghanistan was financed. It was Saudi money, provided by both the state and private citizens, that paid for the defeat of the Soviet 40th Red Army. It was in the palaces of the Saudi royals that the key decisions were made in summits between top Saudi,

Pakistani, and U.S. officials. The principal architect of Saudi policy in the 1980s was Fahd bin Abdulaziz al Saud. Born in 1921, one of the sons of the modern kingdom's founder, Abdulaziz al Saud, Fahd became minister of the interior, a key position, in 1962; upon the death of King Faisal in 1975, he became crown prince. As crown prince, Fahd was the power behind the throne of his brother, King Khalid. When Khalid died on June 13, 1982, Fahd ascended to the throne. Later he began calling himself "Custodian of the Two Holy Mosques," a reminder that he was in charge of the two holiest sites in Islam, Mecca and Medina, and that the kingdom was the defender of Islam everywhere. Despite suffering a debilitating stroke in 1995, Fahd reigned as monarch until his death in 2005. During the critical years of the Afghan war, Fahd called the shots in Saudi Arabia.

Two other princes also played critical roles in the Saudi effort to help Pakistan and the Afghan mujahedin. During the 1980s, Prince Turki bin Faisal al Saud, the son of King Faisal, was the head of the Saudi intelligence agency, the General Intelligence Directorate (GID). The GID handled the kingdom's relationship with foreign intelligence services, including the ISI and the CIA. Turki traveled constantly to keep those relationships on track; he was a frequent visitor to Pakistan and spent an enormous amount of time with General Akhtar and the Afghan party leaders. He was deeply respected by the ISI leadership. Since he represented the king, he had both political and religious authority as well as deep pockets. He would implement Fahd's promise to the United States to match every dollar of U.S. government support to the mujahedin with an equal Saudi contribution, all of it going through the ISI.

The second key prince was then the governor of Riyadh Province, Salman bin Abdulaziz al Saud. Salman, who was born on December 31, 1935, had been governor of Riyadh Province, home of the capital, since 1962. A century ago, in 1911, Riyadh had a population of less than 10,000 inhabitants, and when Salman became governor of Riyadh, it had only 150,000 inhabitants. Today Riyadh is a bustling metropolis in the heart of the Nejdi desert with a population of some 7 million people, and it is one of the fastest-growing cities in the Arab world—a fact that is especially striking given the very arid conditions in the Nejd. Before becoming crown prince in 2012, Salman governed Riyadh for half a century.

It was due to his impressive skills as a top administrator that Khalid and Fahd selected Salman to establish a private committee to raise funds for the mujahedin immediately after the Soviet invasion. The head of the Saudi Wahhabi clerical establishment, Shaykh Abdul Aziz bin Baz, issued a religious order, or fatwa, charging the committee to raise funds from across the kingdom—from both Saudi princes and the public—to fund the jihad in Afghanistan; accordingly, the kingdom contributed both official and "private" money to the war effort.[1] The private Saudi funds were especially critical in the first years of the war, when the United States provided only limited support. The head of the ISI's Afghan cell has written,

> It was largely Arab money that saved the system. By this I mean cash from rich individuals or private organizations in the Arab world, not Saudi government funds. Without these extra millions, the flow of arms actually getting to the mujahedin would have been cut to a trickle [before 1983].[2]

U.S. sources estimated that private Saudi donations through Salman's committee averaged around $20 to $25 million a month.[3]

The Al Saud Wars

The war in Afghanistan came at an especially critical moment in the history of the Saudi state. The original Saudi kingdom was founded in the mid-eighteenth century in an alliance between the al Saud family, which was a prominent tribal clan in the Nejd, a region in the middle of the Arabian Peninsula, and a charismatic Islamic reformer and preacher, Muhammad ibn Abd al Wahhab. In 1744, their partnership combined traditional Bedouin tribal military power with a potent religious message of return to a simple, "pure" form of Islam.[4] Within a few years, the first Saudi kingdom had gained control of much of the peninsula and was conducting raids in Iraq. The Ottomans repressed the Saudis repeatedly in the nineteenth century, ultimately driving the House of Saud into exile in Kuwait in 1891.

In 1902 the founder of the modern Saudi kingdom, Abdulaziz al Saud, seized Masmak Fort in Riyadh from a pro-Ottoman tribe and began to restore the Saudi state. By the 1930s, Saudi Arabia had achieved its modern borders. The oil-rich Eastern Province, along the Persian Gulf, was taken early, and war with Yemen pushed the border further south. The conquest of the Hejaz and control of the two holy cities of Mecca and Medina were the crowning achievements of Saud's career. The Saudis invested considerable resources in expanding the size of the mosques in both cities to allow more of the devout to pray, especially during the pilgrimage, the Hajj, when millions of Muslims come to Saudi Arabia to visit the holy sites.

In November 1979 a conspiracy was hatched to seize the mosque in Mecca, the most holy in all Islam, by a group of extreme Islamic fundamentalists who believed that the redeemer, or Mahdi, had come to proclaim the end of time. Belief in an apocalyptic end of time has a long history in Islam.[5] This conspiracy posed a particular threat to the kingdom, since it amounted to a challenge to the religious legitimacy of the state. The conspirators succeeded in taking control of the Grand Mosque on November 20, 1979, and then held it despite intense military operations conducted by the Saudi National Guard over a two-week period. In the end, the Saudis had to ask the French government for assistance in providing a chemical agent to flush the extremists out of the tunnels under the mosque, and elite French commandoes assisted in the final offensive, in which the holy site was retaken. More than 1,000 Saudis died in the battle.[6] The surviving extremists, who were captured and then executed in January 1980, had formed a multinational force, including 41 Saudis, 10 Egyptians, 6 South Yemenis, 3 Kuwaitis, and one each from North Yemen, Iraq, and Sudan.[7]

The attack on the mosque at Mecca was a profound challenge to the House of Saud and the kingdom's stability. The decision to invite Pakistan to send an armored brigade to the kingdom reflected the royal family's conviction that it had to have a totally reliable force to prevent any repeat of the Mecca revolt. To make matters worse, the internal challenge came in the wake of the collapse of the Shah of Iran's government, across the Persian Gulf. For the Saudi royals, the overthrow of another absolute monarchy was extremely worrisome. They had no great affection for the Shah, who often was a rival in the Gulf, but they were shocked at how his imperial regime had crumbled. Iran's new ruler, Ayatollah Khomeini, called for revolution in Saudi Arabia and encouraged unrest among the kingdom's Shia population, which resides mostly in the oil-rich Eastern

Province and in neighboring Bahrain, a small island connected to the kingdom by a causeway.

Internal and external challenges were mounting, and with the Soviet invasion of Afghanistan in December 1979, it looked as if a perfect storm was hitting the kingdom. For decades the Saudis had relied on their alliance with the United States to ensure their security. The alliance dated to 1945, when King Abdulaziz al Saud met with President Franklin D. Roosevelt in Egypt at the end of World War II and agreed to a strategic security partnership. For the Saudis, the U.S. reaction to the Soviet invasion became a crucial test of the reliability of the United States as a security partner. Both the Saudi royal family and public saw the war in Afghanistan as a contest of good and evil, and support for the mujahedin was high. Islam was under attack by atheistic communists. Securing donations for the war effort was not difficult for Prince Salman. Indeed, some Saudis wanted to do more than give money; they wanted to fight.

Prince Turki was in charge of the Saudi government's war effort and the intelligence partnerships that were at its core. He had something of a role model to follow in funding and assisting the Afghan insurgency: in the 1960s his father, King Faisal, had fought a covert war in Yemen against another Soviet-backed revolutionary regime. Yemen, Saudi Arabia's desperately impoverished and backward neighbor, had been ruled for centuries by the Hamid ud Din royal family, which was overthrown in a coup in September 1962. The coup, which was backed by Egypt's revolutionary leader, Gamal Abdul Nasser, established a republic with close ties to Cairo. The Royalists fled into the mountains and began an insurgency against the Republicans. Cairo and Moscow were determined to back the new regime in Sana'a. The base in Yemen offered an opportunity to destabilize both Saudi Arabia and Britain's colony in Aden—an opportunity recognized by British prime minister Harold Macmillan, who wrote that "the Egyptians mean to use Yemen as a jumping off ground for Saudi Arabia—a great prize."[8]

In October 1962, in the midst of the Cuban missile crisis, Egyptian troops were flown to Sana'a in a massive Soviet airlift to back up the coup. Other Egyptians came via the Red Sea to reinforce the expeditionary force. Soviet pilots flew Antonov transport aircraft filled with troops, equipment, and even MiG-21 jet fighters from Cairo to Sana'a in order to rapidly build up the Egyptian expeditionary forces. At the peak of its effort, Egypt deployed 70,000 soldiers to back up the Republicans, and the Soviets provided pilots and advisers to assist the Egyptian forces. Joint Soviet and Egyptian crews flew bombing missions from Cairo into Yemen, occasionally bombing targets on the Saudi side of the border as well.[9] By 1963 over 1,000 Soviet advisers were in Yemen and at least one Soviet pilot had been shot down and killed.[10]

Saudi Arabia backed the imam, Muhammad al Badr, and his Royalist insurgent army in the mountains of north and east Yemen. Faisal—first as crown prince and after 1964 as king—was the leading player in determining Saudi policy toward the war. He was much more proactive than his predecessor, King Saud,[11] and under Faisal's leadership the kingdom provided money, logistical assistance, and safe haven to the Royalists. A small number of Jordanian troops also were deployed along the border to train the insurgents.[12] The operation was run out of an office on Sloane Street in London, but all of it was paid for by Saudi intelligence,[13] which recruited British, Belgian, and French mercenaries to assist the Royalist tribes. Former British intelligence officers did much of the recruiting. Although the British government gave the operation its tacit support, it kept its role covert.

To get arms to the Royalists, the Saudis and the mercenaries turned to another enemy of the Egyptian dictator, Israel. In early 1964 the Israeli secret intelligence service, the Mossad, made arrangements for the Israeli Air Force to begin clandestine air supply flights down the Red Sea in order to parachute weapons to the Royalists. The mission, code-named Operation Leopard, was approved by the senior leadership of the government and the Israel Defense Forces. The Mossad officer in charge of the covert action was Nahum Admoni, who would go on to become Mossad director in the 1980s.[14] Between 1964 and 1966, the Israelis flew more than a dozen resupply flights to aid the Royalists. Israel had every interest in bogging down the Egyptian army in its own Vietnam-like quagmire. Faisal's intelligence chief, Kamal Adham, a graduate of Cambridge University and a descendant of Turkish and Albanian Ottoman rulers of the Hejaz, supervised the operation on the Saudi side. Direct Saudi-Israeli encounters were kept to a minimum; the British mercenaries shuttled between them.[15] Although the Israelis pressed for direct contact, the Saudis demurred—Adham once agreed to meet the Mossad face to face in London but failed to show at the Dorchester Hotel at the appointed hour.

The Egyptians abandoned the Yemeni war after their catastrophic defeat by Israel in 1967, and the Royalists never succeeded in reestablishing the monarchy. From the Saudi perspective that was unnecessary: the essential objective was to defeat the Egyptian expeditionary force. In that respect, the Afghan war was the same game—defeating the Russian army was the goal; what came next in Afghanistan was secondary.

The Yemeni war was a formative experience for Faisal's son Turki, who was familiar with the details of the campaign from a young age. A book about the Yemeni war written by Turki's deputy Saeed Badeeb and published in 1986 reads like a primer for the Afghan conflict.[16] In a virtual repeat of the situation in Yemen in 1962, Afghanistan looked to Turki and Fahd when the Soviets invaded Afghanistan in 1979, and the Saudis fashioned a response that drew on the earlier campaign.

Prince Turki bin Faisal al Saud succeeded Kamal Adham as intelligence chief in 1978. Turki—a graduate of Georgetown University, an expert in the complex politics of the Middle East, and a smooth operator on the international scene—is a soft-spoken man with a sharp intellect. After more than 20 years as intelligence director, he became Saudi ambassador to the United Kingdom and then to the United States. He had warned Mohammad Daoud Khan in 1978 that a coup was coming in Afghanistan. When Akhtar came to Saudi Arabia immediately after the Soviet invasion, Prince Turki became his partner in the war effort. The two would form a close bond; Akhtar and his ISI team found Turki to be "humble and honest," a man that they could rely on to deliver money and good advice.[17] Turki also would oversee the activities of Saudi private citizens operating in Pakistan in support of the mujahedin. He and his deputy Saeed Badeeb met with them in Pakistan and facilitated their efforts. The GID needed to be confident that the two sides of the Saudi war effort, the government and the private sector, worked in harmony.

The Volunteers

Perhaps the most controversial aspect of the secret war in Afghanistan today is the role played by Muslim volunteers, mostly but not all Arabs, who came to Pakistan in the 1980s to support the mujahedin. Since the most famous of those volunteers was Osama bin Laden, who would go on to create the terrorist group al Qaeda and mastermind the September

11, 2001, attacks against the United States, it has become fashionable to characterize al Qaeda and the 9/11 attacks as "blowback" from the U.S. secret war. The suggestion is that U.S. support for the mujahedin, the ISI, and the Saudis created the environment in which al Qaeda was born and nurtured. Taken to an extreme, that suggests that the 9/11 attack was an unintended consequence of the secret war in the 1980s.

That argument is bad history—pursuing from the future into the past a line of analysis that does not square up with the facts. The Muslims who came to Pakistan in the 1980s to fight with the mujahedin did not come because of the CIA, ISI, or GID, they came because of the Soviet invasion. Decisions made in Moscow are what prompted Osama bin Laden, Ayman al-Zawahiri, and Abdullah Azzam to engage in jihad, not decisions made in Washington or Riyadh or even Islamabad (although Pakistan was the crucial player in allowing the volunteers access to Afghan battlefields). To suggest that there is some inevitable link between President Carter's and President Reagan's backing for the mujahedin and 9/11 is tortured and incorrect logic. It also shows a lack of understanding of the U.S. role in the Afghan war. CIA officers in Pakistan had no interaction with the Arab volunteers, just as they had little interaction with the mujahedin themselves. The business of fighting the war was in the hands of the ISI, not the CIA. If the Americans had interacted with the Arab volunteers, the ISI would have complained. That did mean, of course, that the ISI and the Saudis routinely interacted with the volunteers, who were pursuing their jihad.

Osama bin Laden's case illustrates the reality. Immediately after news broke of the Soviet invasion in December 1979, bin Laden flew to Pakistan to help fight the Russians. He arrived in Peshawar, Pakistan, to support the mujahedin before the first CIA shipment of weapons to arm the insurgents arrived in Karachi.[18] In other words, he was there before significant U.S. aid arrived, and he stayed for the duration of the war, until after the Soviets retreated in defeat.

Osama bin Laden was the son of Mohammed bin Awad bin Laden, the wealthiest construction mogul in Saudi Arabia, who was born in 1908 in Hadramut Province of what was then the British colony of Aden. At the turn of the twentieth century, Aden was among the busiest ports in the world, situated on the shipping line from England to the British colonies of India, Singapore, and Australia. Mohammed bin Laden immigrated to Saudi Arabia, where he began work as a bricklayer, and by 1931 he had amassed enough money to start his own construction company. The business was a great success; it built the kingdom's roads, airports, seaports, and the palaces of the House of Saud and refurbished the mosques in Mecca, in Medina, and (in a contract with the Hashemites in Jordan) in Jerusalem. By the time of his death in a plane crash on September 3, 1967, Mohammed bin Laden had gone from rags to riches and become a multibillionaire.

Mohammed bin Laden was a very pious man. He funded improvements to Jerusalem's Dome of the Rock and the Temple Mount, the Haram al-Sharif, from his own pocket and hosted many pilgrims visiting Mecca at his own home. Among those were prominent Afghans and Pakistanis like Burhanuddin Rabbani, the future president of Afghanistan, and Qazi Hussain Ahmed, the leader of Jamaat-e Islami, Pakistan's leading Islamist party. These men were "common faces" to Osama bin Laden well before the Soviet invasion; he had met them with his father and during their visits to Mecca after his father's death.[19] In 1979, just 22 years old, Osama bin Laden met with the leadership of Jamaat-e Islami immediately after arriving in Pakistan to help the mujahedin cause. He established a close working relationship with the Islamists, who also were close to Zia ul-Haq.[20] At first, Osama's principal duty was to facilitate the flow of private Saudi money from the kingdom's donors to the Afghans in Pakistan. Because he was so well connected through his father's company with the kingdom's powerful and wealthy leadership—and, at the other end, with the Pakistani Islamists and Afghan party leaders—he was perfect for the job. His contacts in the kingdom included not just Prince Turki but the very powerful minister of the interior, Prince Nayef bin Abdulaziz al Saud, a brother of both Fahd and Salman.[21]

For the first few years of the war, Osama stayed in Pakistan and did not venture into the Afghan war zone. But in time he grew ambitious, eager to be more than a financier. By 1985 he had recruited other Saudis to join him in creating an Arab force to fight with the mujahedin inside Afghanistan. With the help of his father's construction empire, bin Laden assisted in the building of the Zhawar base camp and other mujahedin underground fortresses. In late 1985 he built one for his own band, which he called the Lions' Den. Like Zhawar, it was in Paktia Province, Jalaluddin Haqqani's stronghold. On August 17, 1987, bin Laden's small band engaged in an intense firefight with Soviet troops at the camp, known as the battle of Jaji. It was Osama's first time in combat.[22] The battle was a transformative experience for him—he had tasted combat and the danger of war firsthand—and it also helped make him famous in the kingdom.

The Afghan Arabs, as they became known, were a trivial part of the military campaign against the 40th Red Army. Perhaps 500 Arabs and other Muslims died in the war against the Russians in the 1980s, according to the estimate of a senior CIA analyst who worked on the war at the time.[23] In contrast, tens of thousands of Afghan mujahedin died in combat with the Russians and more than 1 million Afghan civilians died in the war. It was Saudi money, not Arab jihadists, that contributed to the victory. But after the fact, the Arab Afghans became important for another contribution to the war effort: the narrative of jihad. The key Arab in this narrative was a Palestinian who was bin Laden's closest partner in the 1980s, Abdullah Azzam. A former head of the Mossad has rightly called Azzam the father of the modern global Islamic jihad.[24] Azzam was born in 1941 in the British mandate of Palestine, near the city of Jenin.[25] His family was a modest one known for its piety, but it was not regarded as extremist. Living in what is now called the West Bank, Azzam suffered through the Palestinian defeat in the first Arab-Israeli war, in 1947–48, known to Palestinians as the Naqba—the catastrophe. When the state of Israel was established and Palestine was divided between Gaza, which Egypt occupied, and the West Bank, which the Hashemite Kingdom of Jordan annexed, hundreds of thousands of Palestinians lost their homes and became refugees.

In 1963 Azzam moved to Damascus, Syria, to attend the Islamic law school at Damascus University, where by 1966 he had obtained a degree. While there he was greatly influenced by faculty belonging to the Muslim Brotherhood, the oldest Islamist party in the Arab world, although he probably was already a member from his youth in Jordan.[26] After graduation he returned to the West Bank, just before the June 1967 Arab-Israeli war. Israel's swift conquest of the West Bank led to another wave of Palestinian refugees fleeing Israeli rule, and Azzam's family joined the exodus to Jordan's East Bank. They settled in a refugee camp outside the city of Zarqa, which would become a hotbed of Islamism for the next half-century. Azzam joined the Palestinian fedayeen resistance movement and participated in their attempts to attack the Israelis across the Jordan

River. He was an active fighter in the fedayeen forces, but he also wanted to continue his studies. He moved to Cairo in late 1968 to study at Al Azhar University, the Islamic world's premier institution of higher learning, where he obtained a master's degree in Islamic jurisprudence, with high honors, in late 1969. He then took a teaching position at Jordan University. He apparently sat out the Jordanian civil war in 1970, not fighting on the side of either the fedayeen or the government and Zia ul-Haq.

In 1971 Azzam returned to Al Azhar to get his doctorate, which he completed in 1973. In Cairo, he became further involved in the underground world of the Muslim Brotherhood and the Islamist movement. Upon graduation he went back to teaching at Jordan University in Amman, and he became well-known in Jordan as an Islamic leader and speaker. King Hussein's government tolerated the Muslim Brotherhood and the Islamists as a counterweight to the more radical nationalist Palestinian movements, but it also closely watched activists to ensure that they did not get out of control and pose a threat to the Hashemites.

Azzam's impressive credentials as an Islamic scholar and his increasingly radical views attracted the attention of the Jordanian intelligence service. When he was pressured to tone down his statements, he refused. Finally, in 1980 he left Amman for a new teaching position at King Abdulaziz University in Jeddah, which had become a stronghold of members of the Muslim Brotherhood and other radicals who had been evicted from their native Arab states but welcomed in the kingdom. In Jeddah, Azzam met and befriended a young Saudi studying at the university, Osama bin Laden. Azzam lived in one of the bin Ladens' homes in the city.[27]

Azzam did not stay long in Saudi Arabia; within a year he obtained a new position at the Islamic University of Islamabad, in Pakistan. There, under the influence of Zia's jihad in Afghanistan, his life would change profoundly. In Pakistan, Azzam became very involved in the mujahedin's cause and began to spend more and more time with the mujahedin in their camps along the border. He began writing pamphlets urging Muslims from all over the world, but especially his fellow Arabs, to come to Pakistan to join the jihad. In 1984 he wrote a crucial book, *The Defense of Muslim Territories,* in which he argued that joining the Afghan jihad was an obligation of every Muslim and that the war in Afghanistan against the Soviet superpower was more important than any other contemporary jihadist cause. Afghanistan was the place to defeat the unbelievers and enemies of Islam, Azzam argued, because the Soviets were the greatest threat to the Islamic world in the 1980s and the pay-off—the defeat of a superpower—would have the greatest influence on Islam's future. Azzam's impressive credentials as a serious scholar with degrees from the most prestigious school in all of Islam made his book a major influence in the entire ummah.

The foreword to the book was written by the leading scholar and religious figure in Saudi Arabia, Shaykh Abdul Aziz bin Baz, the head of the Wahhabi faith there.[28] Baz was a colorful figure, and he was very close to the royal family. He was blind, he believed that the earth is flat, and he opposed allowing women to wear high heels because he considered it too provocative. His endorsement of Azzam was strong support. *The Defense of Muslim Territories* was as important to the Afghan jihad as Thomas Paine's *Common Sense* was to the American Revolution. Azzam would follow it with dozens of other articles and books urging Muslims to support the jihad in Afghanistan. He broke with the Muslim Brother-hood, declaring it too timid, and began spending all of his time in Pesha-war with the mujahedin or traveling around the ummah urging Muslims to join the jihad in South Asia.

To assist jihadis coming from across the ummah to Pakistan, Azzam created the Services Bureau (Maktab al Khadamat) in Peshawar, where they could get food and housing. His co-founder of the Services Bureau was bin Laden, whom he had met in Jeddah. They began by setting up hostels for jihadists in Peshawar and then graduated to setting up training camps for Arabs and others to learn how to fight the Soviets. By 1985 the jihad was attracting many volunteers from across the Arab and Islamic worlds. Azzam traveled extensively to promote the war, including to the United States and Europe. In 1988, for example, he was the featured speaker at the annual conference of the Islamic Association for Palestine (IAP) in Oklahoma City, where he helped raise funds for both the Afghan jihad and Hamas in Palestine. The next year, after his assassination, the IAP conference in Kansas City was dedicated to his memory.[29] He wrote prodigiously to explain his views of jihad, and his lectures were recorded on video and replayed to dozens of audiences. His trips also produced sizable contributions of cash for the jihad.

Azzam's most important idea was that the jihad should be a pan-Islamic war, not just an Afghan or a Pakistani war. Because it divided the ummah, nationalist identity was a part of the problem; all of the ummah should unite together. The ummah, he wrote, needed to become a solid base, or *qaeda sulba,* to fight its enemies and prevent them from stealing Muslim lands, whether in Afghanistan or in Palestine. The jihad was global, not local. All Muslim lands occupied by foreigners, including Afghanistan, Kashmir, and Palestine, were a collective responsibility of all Muslims.

Just as important to Azzam, the jihad would produce martyrs who would be assured of a special place in heaven if they died fighting to repel the outsiders—or, as the foreigners became known, "the far enemy." Azzam's works contributed critically to the creation of the cult of martyrdom in the new jihad. By emphasizing global jihad and encouraging suicide, or martyr, operations, Azzam became the father of the modern global jihad. As he put it in *The Defense of Muslim Lands,* "The mountains of the Hindu Kush are the theater of battles without precedent in the history of the Muslim world."[30] Azzam urged all Muslims to "Join the Caravan" of jihad, as the title of another of his books put it. However, Azzam was not an advocate of taking the war to the enemy's home. Later bin Laden would develop the concept of the far enemy—that is, the United States—which should be attacked to weaken its will to occupy Muslim lands and support corrupt local regimes, the so-called "near enemy." This concept, an essential element of the thinking behind the 9/11 attacks, was not Azzam's, nor was it born during the 1980s war in Afghanistan. It is another example of bad history to trace the idea of attacking the far enemy, the United States, to the mujahedin's war.

Azzam and bin Laden were highly successful in getting other Muslims to come to Pakistan to join the jihad. Thousands came from across the ummah, from Morocco to Indonesia. Some were trained in ISI camps, others joined various mujahedin factions, and some worked with bin Laden in forming an Arab commando unit. As bin Laden later said, "[we] received volunteers from all over the Arab and Muslim countries, the volunteers were trained by the Pakistanis, the weapons were supplied by the Americans, the money by the Saudis."[31] Their military contribution to the mujahedin's war was marginal, but the political implications of their actions and the legitimacy that they gained in the eyes of other jihadis was enormous. The volunteers would become the leaders and role models for the global Islamic jihad that was coming and for al

Qaeda, which took its name, "The Base," from Azzam's idea of a solid base for jihad.

In addition to creating the Services Bureau with bin Laden, Azzam was instrumental in setting up another organization to assist jihad in nearby Kashmir. The Markaz-ud-Dawa-wal-Irshad (MDI) (Center for Preaching and Guidance) was an organization that Azzam helped to create with Hafiz Saeed, a prominent Pakistani Sunni scholar who, like Azzam, had studied in Saudi Arabia in the 1980s. They created MDI to help take the lessons of the Afghan war, which was winding down in 1987 as the Soviets prepared to leave, and apply them to Kashmir and India. Their first priority was to train Kashmiris to fight in Afghanistan with the mujahedin to let them gain combat experience, and camps were set up in Konar Province in Afghanistan for that purpose. Azzam and Saeed were not alone in seeking to start another jihad against India, and the ISI helped the new group set itself up; ISI also trained its operatives. MDI also had a military wing named Lashkar-e-Tayyiba (Army of the Pure), which would become the most effective and the most violent terrorist group fighting India.[32]

Finally, Azzam also played an inspirational role in the creation of one other important organization. Back in Palestine, especially in the Gaza Strip, Azzam's ideas about the urgency of jihad and the importance of martyrdom would help inspire the creation in 1987 of a new Palestinian resistance movement, Harakat al-Muqāwamat al-Islāmiyyah (Islamic Resistance Movement). Better known as Hamas, the group to this day regards Azzam as one of the key ideological influences on its foundation and development. Azzam was directly involved in writing its constitution or covenant, which calls for a jihad to destroy Israel.[33] He also trained Palestinians in Pakistan and sent them back to Gaza and the West Bank to apply their new skills.[34] Hamas leader Khalid Mishal still speaks emotionally about Azzam, especially about his mysterious death. In 2009 Mishal told one interviewer that "Azzam was a great man and we [in Hamas] owe him a lot."[35]

Azzam's call for Muslims to "join the caravan" would ultimately attract thousands to Pakistan. The mastermind of 9/11, Khalid Sheikh Mohammed, a Pakistani who worked briefly as an aide to Azzam in Peshawar, also was among those drawn by Azzam's call. Another jihadist who got training from the ISI in the camps in the late 1980s was Abu

Musab al-Zarqawi, who would go on to lead the al Qaeda war against the U.S. occupation of Iraq.[36] An Indonesian named Riduan Isamuddin but better known as Hambali arrived in 1987. He would go on to help create Jemaah Islamiyah and carry out a wave of terrorist attacks in Southeast Asia, including the bombing of night clubs in Bali, Indonesia, on October 12, 2002, that killed more than 200 people, including 88 Australians and 24 Britons.[37]

Azzam died on November 24, 1989, killed along with two of his sons in a car bombing in Peshawar. In 2009 al Qaeda claimed that he was killed by the Jordanian intelligence service, but the identity of his assassins remains a mystery, like the identity of Zia's. Like Zia and Akhtar, Azzam did not live to see how the foreign volunteers would go on to change the world after the defeat of the 40th Red Army, but he "was a towering figure in the history of modern jihad already in 1989, and he remains so today."[38] Today, in honor of his memory, al Qaeda has named its organization in Lebanon the Abdullah Azzam Brigades.

The CIA estimated that 20,000 foreign fighters had gone to Afghanistan and Pakistan by the end of the war.[39] According to a Pakistani estimate, some 35,000 Muslims from 43 countries received their baptism by fire fighting with the mujahedin, and tens of thousands more obtained their education in the madrassas in Pakistan associated with the war.[40] As noted earlier, the military contribution of the foreign fighters was small, but their ideological contribution was significant. Among the less well-known figures is Abu Mus'ad al Suri. Suri, a Syrian who followed Azzam's call to join the jihad, would train in the camps of the ISI and mujahedin and then write some of the most important ideological books of the modern Islamic jihad. His 1,600-page *Global Islamic Resistance Call* has been rightly described as providing the strategy for the jihad and al Qaeda. Born in Aleppo in 1958, Suri was active in the Syrian Islamist movement, which was crushed in the city of Hama in 1981 by the Syrian government. He went to Peshawar in 1987 and met with Azzam, who convinced him that the struggle in Afghanistan should be a pan-Islamic struggle and should get top attention from Islamists. Suri became a trainer in one of the camps built by the ISI for the mujahedin. After several years of training other Arab volunteers, Suri turned to writing, becoming a major ideological influence in the new jihadist movement that was stirring in the wake of the defeat of the Soviets. He moved to London in the mid-1990s and served as bin Laden's spokesman in Europe, arranging interviews for him and publicizing his works. *Global Islamic Resistance Call* argued that jihad needed to be decentralized and pan-Islamic. It became a jihadi best seller and has been widely read and distributed in the jihadist underground.[41]

The first significant political expression of the Afghan Arabs came in Algeria in 1991, when Algerian veterans returning from the Afghan war played an important part in sounding the call for reform in their country. They helped Islamic parties sweep to electoral victory, only to be forced underground after a coup d'état by the army. The Algerian Afghans then helped to create the violent insurgency that gripped the country for much of the next decade.[42] Other returning volunteers would start making their mark across the Islamic world and beyond as the 1990s progressed. The United States, including the CIA, paid little attention to the Arabs and other Islamic volunteers or to their ideology. CIA deputy director Robert Gates wrote in 1996 that the CIA "began to learn of a significant increase in the numbers of Arab nationals from other countries who had traveled to Afghanistan to fight in the Holy War against the Soviets in 1985. They came from Syria, Iraq, Algeria, and elsewhere."[43] Since the CIA had little direct contact with the mujahedin, it was largely blind to the foreign volunteers. As Gates said more recently, "We missed it, we didn't know and didn't understand [what was going on in the volunteer camps]." As for bin Laden, Gates recalls that his name never came up in any meeting that he attended during the war, either at the White House or the CIA.[44]

The CIA's secret war in Afghanistan did not create the volunteers; they came for their own reasons. Communism and Soviet imperialism had created the provocation that led to the jihad, and Zia ul-Haq and King Fahd provided the venue and the money to make the jihad a reality. The volunteers flocked to join the Afghans.

PART 2

THE U.S. WAR

1-5⁰

CHAPTER SIX

JIMMY CARTER'S WAR

JAMES EARL CARTER, the thirty-ninth president of the United States, was the father of the covert program to aid the mujahedin in Afghanistan in the 1980s. It was Carter who decided that the United States would respond aggressively to the Soviet invasion of Afghanistan in December 1979 and instructed the CIA to begin supplying weapons to the mujahedin. He also orchestrated the creation of the secret U.S.-Pakistani-Saudi alliance that funded and armed what he still calls the "freedom fighters" in Afghanistan. The major U.S. strategic decisions about the war—to arm and fund the Afghan mujahedin, to use Pakistan as a base for the mujahedin, to enlist Saudi help in the war, and to turn Afghanistan into Russia's Vietnam—were made by Carter in the first days of 1980.

Carter has never written or spoken publicly in any detail about those decisions because when he left office in 1981, the war was still in its earliest stages and was still a top-secret project. He published his memoirs before the war ended and rightly kept his part in the war under wraps. So did his key advisers. Both Zbigniew Brzezinski, the national security adviser, and Stansfield Turner, the director of central intelligence, also published their memoirs in the 1980s, so there is little mention of the secret war in their accounts. Turner scarcely mentions Afghanistan at all. Jimmy Carter kept a detailed diary every day of his meetings and decisions as president. A small part of this diary was published in 2010, but most has never been made public. The president was kind enough to give me access to the parts relevant to this book. Carter's role in the secret war in Afghanistan was crucial, and he deserves to be credited with being one of America's most successful presidential spymasters.

George Washington was America's first spymaster. As commander of the Continental Army, he recruited spies, ran covert operations, and produced disinformation to confuse the British. His military victories, from Stony Point to Yorktown, were founded on good intelligence. The newly opened Washington presidential library at Mount Vernon contains his correspondence with Congress requesting funds for his espionage activity. However, it was not until World War II that the first professional U.S. government intelligence organization, the Office of Strategic Services (OSS), was created, by President Franklin D. Roosevelt. Led by William Donovan, the OSS engaged in intelligence collection and analysis and covert operations on a global scale. Americans as different as William Casey, the future director of central intelligence, and Julia Child, the future chef, fought an intelligence war from England to India to Vietnam. Ivy League professors provided analysis for the OSS. U.S. naval intelligence performed an especially critical service in intercepting and decoding Japanese communications. The unique Anglo-American intelligence relationship was created. When the war ended, the OSS was shut down by President Harry Truman, who hoped that the United States would not need a secret intelligence organization. However, the cold war soon required another one, and in 1947 the Central Intelligence Agency was created to manage human intelligence analysis and operations and covert operations. In 1952 the National Security Agency was created to conduct signals intelligence collection.

The 1950s was a golden age for the CIA. Under the leadership of Allen Dulles, the brother of Secretary of State John Foster Dulles, it became a global intelligence service engaged in intelligence collection and analysis as well as covert operations. The CIA's Directorate of Plans, as it was called before becoming the Directorate of Operations (DO), had some notable successes in covert operations. Perhaps the most successful was Operation Ajax, in which the government of Iran was overthrown in 1953 and the Shah put back on his throne. The operation was engineered by the DO's Near East Division (NE), and its success established NE as the elite division of the DO. Such covert operations were a major part of the NE mystique, and within the CIA the chiefs of NE were considered barons of an espionage empire ranging from North Africa to South Asia. In the late 1950s the intense U.S. espionage relationship with Pakistan began, and the CIA started to fly U-2 spy missions out of Pakistan. In the Middle East and South Asia, many leaders as well as average citizens believed that the CIA was capable of anything and responsible for everything.

The agency's analysts also produced high-quality finished assessments for the White House of the many issues facing U.S. policymakers in the cold war, drawing on all the sources of intelligence available. Agency intelligence found the Soviet missiles in Cuba before the Russians were ready for a crisis, giving President John Kennedy time to negotiate a deal to remove them. In 1967 the agency correctly predicted that Israel would rapidly defeat its Arab enemies, strengthening the standing of Director Richard Helms in President Lyndon Johnson's eyes. During the Vietnam War, the CIA expanded greatly in size. It engaged in huge covert operations in Southeast Asia, running its own air force in Laos and a major counter-guerilla program (Operation Phoenix) to eliminate Viet Cong in South Vietnam.

The 1970s were not as good to the CIA as the two previous decades had been. In 1973 the agency disastrously listened to Israeli intelligence, which had said that no war was coming, and was caught by surprise when the Arabs attacked Israel on Yom Kippur. As Vietnam collapsed in 1975, the CIA had to abandon its largest overseas station, under fire. In the mid-1970s a series of scandals occurred over the illicit collection of information on Americans at home and botched covert operations abroad, damaging the agency's reputation. President Gerald Ford brought in a political overseer, George Bush, to fix the problem, but Bush served only a year as the CIA's director.

A Very Difficult Start

The CIA that Jimmy Carter inherited in 1977 was in trouble. It was bloated with Vietnam veterans that it could no longer use effectively, it was accused of malfeasance in collecting information on American citizens illegally, and it was still recovering from the 1973 Yom Kippur disaster. Bush tried to persuade Carter to keep him on as director, but Carter wanted his own man. At first he choose Theodore Sorensen, who had served in President Kennedy's administration as a speechwriter and political adviser, but Sorenson withdrew his name a few weeks after being nominated in the face of serious criticism that as a young man he had been a conscientious objector and that he was far too political for the job.[3]

Sorenson later wrote that his nomination had been sabotaged by agency officials, past and present, who smeared him in the press to prevent his appointment.[4] Carter turned to a navy officer, Admiral Stansfield Turner, to try to set things right. The two had been students together at the U.S. Naval Academy, but they were not close. Turner was an outsider, and his decision to retire more than 800 Vietnam-era case officers soon after arriving at CIA headquarters in Langley, Virginia, cost him the trust of the clandestine service. He would have a stormy tour as director of the CIA.[5]

Afghanistan was not high on the agency's list of priorities when Turner took over. As seen in chapter 1, the United States had recognized Afghanistan as an independent country only after the Third Anglo-Afghan War, in 1919. Kabul sent an ambassador to Washington in 1922, but Washington did not send an ambassador to Kabul until 20 years later, after Pearl Harbor. During the first decades of the cold war, while it sought an alliance with Pakistan, Washington kept Kabul at arm's length. Although Eisenhower had visited Afghanistan in 1959 and King Zahir had come to the United States in 1963, high-level interaction between Washington and Kabul was rare. When Carter traveled to India and Iran in late 1978 and early 1979 on a whirlwind tour that also included Saudi Arabia, he skipped Afghanistan. He also flew over Pakistan. His diary shows no mention of Pakistan during his trip or of its ruler at the time, General Zia ul-Haq. Carter's relationship with Zia and Pakistan, which traveled a remarkable road from hostility to partnership, would come to define the U.S. role in the Afghan war. In the end, an initially very skeptical Carter came to see in Zia not only an essential partner but a man whom he "liked" when they finally met face to face and whom he described in his private diary as "calm, very courageous, and intelligent."[6]

Carter's relationship with Zia did not start out that way. In 1977, at the traditional July 4th party of the U.S. Embassy in Islamabad, Arnie Raphel, one of the embassy's officers, asked General Zia whether they could meet the next day. Zia replied that he would be "very busy" on July 5 and regretfully had to decline. About twelve hours later, at midnight, Zia launched a coup to overthrow the elected government of Zulfikar Ali Bhutto.[7] The coup, code-named Operation Fair Play, was a direct challenge to Carter's determination as president to move the United States away from its support of dictators during the cold war and toward a policy of supporting human rights and democracy. Carter had campaigned in 1976 as a new face in America, eager to break with the old cold war paradigms that had led the country into the Vietnam quagmire. All too often in the past, Washington had backed military dictators like Zia to fight communism and Soviet expansionism, only to see them exploit their people and thereby nurture anti-Americanism. Pakistan was a textbook example. The United States had backed the country's first two dictators and was widely unpopular for doing so.

At first Zia promised that the coup would be only a temporary interruption of the Pakistani democratic process. However, he soon changed his tune, and in October 1977 he put Bhutto on trial for allegedly authorizing the murder of a political opponent. The judicial process dragged on for months. Carter and many other world leaders appealed to Zia to show clemency and not execute his predecessor. Zia's responses were evasive. In March 1978 the Lahore high court found Bhutto guilty of murder and sentenced him to death. Bhutto appealed. On February 2, 1979, Pakistan's supreme court rejected the appeal. Carter again wrote to Zia asking for clemency, and Congress passed a resolution asking for clemency as well. A third Carter appeal followed in March. On April 4, 1979, Bhutto was hanged. The general had rebuffed the president and most of the rest of the world.

Relations between the United States and Pakistan also were troubled by Pakistan's pursuit of nuclear weapons. After India defeated Pakistan in their 1971 war and tested an atomic bomb in 1974, Bhutto had embarked on a major program to build a bomb for Pakistan. Zia was even more determined to catch up with India. Even before Zia's coup, Carter had canceled a deal to sell Pakistan 110 fighter-bombers because of the Pakistani nuclear program; he also succeeded in pressing France to cancel a deal to build a nuclear reprocessing plant in Pakistan. Zia made the issue worse by telling a Saudi newspaper that "if Pakistan possesses nuclear weapons, it would reinforce the power of the Muslim world." The U.S. ambassador in Islamabad, Arthur Hummel, told Washington that it was just a "gaffe" and should not be given importance. Then Zia said the same thing to the *Washington Post*. "The West has got it," he said. "In the East, Russians have got it. The Chinese have got it. The Indians have got it. The Jews [Israel] have got it. Then, why should Pakistan, which is considered part of the Muslim world, be deprived of this technology?" Zia never used the word "weapon," but his intent was clear.

Throughout the Carter administration and the Reagan years as well, the U.S. intelligence community continued to report to the White House on the steady development of the Pakistani weapons program. For example, in response to a request from the National Security Council, on December 7, 1979, the eve of the Soviet invasion of Afghanistan, the CIA sent the White House "A Review of the Evidence of Chinese Involvement in Pakistan's Nuclear Weapons Program." The review concluded that Pakistan had been seeking Chinese assistance for its weapons program since at least 1974. Despite Chinese denials of any role in the program, the CIA concluded that "China has almost certainly been involved" but was uncertain of the "precise nature" of Chinese assistance. It is now known that China provided considerable help to Pakistan in developing its bomb.[10] Faced with the evidence of Pakistan's progress in achieving its nuclear ambitions and the rebuff of U.S. appeals for clemency for Bhutto, the Carter administration suspended aid to Pakistan two days after Bhutto's execution in April 1979. Zia blamed the suspension on the influence of the Zionist lobby in Washington and denied that Pakistan had any intention of making a bomb. He accused Carter of applying a double standard, treating Israel and India differently from Muslim Pakistan. Relations between Pakistan and the United States were at a deep low, and they would get worse.

Nonetheless, it is clear from Carter's unpublished diary that he was determined to keep the bilateral relationship from foundering and breaking apart completely. In 1978, as events such as the Saur Revolution and the growing unrest in Iran weakened the U.S. posture in the Persian Gulf and South Asia, Carter realized Pakistan's increasing strategic importance. According to his diary, late in 1978 Carter wanted to find a way to improve relations with Pakistan despite all the difficulties. At Camp David on December 29, 1978, Carter "told [Secretary of State] Cy Vance to bend over backwards to strengthen our ties with Pakistan" and asked the National Security Council "to assess thoroughly how we can improve our ties with Pakistan."[11] On January 1, 1979, Carter met with his foreign policy team: "I directed Cy and Zbig [Zbigniew Brzezinski, the national security adviser] to start an all-out effort to repair our relationships with Pakistan and to give me an analysis of both Pakistan and Afghanistan without delay." This directive came after a "long discussion about Iran."[12]

The president and his team also began pressing key U.S. allies to work with Zia. In early January, at a summit of key Western leaders in Guadeloupe, Carter impressed on them "the importance of keeping Pakistan with the West." Later in the month he made the same argument about Pakistan's importance to Chinese leaders, who would not want to see the Soviets increase their range or power.[13] Brzezinski was making the same case to skeptics in the State Department and elsewhere within the administration who were focused on the nuclear issue. In May 1979 he warned the president that "if the Soviets came to dominate Afghanistan, they could promote a separate Baluchistan, which would give them access to the Indian Ocean while dismembering Pakistan and Iran."[14] Increasingly concerned, Carter received briefings from the CIA on April 4, 1979, and May 23, 1979, on the situation in Afghanistan. The April briefing focused "primarily on Afghanistan, with detailed maps showing the spread of dissident [mujahedin] strength and the interrelationships between the Soviet Union, Afghanistan, Pakistan, Iran, and the ethnic groups in the Soviet Union." In May the CIA reported again on the "growing opposition to the communist regime, and whether or not the Soviets would intercede directly if and when the Taraki government might be overthrown." As discussed previously, the CIA's judgment was that the Soviet would not intervene directly.[15]

After consultations with his national security team on July 3, 1979, Carter authorized a limited CIA covert action to start providing non-lethal assistance to the Afghan mujahedin, or as Carter calls them, "the freedom fighters."[16] The project was to include propaganda and psychological warfare operations only; no weapons were to be provided. Carter allocated a half-million dollars to the project, which was spent in six weeks. That modest start marked the beginning of the CIA partnership with the ISI to back the mujahedin. So, by the fall of 1979, in response to the Soviet threat in Afghanistan and the fall of the Shah, the U.S. ally in Iran, President Carter was trying to repair the fractured U.S. relationship with Pakistan and his own relationship with Zia. Strong support for his effort was coming from cold war hawks in both the Republican and Democratic parties. Inside the administration, Brzezinski was the leading advocate of taking a tougher line on Moscow and of finding a path to improving ties with Pakistan.

Then disaster appeared to strike. First the U.S. Embassy in Tehran was overrun by a mob of students protesting Carter's decision to allow the deposed Shah to come to the United States for medical treatment. Initially Carter hoped that the occupation of the embassy and the detention of the hostages, including both U.S. staff and local employees, would be short lived. The embassy had been overrun before, in February 1979, but only for a few hours; the Iranian government had quickly rescued the American staff. Coincidentally, the U.S. ambassador in Kabul, Adolph Dubs, had been shot to death at the same time in a botched rescue attempt by the Afghan communist army after he was kidnapped by leftist extremists.[17]

However, Iran had changed considerably by November 1979, and not for the better. Extremists were eager to exploit the embassy takeover. In the midst of the tensions in Tehran that November, the Grand Mosque in Mecca was attacked by Islamic extremists. The Iranian government, now under the control of Ayatollah Khomeini and his supporters, blamed the United States for the attack on Islam's holiest site. On November 21, U.S. embassies in several countries were attacked by mobs inflamed by the Iranian accusations. The worst incident occurred in Islamabad. At noon on November 21, student demonstrators from nearby Quaid-i-Azam University began to gather outside the embassy, some arriving in buses. At first it looked like a peaceful demonstration, and the embassy accepted a delegation, which made a protest statement. The demonstration appeared to be winding down when more buses arrived and a much larger crowd formed. The ambassador, Hummel, who was in his residence, began calling the Pakistani authorities for help. The crowd rushed the embassy at 1:40 p.m. and broke inside. One Marine guard was killed in the first clashes with demonstrators, and the American staff and some of the Pakistani employees—137 people in total—barricaded themselves in a secure vault to avoid being taken hostage like their counterparts in Tehran. Hummel continued to call for help from the Pakistani government while the mob ransacked the embassy and set it on fire. To help stoke the fire, gasoline was drained from the cars in the parking lot. The temperature in the vault was rising fast, and the smoke started to enter the secure area.[18]

At 4:00 a.m. Washington time, Carter was awakened by a call from Secretary Vance with the news that the embassy had been attacked and that one Marine was injured. Vance called back shortly afterward to report that the situation was getting much worse: the Marine was dead and the air supply in the vault was getting dangerously low. Vance said that Hummel and the State Department were pressing Zia and his staff for help.[19] In a public relations stunt to encourage the use of bicycles, Zia was cycling through the city of Rawalpindi, Pakistan's military capital, fifteen miles from Islamabad. His staff later claimed that they were slow to react because of poor communications. At first two Pakistani army helicopters flew over the embassy, but they could not see much due to the smoke; only at 5:30 p.m. did an army unit finally arrive on the scene. By then, most of the mob had already left and the trapped staff had opened the doors to the roof and gotten fresh air. Two Americans and two Pakistani employees were dead, and the embassy was a charred ruin. The staff had to be moved into the British and Canadian embassies before being flown home.

It had taken the Pakistani army four hours to respond. In Zia's coup, Operation Fair Play, the army had traveled the same ground in July 1977 in less than thirty-five minutes.[20] Many of the Americans trapped in the burning building believed that the army had deliberately left them there to die; some suspected that the entire attack was orchestrated by the ISI. Even today many believe that the Pakistani government, at some level, actively colluded in the attack.[21] The U.S. consulates in Karachi and Lahore had also been attacked, but without any loss of life. Carter and Zia spoke by phone at 10:00 a.m., Washington time, after the danger had passed. Carter's diary shows that he thanked Zia for his help in saving the embassy staff and employees but that Zia "said he deserved no thanks." Zia said that "he was personally responsible for their protection," and he offered to pay to rebuild the damaged embassy. He blamed the false reports of U.S. involvement in the attack on the mosque at Mecca not on Iran but on India: "This report originated in India," he claimed. However, U.S. intelligence officials assured Carter that Iran, not India, was behind the false broadcasts blaming the United States for the attack.[22] U.S. relations with Pakistan were badly damaged by the incident, but Carter was determined to not let his emotions sway his judgment about Pakistan's strategic importance. He accepted Zia's offer to pay for the damages, and Pakistan paid $23 million dollars in compensation. He did not blame the Pakistani government for the incident and publicly thanked Zia for his help, much to the anger of many of the embassy employees. Carter sensed that the embassy attack was only a part of the larger U.S. struggle with Iran. His instinct to maintain his ties to Zia would soon pay off.

Carter Develops the Plan to Defeat Moscow

As discussed in chapter 2, the Soviet invasion of Afghanistan on Christmas 1979 came as a surprise to President Carter. The CIA's assessment that Moscow would not put a significant number of its own boots on the ground in Afghanistan had proven dead wrong. As Bob Gates, the future director of the CIA, later wrote, "CIA's Soviet analysts thought that the Soviet leaders thought as they did. It was not the first or the last time they would make this mistake."[22] In an interview with me decades later, Carter was still disappointed that he had been provided poor intelligence.[23]

Hamilton Jordan, Carter's White House chief of staff, had gone to Georgia for the holidays. He got an urgent call from the White House Situation Room after Christmas informing him that the president wanted him to know that the Soviets were invading Afghanistan. Incredulous, Jordan replied, "What?" When he called the president at Camp David, where Carter was staying for the holiday, Carter told him that the new Soviet crisis was much worse than the Iran hostage crisis: the hostage crisis had been the act of a "bunch of radicals condoned by a crazy old man," but invading Afghanistan was an act of aggression that "raised grave questions about Soviet intentions," destroyed any chance for a new arms control treaty, and increased the prospects for "nuclear war."[24] Carter scheduled a National Security Council meeting at the White House for December 28. The meeting would prove decisive in decisionmaking for the CIA secret war in Afghanistan.

Brzezinski set the stage with a memo, which he sent to the president the day before the meeting, arguing that whatever Moscow's motives for the invasion, once the Soviets were in Afghanistan, their ambitions might grow, given the instability in Iran and Pakistan. The invasion, he wrote, "could produce a Soviet presence right down on the edge of the Arabian and Oman Gulfs." To stop the Soviets, it was essential to provide "more money as well as arms shipments to the rebels" in Afghanistan, in "concert with Islamic countries in a covert action campaign to help the rebels." China should be enlisted as well as European allies such as the United Kingdom and France; military and economic development aid to Pakistan must be restored as well.[26] Zbig became the architect, with Carter, of a new policy toward Afghanistan and Pakistan.

According to Carter's diary, the president and his team decided to regard the Soviet invasion as "a radical departure from the reticence which the Soviets had shown for the last ten years since they overthrew the government of Czechoslovakia" and "to make this action by the Soviets as politically costly as possible." Carter "sent on the Hot Line the sharpest message that I have ever sent to Brezhnev, telling him the invasion of Afghanistan would seriously and adversely affect the relationship between our two countries." The president decided to impose economic sanctions on Russia, interrupting grain sales and technology sharing; canceling fishing rights; restricting negotiations on culture, trade, commerce, and other bilateral exchanges; canceling visits to the Soviet Union; and establishing different standards in trade and technology transfer that would benefit China at the Soviets' expense. The sanctions were announced in January 1980.[27] The president also decided to authorize a new covert action by the CIA to supply lethal weapons to the mujahedin through the Pakistani government, and he signed the authorization on January 29, 1980.[28] Congress, which was notified of the covert action so that it could conduct oversight, authorized $50 million in annual funding for the program.[29]

At the time, the chief of the Near East Division in the Directorate of Operations was Charles Cogan, a longtime veteran of the CIA with years of experience in clandestine activity. Cogan, who had just become chief in the summer of 1979, would stay in that key post until 1984. Cogan quickly turned the authorization into action. His officers were ready to act. As he relates it, "the first arms—mainly .303 Enfield rifles—arrived in Pakistan on January 10, 1980, fourteen days after the Soviet invasion." The initial goal was "harassing the Soviet occupation forces in Afghanistan." The non-lethal program begun six months before now became a war to bleed the Soviet Union dry.[30] The arms would be carefully chosen so that they could not be traced to the United States, thereby allowing the operation to remain secret and giving the president "plausible deniability" that a secret war was under way. Carter wanted weapons of Soviet origin so that if they were found in the possession of the mujahedin, it would appear that they had simply been captured on the battlefield. The CIA's leaders saw the same need to keep the CIA's hand hidden.

Pakistani cooperation was essential to Carter's plan to resist the Soviet takeover. Indeed, the president and his advisers were worried that Pakistan and Iran were next and that the Soviets intended to use Afghanistan as a stepping stone on their march to the Indian Ocean and the Persian Gulf. Surprised at Moscow's decision to use Russian troops to control Afghanistan, the White House prudently feared that it might miscalculate Moscow's intentions again. Carter had called Zia after the conclusion of the December 28, 1979, National Security Council meeting to ask him to receive Deputy Secretary of State Warren Christopher, who had an urgent message to convey. According to Carter's diary, Zia was "reluctant" to have Christopher come immediately as the situation in Pakistan was "delicate, tragic and sensitive," but he made clear that he wanted U.S. aid for Pakistan and the Afghan resistance. Zia told Carter that Pakistan now faced an "onslaught" by the Soviets and that Pakistan was determined to resist. Zia also wanted plausible deniability of the ISI's role in the undertaking, just as Carter did for the CIA's. In that call, the basis of U.S.-Pakistani covert cooperation was established.[31]

The president wanted to build as large a global alliance as possible to censure the Soviets and to support Pakistan and the Afghan mujahedin. With its veto, Moscow blocked any significant action in the United Nations Security Council, so the UN General Assembly was urgently convened. There are no vetoes in the General Assembly. Pakistan's foreign minister, Agha Shahi, led the campaign to condemn the Soviets in the assembly, with strong support from Saudi Arabia. In a stunning diplomatic defeat for Moscow, the assembly voted 104 to 18 to condemn the Soviets, with 14 abstentions. The Soviet bloc states backed Moscow, of course, but India was the only democracy not to condemn the invasion, a fact that Zia quickly pointed out to Carter. Indira Gandhi did not want to sacrifice the treaty of friendship with Moscow that she had negotiated in 1971 for the sake of Afghanistan, and U.S.-Indian relations suffered as a result.

On January 4, 1980, President Carter convened another meeting in the White House to review aid to Pakistan and the Afghans. His diary notes that his "preference was to send them the kind of weapons they could use in the mountains in a portable condition, primarily against tanks and armored personnel carriers. We need to get as many other nations as possible to join us in a consortium so that the Paks won't be directly seen as dependent on or subservient to us." That evening Carter addressed the nation on television to explain his new policy. He announced the sanctions on Russia, promised aid to Pakistan to deal with the threat "from the north," and committed the United States to the defense of the Persian Gulf from outside aggression. The United States would also boycott the summer Olympics in Moscow as a symbol of its determination to condemn the invasion.[32] British prime minister Margaret Thatcher was an early and enthusiastic supporter of arming the mujahedin and boycotting the Olympics. Declassified British documents show that she and her cabinet encouraged Carter's robust response and pushed early for supplying arms to the insurgency. In a January 1980 briefing on the Saudi role, Thatcher was informed that "Muslim money is already flowing and may be sufficient." The British were less worried than the CIA that Moscow might invade Pakistan. The Joint Intelligence Committee, which produces British finished intelligence reports, concluded in March 1980 that the CIA was being too alarmist about the Soviet threat to Pakistan.[33]

Shahi was invited to visit Washington after the vote at the UN General Assembly. Carter and Zia spoke by phone again on January 8, 1980, and Carter met with Shahi on January 12 in the Oval Office. Carter proposed a $400 million aid package in combined economic and military assistance over a two-year period. Carter recounts in his diary that Washington would also ask for aid for Islamabad "from the Saudis, European allies, and Japan." He urged Pakistan to "work closely with the Indians in resolving their bilateral differences." He thought the meeting was "surprisingly good."[34] The State Department provided the details on the aid package to Congress on January 14.

However, the package was not enough for Zia, who was well aware of both the dangers that he faced from the Soviets and Indians and the strong card that he held with the United States. In the media, he called the U.S. offer "peanuts," a too-clever reference to Carter's days as a peanut farmer in Georgia. But Carter was again determined not to let his emotions interfere with policy. He ignored the remark and proceeded as if it had never been uttered, and Christopher and Brzezinski went to Islamabad to sell the package to Zia. As he related in his diary, Carter wanted to "keep the Paks responsible for their own future as much as possible"; if they rejected $400 million as too little, that "suits me fine" for now.[35] A little public friction helped preserve the covert entente.

The two U.S. envoys presented Zia with a broad overview of Washington's post-invasion strategy. On December 30, 1979, Brzezinski had said in a carefully orchestrated interview on national television that the United States was committed to defending Pakistan from Soviet aggression, thereby providing major reassurance to Zia. Christopher and Brzezinski repeated the message in Islamabad. When Zia asked for similar reassurance regarding Indian aggression, especially with Indira Gandhi back in office, the envoys responded that the commitment applied only to the Soviets, not to India. Zia then said that he welcomed U.S. backing but would leave some distance publicly between Washington and Islamabad. Brzezinski told Zia that Carter was fine with that approach since it helped preserve the secrecy of the covert operation. Zbig found Zia very self-confident and self-assured despite the dangerous waters around Pakistan.[36] The details of the covert war were left to the CIA to work out with the ISI. Brzezinski was careful not to tamper with Turner's responsibility to manage covert operations. The grand strategy was the key issue; the logistics could be left to the experts.[37]

The Christopher and Brzezinski mission was a success in both Islamabad and Riyadh. The Saudis agreed to match U.S. funding for the mujahedin, and the ISI-CIA-GID partnership was established. "Zbig reported privately to me that his trip to Pakistan and Saudi Arabia was successful," Carter wrote in his diary on February 6, 1980. Both Zia and the Saudis wanted U.S. "protection," but they wanted it kept private. In public, the two would be defended from Moscow by "unanimity among the Muslim world"; the secret war would stay behind the scenes.[38] But secret wars are hard to keep secret. As the president was jogging on February 12, 1980, his press secretary, Jody Powell, interrupted his run to tell him that the *Washington Post* had a story in the works about the CIA's operation to feed arms to the mujahedin rebels through Pakistan. In short, less than a month after the first arms arrived in Karachi, the secret was about to be published in the media. As Carter noted, the Pakistanis "would be highly embarrassed." Secretary Vance appealed to the *Post* to hold the story, but it ran a few days later, watered down a bit.[39] Zia did not back off from the secret war despite the press leaks. While the covert war was starting, U.S.-Pakistani negotiations on a large assistance package stalled. Zia wanted more than Carter was prepared to offer, and Carter was in no hurry to provide a more generous offer. Senior delegations were exchanged back and forth without reaching agreement.

Brzezinski focused on another angle, the Chinese. Earlier in the administration, he had been at the center of Carter's opening to China. Now he sought to get China to provide aid to the mujahedin. Zia too was eager for the Chinese to help since it would signal to both Moscow and New Delhi that Pakistan had two powerful patrons, Washington and Beijing. China agreed, and by the end of the war Chinese aid had exceeded $400 million. Some 300 Chinese advisers helped train mujahedin in ISI camps in Pakistan. Brzezinski recalls that some Afghans got advanced training in China.[40] The Chinese used weapons systems that were almost identical to Soviet weapons and thus in keeping with the doctrine of plausible deniability.

As 1980 proceeded, the Carter administration became increasingly consumed with the Iran problem. A rescue mission to free the hostages failed disastrously on April 24, 1980, and eight U.S. soldiers were killed in the attempt. The hostages were immediately removed from the embassy compound, where they had been incarcerated since November, and dispersed in small groups around Iran, making another rescue attempt impossible. The Iranians secretly brought them back to Tehran during the summer and put most of them in Komiteh prison, where they were held until their ultimate release in January 1981.[41]

During the summer of 1980 the Soviets had secretly conducted a major military command post exercise (CPX) to practice an invasion of Iran. It was entirely a headquarters exercise—no troops were actually deployed—but it caused serious worry in Washington. It was unclear then whether the CPX indicated a new Soviet interest in a possible invasion or whether it was simply a routine military drill.[42] A special national intelligence estimate prepared in August 1980 concluded that "the Soviets are indeed developing plans for military contingencies in Iran." The CPX involved an invasion force of sixteen divisions, including elements of the 40th Red Army in Afghanistan. Brzezinski pressed for an explicit warning to Moscow that "any Soviet military action in Iran would lead to a direct military confrontation with the United States."[43] Again, most analysts at the CIA thought an invasion unlikely, but the exercises and modest increases in the readiness of Soviet forces in Turkmenistan and the Caucasus region were worrisome.[44] This time, however, there was much less certainty in the CIA's estimate of Moscow's intentions.

Then, in September 1980, after a series of border clashes, Iraq invaded Iran. The intelligence community had seen this war coming.[45] It was the largest conventional war since the Korean War, and hundreds of thousands would be killed before it ended eight years later. For weeks the Carter administration was preoccupied with containing the war to keep it from spreading throughout the Persian Gulf. Oman seriously considered allowing Iraq to stage bombing raids from its territory into Iran, and the Carter team had to persuade the sultan that such a move would only expand the war.[46]

In the midst of the ongoing Iranian crisis and the approach of the U.S. presidential election, Zia made his first visit to the White House. On October 3, 1980, Zia and Carter met face to face for the first time. Much of the conversation was devoted to the Iran-Iraq war, which Pakistan was trying to mediate to secure a cease-fire. Carter had decided to up the ante for Pakistan's aid and agreed to include F-16 fighter jets in the package. However, Zia did not respond directly; the Pakistanis had concluded that they could wait for the outcome of the U.S. election. If Carter won, the offer would still stand; if he lost, the Republican challenger, Ronald Reagan, would likely be more favorable to Pakistan's requests and they could do better for themselves. "A careful forecast of the American elections outcome" and the advice of Saudi Arabia convinced Zia that Carter would lose.[47] Nonetheless, the meeting went well, and the two men enjoyed each other's company. Zia had told the CIA before the meeting that he was "pleased with the level of assistance and the level of resistance in Afghanistan [which] Zia thought was just about right.[48] Carter found that he "liked Zia very much. He's calm. I think very courageous. Intelligent.[49] Carter did lose in November. After leaving the White House, he would continue to work with Zia in a private capacity. His Carter Center in Atlanta sponsored disease eradication programs in Pakistan in the 1980s that helped eliminate a waterborne eye disease that had plagued Pakistani children for centuries. The two engaged in correspondence until Zia's death.

In retrospect, it seems that Carter probably exaggerated the danger of a Soviet move into Pakistan or Iran from Afghanistan after December 1979. The more cautious CIA analysts who thought that scenario unlikely and their counterparts in London's Joint Intelligence Committee were proved right. But that is hindsight. Prudent policymakers in 1980 had to consider the worst. Carter was also very mindful of U.S. dependence on Persian Gulf oil. The 1973 and 1978 oil shortages, which had created high prices and empty gas stations, were very much on his mind. If the Soviets occupied the north shore of the Gulf of Oman, what would be the impact on global energy flows? Reagan, Carter's successor, was, of course, even more alarmist about Soviet intentions and much more dismissive of any CIA analysis that suggested that Moscow might have limited ambitions.

By the end of the Carter presidency, the secret war in Afghanistan was well under way. All the strategic fundamentals were in place, and the CIA, ISI, and GID, along with the British and others, were actively assisting the "freedom fighters" in their war against the Soviets' 40th Red Army. As noted, Carter was the father of the covert program to aid the mujahedin. He had created a covert war to defeat Moscow's venture in Central Asia and had done so without a major commitment of aid to Pakistan. Bob Gates, who worked closely with Brzezinski at the White House, has rightly written that historians and the public have tended to underestimate Carter's role in winning the cold war. Nonetheless, as Gates observes, "the key alliances were established with Saudi Arabia and Pakistan, and the first elements of an extraordinary logistics pipeline from suppliers around the world were assembled" by Carter.[50] For his part, Reagan would ramp up the war and embrace Zia and Pakistan much more fully.

CHAPTER SEVEN

REAGAN AND CASEY

DIRECTORS OF THE Central Intelligence Agency travel abroad in great secrecy; only a select few individuals know their itinerary. In the 1980s they flew in unmarked C-141 Starlifter aircraft provided by the U.S. Air Force that were outfitted with the latest in electronic systems to deflect missile attack. On board, a complete communications package allowed them to remain in constant contact with the CIA operations center at headquarters in Langley, Virginia. Unlike presidents and cabinet members, they fly without a media entourage, and no journalists meet them at the airport. Their meetings with foreign leaders and other spymasters were and are top secret. In the 1980s, Ronald Reagan would send his director of central intelligence (DCI) around the world year after year to fight a global war against the Soviet Union. The fortieth president of the United States, Reagan was inaugurated on the day that the American hostages in Iran were finally released from captivity. They flew to West Point by way of Germany, where Jimmy Carter met them to escort them home. Their freedom meant that Reagan could focus on foreign policy without their fate hanging over his head.

Like George W. Bush in 1977, Stansfield Turner hoped to stay on as DCI after Carter's defeat in the November 1980 presidential election. Admiral Turner believed that in bringing the CIA back from the dark days of the mid-1970s, when it was under attack at home and morale was low, he had done a difficult job well. In his mind, he had cut the clandestine service of much dead wood and begun to reorient the agency toward the future. He told the president-elect that the CIA was still too timid, too scared by past episodes in which after the president had moved on, agency foot soldiers were left to bear the blame for actions that the White House had ordered.[1]

Turner also was disappointed that his access to the Oval Office had dried up during Carter's term. When he started in 1977, he had met with Carter three times a week; later the meetings were held just once a week and finally just once every other week. Turner blamed Brzezinski for shutting him out. From the very beginning of Carter's administration, Zbig had turned the daily intelligence briefing on Carter's calendar into a national security briefing, making himself, not Turner, the central figure. Proximity counts in the White House, especially when a strong national security adviser is only steps away from the Oval Office. The botched CIA analysis of the Soviet invasion of Afghanistan, which had undermined the White House's confidence in Turner and his agency, did not help increase Turner's access to the president.[2]

Casey and Zia's War

Reagan had someone else in mind to run the CIA: William J. Casey, the man who had managed his campaign for the presidency. Casey was not a longtime Reagan intimate. Reagan had asked him to join his campaign in 1979, and Casey had raised hundreds of thousands of dollars in campaign contributions, especially in his native New York City. Reagan made him campaign manager in 1980. Casey was born in Queens, the son of Irish Catholic immigrants. He would remain a devout Catholic all his life, and his firm religious convictions were a major factor in his world view. He believed deeply that the cold war was a contest of good against evil, of God versus the devil. Reagan saw the conflict in similarly black-and-white terms.

Casey had served in the CIA's predecessor, the Office of Strategic Services (OSS), in Europe during World War II. By the end of the war, Casey was chief of OSS intelligence in Europe and had acquired real hands-on experience in running agents behind enemy lines and conducting covert operations against the Germans. He went on to become a lawyer and venture capitalist after the war, specializing in tax law (he has been labeled the inventor of the tax shelter). During the Nixon administration, he was chairman of the Securities and Exchange Commission, undersecretary of state for economic affairs, and president of the Export-Import Bank of the

United States. He was on a multitude of boards and advisory commissions, such as the President's Foreign Intelligence Advisory Board and the Fordham University Board of Trustees. In Republican Party circles, especially in New York, he was a major behind-the-scenes operator and player.[3]

Casey also was an amateur historian and a prolific writer. He published a book on the American Revolution in 1976, the bicentennial of the war,[4] and he was the author of numerous books on tax policy. Casey had hoped Reagan would make him secretary of state, but he was very pleased to be appointed director of central intelligence instead. Reagan sweetened the deal by elevating the DCI to cabinet status, a promotion unique in the history of directors of central intelligence. Casey also got an office suite in the Old Executive Office Building, part of the White House complex, which gave him easy access to the Oval Office. Reagan and Casey wanted to use the CIA to wage a global war on the "evil empire." Their goal was not just to pay the Soviet Union back for Vietnam or to bog it down in quagmires—they intended to win the cold war, defeating the Soviets for good. Reagan had criticized Carter's response to the Soviet invasion of Afghanistan as too weak, not as too strong. He had lampooned the sanctions on grain sales, saying that "pigs, cows, and chickens" had not invaded Afghanistan and arguing that American farmers should not pay the price of fighting Russia.[5]

Casey soon discovered that Turner was right about the timidity of the agency. The Directorate of Operations (DO) was risk averse, he thought, and gun-shy. Even worse, he thought that the Directorate of Intelligence—the analyst wing—was soft on the Soviets and blind to the extent of Soviet involvement in supporting international terrorism. Casey was convinced that the Soviets had been behind the attempted assassination of Pope John Paul II, for example, and was frustrated that the CIA analysts were unable to find evidence to support his conviction. A few months after taking office in May 1981, Casey wrote a private memo to Reagan entitled "Progress at the CIA," in which he laid out his views of the organization. He said that the CIA was a "good outfit with some dedicated people" but that it had been "permitted to run down" and had been "kicked around by the press and Congress" and by "Turner's wholesale firings." The Directorate of Intelligence was in the worst shape. Its analysis was "academic, soft, and not sufficiently relevant and realistic," and he was changing up its leadership. He would even move the Soviet analysis office outside the headquarters building for a time—a kind of mass exile for its soft approach to the Soviets. Casey told Reagan that the operational side, the DO, also needed a shake-up and new leadership. He concluded the memo by noting that the "Soviet service outnumbers us three to one around the world."[6]

The goals of the Afghan covert operation were still modest. The CIA officers who ran it in the early 1980s were focused on harassing and wounding the 40th Red Army, not defeating it. Frank Anderson, a career officer in the Near East Division of the DO who went on to become chief of the division, has said that until about 1985, the CIA's Afghanistan team "believed a superpower had conquered yet another third-world nation and that was an irreversible fact. We had no hope that they [the mujahedin] could expel the Soviets." Instead, the goal was to increase the cost of the occupation, not to end it. Some inside the agency worried about "the morality of fighting a losing war to the last Afghan," but the majority wanted revenge for Vietnam.[7]

In April 1982, a year after becoming DCI, Casey traveled to Pakistan and Saudi Arabia to take a first-hand look at the secret war in Afghanistan. Charles Cogan, the chief of the Near East Division, accompanied him on the trip. Casey and Cogan flew to Pakistan in an unmarked air force jet to meet with Zia in his bungalow at General Headquarters in Rawalpindi. Zia had refused to move into the president's quarters in Islamabad, preferring his more humble military accommodations; residing there also allowed him to stay closer to his fellow generals. Akhtar lived in the next bungalow. As Cogan describes it, "at their first meeting Zia more than impressed Casey, who came away muttering at how the American press had distorted the image of the man. (Casey was struck in particular by the affection and patience Zia showed toward his handicapped daughter, who kept wandering into the living room.)" Zia had no doubts about Soviet intentions in Afghanistan. He "had a red template, a rough triangle, which he placed on a large area map spread out on his coffee table. The template covered the southern third of Afghanistan, and its tip was placed on the point where the Afghan border meets that of Iran and the Pakistani province of Baluchistan. The tip was only three hundred and fifty miles from the Indian Ocean—graphic testimony to Zia's reading of Soviet aims."[8] As Cogan writes, Zia was a "believer" and so was Casey.

Casey's first trip began a cycle of annual visits each spring to see Zia in Pakistan and King Fahd in Saudi Arabia. Casey fully agreed with Zia's and Fahd's assessment that Moscow's goal was to reach the Indian Ocean and control the flow of oil out of the Persian Gulf. As Casey's biographer Joseph Persico notes, "Casey believed that Afghanistan fit another ancient Russian dream, not just of the Communists but of the Czars: a warm-water port on the Indian Ocean. Afghanistan put that goal a tantalizing 350 miles away.⁹

Over time, Zia and Casey became close. Both were taciturn men—during their meetings, they didn't engage in small talk, they discussed business. Casey would open the meetings with the latest U.S. intelligence on the Soviet Union, its global activities, and the status of the 40th Red Army. Casey would also brief Zia on U.S. intelligence about India's military strength, a subject in which Zia was deeply interested. The sessions ran all morning and into the afternoon. "The last item was always the same: Zia would bring the subject around to the real enemy, not the communist regime in Kabul, not the Soviet Union, but India." Zia would tell Casey that India was Moscow's ally and that "the Soviets might well provoke an Indian invasion of Pakistan just to distract the Pakistanis from helping the Afghans. So he needed more weapons to defend Pakistan against India. And Casey agreed.¹⁰ Zia's message also was cautious. Casey's deputy Bob Gates wrote later that Zia made clear during the first term of the Reagan administration that "our objective in Afghanistan should be to 'keep the pot boiling but not boil over.'¹¹ Zia feared that providing overly aggressive support to the mujahedin could end in his nightmare scenario, a joint effort of the Soviet Union and India to dismember Pakistan. Of the two, Zia feared India more, especially with Indira Gandhi as prime minister. Casey's stops in Riyadh also followed a consistent pattern. He would meet with Fahd late in the evening in the royal palace. Fahd would reaffirm the Saudis' commitment to match U.S. spending on the mujahedin from their government accounts; private donations added a considerable additional bonus. Fahd would also support Zia's requests for more aid, especially weapons.

For the first several years of the Reagan administration, Zia did not press Washington and Riyadh for an expansion of the Afghan war effort. Casey kept the aid for the covert operation at roughly the same level that

Carter had approved in 1980. About $60 million in funds was provided to buy weapons for the mujahedin and to send them to Karachi in 1981, 1982, and 1983; the amount increased to $100 million in 1984. Casey also continued Carter's policy of sending only arms that could be plausibly argued not to be of U.S. origin.[12] The war would simmer, not boil over, just as Zia wanted. In time Casey would become "an early advocate of the idea that maybe we can push for victory" in Afghanistan, but in the early 1980s, Casey followed Zia's lead.[13]

Shortly after taking office, Reagan ordered a review of Pakistan's requests for assistance. Unlike the CIA project, which enjoyed broad and growing congressional support and for the most part was kept out of the media, military and economic aid to Pakistan was controversial in the media and in Congress. Zia was a military dictator who brutally repressed any opposition. He kept Benazir Bhutto in prison for several years. He promoted harsh and extreme interpretations of Islamic law. Human rights violations were a constant source of friction. Nonetheless, aid to Pakistan would dramatically increase.

Another point of friction was the nuclear issue. Zia was determined to build a bomb and was actively pursuing a number of ways to do it— among them the effort of A. Q. Khan to make use of centrifuge technology stolen from European sources. Pakistan also was working closely with China on developing a bomb. The Reagan team knew that it had to move carefully to avoid having the nuclear issue, in particular, upset the entire bilateral relationship. There was interest, particularly in parts of the bureaucracy, in trying to slow down if not halt Pakistan's nuclear program. Casey probably did not share that concern himself, but he was smart enough to recognize that the bomb issue could blow up his secret war if it was not handled with care.

In February 1981, just after Reagan took office, the administration prepared a five-year aid proposal worth $3.2 billion, a substantially larger offer than Carter's. In March, U.S. ambassador Arthur Hummel previewed it privately with Zia in Islamabad. When Foreign Minister Shahi came to Washington in April, he gave the White House implicit reassurance that Pakistan would not test a bomb. The administration, in turn, told Shahi that Pakistan's internal problems and policies were not an issue for it to judge.[14] The negotiations on the specifics of the deal were lengthy but positive. Pakistan accepted the package, which included equal amounts of economic and military assistance, including forty advanced F-16 aircraft. The F-16s were the top selling point.

In November 1982, in preparation for a visit by Zia to meet Reagan face to face in Washington, the intelligence community prepared a special national intelligence estimate (SNIE) entitled "Pakistan: The Next Years." The SNIE provides a useful snapshot of how the U.S. intelligence community viewed Pakistan in the midst of the secret war. The document highlighted that "the primary factor in Pakistan's foreign policy is suspicion of India"; Zia knew that he could not rely on "U.S. support against India" and therefore had to have "nuclear capability as his ultimate deterrent."[15] Based on Casey's discussions with Zia, the SNIE reported that "Zia and his senior generals fear the Soviets will not leave Afghanistan and believe Moscow intends to eventually reach the Indian Ocean by creating further client states in Southwest Asia" and that their "worst fear is of a future Soviet and Indian collaboration to dismember Pakistan." The estimate reported on Soviet contacts with Baluchi and Pashtun separatists and Pakistan People's Party leftists and anticipated more hijackings of Pakistani civilian aircraft like that carried out by Zulfiqar.[16]

The SNIE, which represented the collective opinion of the entire intelligence community, concluded that the Pakistanis fundamentally did not trust "the reliability of U.S. commitments and U.S. steadfastness in times of crisis." China was seen as Pakistan's most reliable ally, and Pakistan was already sharing sensitive French weapons with China. The estimate predicted that Zia would do the same with U.S. weapons supplied to Pakistan and concluded that "Pakistani decision makers, at a minimum, probably want the option to explode a nuclear device and/or to establish a nuclear weapons stockpile on short order, despite U.S. opposition." Pakistan was continuing to produce fissile material and to develop a bomb design despite the risk that as a result the United States might cut its aid to Pakistan.[17] The 1982 SNIE was a sober and cogent assessment of the Zia government and its policies. It left no doubt that Pakistan would never abandon its nuclear program in order to maintain its ties to the United States. U.S. policymakers, including Casey and Reagan, knew what they were doing in backing the ISI and the mujahedin; nonetheless, they judged it to be the right policy given the ongoing cold war.

Zia came to Washington on December 6, 1982, and met with Secretary of State George Shultz. The next day Zia went to the White House to see Reagan. The two met alone in the Oval Office for twenty minutes, then they had a larger group meeting in the Cabinet Room. The one-on-one talk focused on the delicate nuclear issue. What transpired in the Oval Office is unknown; all that the White House said later was that Reagan was satisfied that Zia was telling the truth—that Pakistan's nuclear program was strictly "for peaceful purposes." Zia repeated his commitment not to seek nuclear weapons in meetings with Congress and the press, and the visit was considered a big success for both sides.[18] Reagan never traveled to Pakistan himself, but he did send Vice President George Bush in May 1984. Again Zia promised that the nuclear program was strictly peaceful. "You have my personal assurance," Zia told Bush.[19]

Zia also pursued a desultory diplomatic track on Afghanistan. After securing an overwhelming vote in the UN General Assembly in 1980 to censure Moscow for invading Afghanistan, Pakistan and Saudi Arabia achieved an even more lopsided majority in 1981 that condemned the occupation again and proposed that the United Nations try to negotiate a Soviet withdrawal. An Ecuadoran diplomat, Diego Cordovez, headed the effort. After shuttling between Moscow, Kabul, Islamabad, and Tehran, he opened a dialogue in Geneva in June 1982. Pakistan would not recognize the legitimacy of the Babrak Karmal regime, so Cordovez held "proximity talks" with the Afghan communists and the Pakistanis separately. The Russians refused to discuss withdrawal and demanded that all outside interference in Afghanistan—meaning the CIA-ISI covert war—be halted. The Reagan administration did not participate in the Geneva talks at that point. As Reagan ran for reelection in 1984, the Geneva process stalled.

The Pot Boils

Reagan's second term would see a fundamental escalation in the secret war. After four years of stalemate, the Americans, Pakistanis, and Saudis decided in the mid-1980s to intensify the pressure on the Soviets and increase significantly their support for the Afghan resistance. Several different developments converged to produce that change, which would determine the outcome of the war. First and most important, Zia changed his mind. In 1985, he decided to escalate the conflict. Since neither Zia nor Akhtar ever wrote his memoirs, what constellation of factors convinced them that they could pursue a more provocative policy can only be surmised. Probably five years of war had been sufficient to convince Zia that the risk of Soviet invasion had passed. The 40th Red Army's strength had stabilized, and the Soviets were too preoccupied with the mujahedin to seriously consider an invasion of Pakistan. Thanks to U.S. intelligence, Zia knew that there was no Soviet buildup in Central Asia. Gorbachev had come into power in March 1985, after Chernenko's death, and seemed unlikely to pursue an aggressive invasion.

On Pakistan's other front, Indira Gandhi was assassinated on October 31, 1984, by her own Sikh bodyguards. Her son Rajiv succeeded her. Zia regarded Indira as a formidable opponent, for good reason. She had dismembered Pakistan in the 1971 war. Her son, however, was not so formidable; in fact, Zia regarded Rajiv as a playboy and lightweight. So what had always been Zia's worst fear—a two-front war in which the Soviet Union and India dismantled Pakistan—seemed significantly less likely to materialize after 1985. In addition, Reagan's reelection probably boosted Zia's confidence. He had come to trust the president and Casey and expected them to be in office for another four years. Zia undoubtedly still distrusted long-term U.S. staying power and reliability, but he had reason to believe that Reagan and Casey could be relied on for the time that they remained in office.

As discussed in chapter 4, in 1984 Zia authorized the ISI to explore missions into Soviet Central Asia, and in 1985 he authorized sabotage raids north of the Amu Darya River into the Soviet Union. The CIA declined to help the ISI conduct cross-border missions. Zia was getting bolder. In 1985 Zia also authorized the ISI to use the British Blowpipe surface-to-air missile system to help the mujahedin. It didn't work. However, by authorizing the delivery of the missiles to the battlefield, even in small numbers, Zia had broken with his own policy of plausible deniability: a British-made shoulder-fired missile was obviously not a weapon captured on the battlefield. In using Blowpipe missiles, Zia was taking a risk that the ISI's hand in the war would be discovered. Zia became more aggressive throughout 1985. Then, in January 1986, he surprised the United States by asking for Stinger surface-to-air missiles.

The request came at Zia's bungalow in Rawalpindi in a meeting with a visiting U.S. senator, Orrin Hatch from Utah, and the CIA's chief in Islamabad, Bill Piekney. After months of rebuffing requests for the Stingers from Mohammad Yousaf, his own Afghan branch chief, Zia told Hatch and Piekney that he would use them if the Unites States would supply them. As Piekney's successor, Milt Bearden, later wrote, "Hatch's meeting with Zia turned out to be a watershed event in American support to the Afghan rebels. With Zia's approval, opposition within the Reagan administration to the direct infusion of American arms collapsed.[20] When Casey visited Pakistan a few days after Hatch's visit, Zia told him that "this is the time to increase the pressure" on the Soviets. Casey replied that Washington was close to a decision to provide Stingers. The next month, Casey informed Zia that 400 missiles would be sent in a first installment[21] The old U.S. policy of plausible deniability in providing only weapons of Soviet origin to the freedom fighters had ended.

Zia's increased willingness to take risks was matched by a new mood in Washington. In a case of true bipartisan decisionmaking and cooperation, both the administration and Congress sought to do more. The U.S. Afghan war effort enjoyed genuine bipartisan support and, as required by law, was fully transparent to Congress. The Hollywood movie *Charlie Wilson's War* immortalized one of the key figures in the change in Washington, Charlie Wilson, a flamboyant Democratic congressman from Texas. He was elected to the House of Representatives in 1972, and his first foreign policy cause was to garner support for Israel during the 1973 war. Although he was not Jewish, Wilson developed a passionate commitment to the Israeli cause and a hatred for the Soviet Union. The Israeli embassy quickly saw the advantage of having the support of a congressman from Texas, a state with few Jewish voters, and a close friendship developed between Wilson and Zvi Rafiah, the embassy's congressional liaison officer[22]

Wilson's next foreign policy cause was to elicit support for Afghanistan and Pakistan in the Afghan war. One of his key fundraisers was a Texas millionaire named Joanne Herring, who was passionately anticommunist. She had been a supporter of Pakistan since the late 1970s, when Pakistan had few friends in Washington. The Pakistani ambassador, Sahabzada Yaqub Khan, who went on to become foreign minister, made her honorary consul in Houston. Herring converted Wilson to the

Afghan cause and convinced him to back Zia. As a member of several key committees, Wilson played an increasingly powerful role in pushing for an escalation of the war. He could secure increased appropriations for the CIA program in the House by virtue of his position and his contacts with other members. But he was not alone; Republicans like Orrin Hatch also were pushing for more money to fight the Soviets and for loosening restrictions on the kind of weapons that could be provided. There was a fairly broad bipartisan consensus for turning Afghanistan into the Soviet Union's Vietnam.

Two other CIA covert operations in the mid-1980s provide a striking contrast to the Afghan operation. The first was the covert war in Central America. Casey had been eager to assist anti-communist guerillas in Nicaragua from the first days of the Reagan administration; however, the anti-communist guerillas were seen by many as right-wing death squads, and Congress—especially the Democrats—was much less eager. Casey failed to build a consensus on the Hill in favor of his covert war in Central America. Worse, Congress tied his hands by ordering a stop to the operation. Casey also was deeply involved in another top-secret covert operation—the deal to provide arms to Iran, still at war with Iraq, in return for freeing American hostages in Lebanon held by Iran's terrorist organization Hizballah. Congress was never briefed on this covert action at all. In violation of the law, Casey and Reagan had sold arms to the Iranians and then used the money to fund the secret war in Nicaragua. The scandal following the discovery of the Iran-Contra affair resulted in the demise of Casey.

In contrast, bipartisan support in Congress increased the pressure on the Reagan administration to do more, not less, to help the mujahedin in Afghanistan. But the Hill was pushing on an open door at the White House, especially after the Pakistanis decided to turn up the heat. Both the State Department and the Defense Department also wanted to do more. In March 1985, the CIA professionals who wanted to maintain plausible deniability by refusing to provide U.S.-made arms were overruled when Reagan signed National Security Decision Directive 166, "which set forth a new American objective in Afghanistan: to win. To push the Soviets out."[23]

The Stinger missile system was at the center of the debate about how to do more. The missile had already been provided covertly to anti-communist insurgents in Angola, so its use in a guerilla war was not unprecedented.[24] Wilson and other hawks wanted to use the Stinger to defeat Soviet air superiority; however, the U.S. military, fearing loss of the technological advantage conveyed by its state-of-the-art weapons system, was reluctant to use it in an operation that did not directly protect U.S. troops. Many feared that once the mujahedin had the Stingers, the Soviets and Iranians would get some (and they did). Some in the CIA worried that supplying the Stinger system would destroy any pretense of plausible deniability for the covert program, that "whatever fig leaf we had" of cover would be gone. Others worried that Stingers would end up in the hands of terrorists outside Afghanistan. The potential for missiles being used by terrorists was a "serious and a valid concern," as one CIA officer said later.[25]

Nonetheless, Zia's change of mind on the missile question ended the debate. Casey was certain that Zia was right. The coming of the second Reagan administration also saw some important changes inside the CIA with respect to the war effort. Charles Cogan, whom Wilson had criticized as being too cautious, finished his tour as chief of the Near East Division in 1984 and went to an important overseas posting.[26] His successor was Tom Twetten, another career intelligence officer with years of experience in the Middle East. Casey and Twetten did not object when Wilson pushed for a substantial increase in funding—from $60 million to $100 million—for the Afghan covert action program in 1984. Just before Reagan's reelection in 1984, Casey pushed for an even larger increase in funding for 1985. Casey, with solid backing on the Hill from Wilson and others, suggested to the Pakistanis and Saudis an increase in the U.S. budget for the covert war to $250 million. The Saudis agreed to match the U.S. increase. As Gates wrote later, "the character of U.S. policy toward Afghanistan changed dramatically. Thanks mainly to pressure from Charlie Wilson and Casey's embrace of his support the size of the CIA's covert program to help the Mujahedin increased several times over.[27]

Wilson also wanted to get Israel involved in the Afghan war. In one of his frequent trips to Israel, he asked Israel Military Industries (IMI), the country's main armaments company, to build a mortar for the mujahedin that could be easily broken down for transport by mules over Afghanistan's harsh terrain. IMI did some design work on a project that it called CHARLIE HORSE. But the next time that Charlie came through Tel

Aviv, he had to tell IMI that the deal was off. The Saudis had told the CIA that Israel was to have no hand in the Afghan war. The CIA agreed with the Saudis that the operation was too sensitive to include Israel.[28]

Casey brought in another key figure to run the expanded CIA program in Pakistan—Milt Bearden, who replaced Bill Piekney in the summer of 1986. Bearden had joined the CIA in 1964. Casey had been impressed by Bearden when he met him in Lagos, Nigeria, in 1981 on one of Casey's early trips abroad. After his stint in Lagos, Bearden had served in Sudan in the mid-1980s, where he supervised a very sensitive operation to protect a team of Mossad officers and spirit them out of Khartoum and home to Tel Aviv while the Sudanese government tried to track them down. As Bearden wrote later, the operation "had caught Bill Casey's imagination."[29] Before leaving for Islamabad, Casey gave Bearden his marching orders in a meeting in the director's office on July 12, 1986. Casey spoke fondly of his friends Zia and Akhtar and urged close cooperation with the ISI. Then he told Bearden, "You do whatever it takes to win out there. I want to win the whole thing; Afghanistan is only a part of it. I will give you anything you'll need." The CIA program would be funded for 1987 at a half-billion dollars, meaning that with matching Saudi funding, it would be a billion-dollar effort. The covert action budget had expanded to ten times its original size in 1980.[30] Bearden would arrive in Islamabad with both an imminent tenfold increase in funding and the Stingers.

In 1987, another career officer, Frank Anderson, became chief of the task force running the Afghan war effort in Near East Division. Anderson later noted that the "Stinger coming in late 1986 just as the volume of weaponry that was being provided to the mujahedin went up ten times had the effect of making it go up twenty times."[31] To increase the pressure even more, Anderson kept looking for other new weapons. In 1987 the CIA began providing the ISI with French-made Milan anti-tank missiles for the mujahedin, followed by Soviet-made SPG-9 73-mm recoilless rifles, also for use against tanks. As Soviet morale plummeted, the morale of the freedom fighters jumped.[32] The pot was boiling.

Changes also were under way in Moscow. Gorbachev, unlike his predecessors, had no role in the decision to invade Afghanistan in December 1979. He also was much more aware than the men who had preceded him of the weaknesses of the Soviet system, especially its economy. He saw the war as a drain on Soviet military and economic resources that needed to be resolved, one way or another. But not all of his colleagues in the Kremlin agreed. So his first response was to give the military a chance to prove that it could win. The result was the large military offensive in 1987 (described in chapter 3) to defeat the mujahedin around Khost. As Gates later recalled, it was the last surge to prove whether the war was winnable. It also coincided with the arrival of large numbers of Stingers and Milans and the increase in the CIA's budget.[33]

Gorbachev was setting the stage to get out of Afghanistan or, at least, to bring home the 40th Army. The Soviet archives indicate that in October 1985 Gorbachev summoned Babrak Karmal to Moscow to tell him that the Soviet army was going to withdraw and that the Afghan communists needed to be ready to defend themselves without Soviet combat troops. In April 1986 Gorbachev meet Karmal again in Moscow and urged him to retire. Initially, Karmal refused, but under intense Soviet pressure he stepped down in May 1986. Najibullah, the secret police chief and Abdul Rashid Dostum's boss, replaced him.[34] A year later, in September 1987, Gorbachev's foreign minister, Eduard Shevardnadze, told Secretary of State Shultz privately that the Soviets would leave Afghanistan within a year. The Soviets had already told the Afghan communists that they were departing, but Washington didn't know that. In December 1987, at a summit with Reagan in Washington, Gorbachev announced publicly that the Soviets would be leaving over a twelve-month period. He sought an end to external aid to the mujahedin but did not insist on a political settlement to leave the communists in power before the 40th Army left.

A comprehensive review of the Soviet archives and Gorbachev's papers by a leading scholar, Artemy Kalinovsky, concluded that while Gorbachev probably wanted to get out of the war from the beginning of his term, he was very reluctant to do so if getting out meant a clear-cut Soviet defeat. The implications of a "botched withdrawal" for other Soviet global commitments deterred Gorbachev from an early and hasty departure from Afghanistan. Among the commitments that weighed heavily on Gorbachev's mind was the commitment to India, Moscow's key ally in South Asia. Gorbachev had an excellent relationship with Rajiv Gandhi, who did not want to see "a triumphant, resurgent Pakistan, confident it had won an ideological victory and helped defeat the mighty Red Army, which would surely start causing more trouble for India." Indeed, when Gorbachev met Rajiv shortly after Gorbachev's summit with Reagan in

Iceland in October 1986, the Indian prime minister told him, referring to the CIA and ISI covert war against the Soviets, that "it will be much worse for the region if imperialism succeeded in strangling the [Saur] revolution in Afghanistan."[35]

Making Gorbachev's effort to withdraw even more difficult, many in the Reagan administration were still skeptical of Gorbachev, even when he signaled his desire to get out to Shultz. Bob Gates was among the most skeptical. Nonetheless, Reagan had developed a relationship with Gorbachev and was ready to work with him. The two had met in Geneva in November 1985 and then again in Reykjavik, Iceland, in October 1986. The meeting in Hofoi House in Reykjavik was devoted almost entirely to arms control issues and produced no results on that score, but it did help to create a bond between the two leaders. As Cogan described it later, "by the time of the Reykjavik summit it was clear that we had something going here and Gorbachev was the key figure."[36]

The hitherto stalled talks in Geneva on Afghanistan acquired new importance as Moscow opened the door to withdrawal. Gorbachev pressed for a deal that would end all outside military aid to the fighting forces in Afghanistan. U.S. and Pakistani differences also became more apparent. Washington wanted to get the Soviets out of Afghanistan as quickly as possible, and while Zia also was eager to get them out, he naturally was more interested than the United States in what would come next in Kabul. Zia wanted as much commitment as possible that the communist regime would go too. Moscow refused. As a result, the Geneva talks focused almost entirely on whether there would be any constraints on the flow of arms to the warring parties after the Soviets left the country. Reagan insisted that the flow of arms to the mujahedin continue after the Soviet combat forces left. In December 1987, he dismissed the possibility of any aid cutoff in a public statement, arguing that "you can't suddenly disarm [the mujahedin] and leave them prey to the other government."[37] Thus 1987 was a critical year for Gorbachev, who finally had to accept that withdrawal would mean that the Afghan communists would be left to "face ultimate defeat." Soviet global credibility would suffer and there would be little political cover to hide the reality of the setback for the Red Army.[38]

On April 14, 1988, Shevardnadze, Shultz, Pakistani foreign minister Zain Noorani, and an Afghan envoy separately signed the Geneva

Accords under the auspices of the United Nations. The four delegations never met together. The agreements included some hortatory promises by Afghanistan and Pakistan to respect each other's sovereignty and territorial integrity. The main document outlined a promised Soviet troop withdrawal to begin on May 15, 1988, and conclude by February 15, 1989. A UN team, the UN Good Offices Mission in Afghanistan and Pakistan (UNGOMAP), would oversee the withdrawal. There was no agreement on halting either Soviet military and economic aid to the Afghan communists or CIA aid to the mujahedin.

UNGOMAP was set up in April 1988 to monitor the Soviet withdrawal. Fifty military officers from ten countries were sent to Kabul and Islamabad to serve as observers, most posted inside Afghanistan at its northern border exits to oversee the withdrawal. A Finnish major general, a choice judged to be neutral by Washington and Moscow, was put in charge. The UNGOMAP teams inspected Soviet installations to ensure the complete withdrawal and departure of the 40th Red Army. On crossing the bridge on the Amu Darya River on February 15, 1989, Lieutenant General Boris Gromov officially terminated the Soviet occupation of Afghanistan. Shortly afterward, the 40th Red Army ceased to exist. The Soviet Union had been defeated; the covert war was a success. The war between the Afghans, however, continued.

The mujahedin did not interfere seriously in the Soviet withdrawal, and the retreating forces were largely left undisturbed on their way out. Many of the mujahedin commanders, including Massoud, were already more focused on what would come next, and they wanted to save their resources and firepower for the battle for Kabul. In a back-door effort that infuriated their client Najibullah, the Soviets worked discreetly with Massoud to ensure that their withdrawal was as quiet as possible. To keep Najibullah happy, Soviet economic aid was increased in 1988 and 1989, more arms were delivered, and Soviet specialists and advisers remained behind in Kabul and other cities to assist the Afghan communist regime. But the combat forces were gone.[39]

The U.S. intelligence community had prepared a special national intelligence estimate in March 1988 predicting that the "Najibullah regime will not long survive the completion of Soviet withdrawal, even with continued Soviet assistance. The regime may fall before withdrawal is complete." The SNIE expected the mujahedin to fight among themselves but nonetheless stated that "we believe the resistance will retain sufficient supplies and military strength to ensure the demise of the communist government." The possibility that infighting among the mujahedin would be so intense that the communists could survive for a protracted period was considered less likely: according to the SNIE, "the odds of this outcome, in our view, are very small." Both Bearden and Anderson agreed with that assessment, which proved to be wrong.[40]

Some scholars have suggested that Gorbachev would have left Afghanistan even without the introduction of the Stinger in 1986 and the other weapons systems that followed, citing the meeting with Babrak Karmal in 1985 as evidence. That may be, but it is likely that Gorbachev's initial desire to find a way out was reinforced significantly by the Soviet setbacks on the battlefield that resulted from the escalation of the war in 1986 and 1987. The process was cumulative and reinforcing. According to the official Soviet count of casualties, more than 2,000 Russian soldiers died during the Gorbachev phase of the war, underscoring the fact that serious fighting went on under his command.[41] Indeed, the biggest battles of the war in Zhawar took place in the last years of the Soviet occupation.

Well before Gromov's televised departure, many of the main figures in the saga had passed away. Zia and Akhtar died in a mysterious plane crash on August 17, 1988. Even before the plane crash, Hamid Gul had replaced Akhtar as head of the ISI. Benazir Bhutto had become prime minister, and she and her civilian government were on a collision course with the military. Pakistan was a house divided against itself. Long before that, Casey had been caught in the webs of lies spun around his other covert operations, the ones that did not have solid support on Capitol Hill. In November 1986, the Iran-Contra scandal broke in the American media. Demands for Casey to step down began to be heard, and Reagan also faced sharp criticism. On December 15, 1986, Casey suffered a stroke in his office at the CIA and was taken to Georgetown University Hospital. The Pakistanis learned of the news from Bearden, in the midst of the crisis over Operation Brass Tacks, India's military maneuvers on the Pakistani border. Akhtar was deeply worried that Pakistan had lost its best friend in Washington just as the Indians were getting ready to strike.[42] Fortunately, as discussed previously, India and Pakistan backed away from the conflict. Casey died on May 6, 1987, from a brain tumor and was succeeded as director of central intelligence by William Webster. Reagan survived the Iran-Contra scandal and finished his term in office in January 1989. His successor and former vice president, George Bush, would officially preside over the last days of the war against the 40th Army.

As the last Soviet soldiers crossed the bridge home, Milt Bearden, the CIA chief in Islamabad, cabled Langley a terse message. The subject line read "Soviet Occupation of Afghanistan," and the text said simply "WE WON," in page-size letters. That night Bearden also ended a ritual. Since his arrival in Pakistan, he had left a table lamp in his office on twenty-four hours a day. The Soviet Embassy in Islamabad had a straight line of sight to his office. The KGB had told the CIA that they noticed that his office light always seemed to be on and that he seemed to be working around the clock. That night Bearden turned the light out.[43]

CHAPTER EIGHT

ENDGAMES WITHOUT END

THE AFGHAN WAR went on without the Soviet army. Moscow and Washington provided arms to the communists and mujahedin for another three years, then both lost interest. Afghanistan would descend into a bloody and endless civil war among the various mujahedin factions, with Abdul Rashid Dostum as a key participant. Later a new movement, the Taliban, would emerge and take over most of the country. Endless strategies to win the war would be devised by one side or another, but none succeeded and resulted in a real endgame. Then the 9/11 attacks brought the United States back to Afghanistan and into yet another long war without an endgame. The tangled history of Afghanistan after 1989 is beyond the scope of this book, which focuses on the covert war in the 1980s. Nonetheless, some review of the last two decades of war in Afghanistan is needed to understand why the CIA war in the 1980s succeeded and to determine what lessons the war offers for the future.

Bush's War

George Bush inherited a world in transition, one that was changing at a dizzying pace from the world of Ronald Reagan. The cold war, which had dominated global politics for a half-century, was coming to a rapid end. Bush came into office with impressive credentials for the job: he had been director of central intelligence, ambassador to China, and ambassador to the UN as well as a congressman and vice president of the nation. He assembled a solid team to run his foreign policy from the White House, including Brent Scowcroft, an experienced air force officer, as national security adviser and Bob Gates, from the CIA, as deputy national security adviser.

Afghanistan was still a key issue in early 1989, when the Soviet withdrawal and the covert war were still under way. But, as usual, it was Pakistan that commanded more attention in Washington. On November 16, 1988, Benazir Bhutto won Pakistan's first relatively fair and free elections in a decade, becoming prime minister at 35 years of age. She inherited from Zia an army and an ISI that were deeply suspicious of her. She, in turn, was deeply suspicious of the army and the ISI, which she despised for her years in prison and exile after her father's execution. She felt that her victory had come despite a concerted effort by the ISI and Osama bin Laden to defeat her and elect her opponent, Nawaz Sharif.[1] She was right.

After she took office, the ISI told her that the mujahedin would sweep to victory quickly once the last Soviet soldier left Afghanistan in 1989. The CIA gave President George Bush the same estimate.[2] However, it did not turn out that way. The communist government in Kabul, which did not fall from power until 1992, outlived the Union of Soviet Socialist Republics. Early in his administration, Bush invited Bhutto to Washington for a formal state visit, the first of his administration and the highest honor that he could pay a visiting foreign leader. He assured her that the CIA would continue to provide arms for the mujahedin and that Pakistan would continue to have the backing of the United States. U.S. policy, which had helped defeat the Soviets, stayed on autopilot, determined to quickly defeat the Afghan communists next. It failed.

The key reason for the failure was a strategic miscalculation by Hamid Gul, the new ISI director. Gul decided that since the Soviets were gone, the mujahedin should move from guerilla to conventional warfare, and the CIA agreed to support that strategy. The first target would be the city of Jalalabad, on the road from the Khyber Pass to Kabul. The siege that followed would be a terrible mistake. The mujahedin were simply not ready to conduct a conventional military siege against an enemy with artillery, tanks, Scud missiles, and air power. The Afghan communist army held off the mujahedin, and the stalemate led to bitter recriminations among the mujahedin factions. After that debacle, Bhutto engineered Gul's removal from his position as director of the ISI. Gul would go on to become a public advocate for the Taliban, the Kashmiri insurgency, and Osama bin

Laden. After the 9/11 attacks, he would say that they were the work of the Israeli intelligence service, the Mossad, and an excuse for U.S. intervention in Afghanistan.⑤ Just before her assassination in 2007, Benazir Bhutto claimed that he was plotting her murder.④

While the Afghan insurgency stalled, the Kashmiri insurgency blossomed. Much of it was the result of the anger of indigenous Kashmiri Muslims over years of heavy-handed oppression by India. In 1988, 1989, and 1990, the bottled-up anger of the Kashmiris exploded into riots and violence, with the number of incidents of violence rising from 390 in 1988 to 2,100 in 1989 and almost 4,000 in 1990.⑤ By August 1989 India was reinforcing its already large troop presence in the province to suppress the unrest, using a very heavy hand, and the growing tension in Kashmir exacerbated Indo-Pakistani tensions. New Delhi accused Islamabad of helping the insurgents. In December 1989, Pakistan responded with a massive military exercise, deploying 200,000 ground troops and virtually the entire Pakistani air force in a display of its might and determination to aid the Kashmiri resistance.⑥ The rhetoric on both sides heated up as well. On March 13, 1990, Benazir declared that Pakistan would fight for a "thousand years" to free Kashmir. The two countries seemed to be heading toward war. To try to calm things down, President George Bush dispatched Bob Gates, the deputy national security adviser, and Richard Haass, the senior director for Near East and South Asia affairs in the National Security Council, to the region in May 1990. By the end of their trip, tensions had begun to abate.

After the crisis had passed, the army and Pakistan's president, Ghulam Ishaq Khan, moved to oust Benazir Bhutto, citing alleged corruption by Bhutto and her husband, Asif Ali Zardari. New elections were called, and the ISI worked actively to help elect Nawaz Sharif, a prominent Punjabi politician. According to Husain Haqqani, Pakistan's future ambassador to the United States, Hamid Gul ran the anti-Bhutto campaign for the army, which included allegations that Bhutto had "strong Zionist links" and was too pro-American.⑦ Before Sharif took office, the bottom fell out of the U.S.-Pakistani relationship. In October 1990, President Bush reported to Congress that he could not certify that Pakistan was abiding by U.S. requests not to cross the nuclear threshold, saying, in effect, that Pakistan had a nuclear bomb. Under the terms of the Pressler Amendment, all U.S. foreign assistance to Pakistan had to be halted immediately;

even equipment that had been paid for, like the F-16 fighter jets, could not be delivered. The spring 1990 crisis between Pakistan and India and the Gates and Haass mission had contributed to the growing sense in Washington that Pakistan did in fact have a bomb—after all, if Pakistan didn't, why was Bush worried about a possible nuclear exchange in South Asia?

The Pakistanis argued that because the Soviets were in retreat, the United States simply did not need their country anymore. Many, if not most, felt then and now that the United States had just used the nuclear issue as a means to dispense with helping Pakistan; the United States had known of Pakistan's nuclear ambitions under Zia but pretended that Islamabad had not crossed the threshold. Other Pakistanis would say that the Afghan war had provided Zia with crucial cover in Washington in the early and mid-1980s, allowing Pakistan to build the bomb without U.S. sanctions. A. Q. Khan, the self-described father of Pakistan's bomb, has said that he urged Zia to test a bomb in 1984 but that Zia told him to wait while the war continued. Khan concluded that "had the Afghan war not taken place, we would not have been able to make the bomb as early as we did given the U.S. and European pressure on our program."[8]

The new prime minster, Nawaz Sharif, was a protégé of Zia, who had hand-picked him to be governor of the Punjab. He found himself inheriting the jihads in Afghanistan and Kashmir but without the U.S. support that Zia and Benazir had enjoyed. He was highly dependent on the ISI and the army as well as the religious parties for his position. Sharif had a new ISI commander, Lieutenant General Javid Nasir, a self-proclaimed Islamist who was very eager to prosecute the wars east and west and pushed Sharif to pursue both jihads.

The Afghan war came to a head in April 1992, when Abdul Rashid Dostum, who was now the key commander in the communist army, defected to the mujahedin. The communist government collapsed quickly from within, and the mujahedin finally took Kabul. After 12 years it appeared that Zia's jihad had triumphed, but it was an empty triumph. The mujahedin fell to fighting among themselves, and the brutal and bloody civil war that followed continues to this day.

With the suspension of U.S. aid to Pakistan and the collapse of the communist government in Kabul, the CIA's covert war in Afghanistan came to an end. Funding for the mujahedin also ended, and the CIA's

Afghan task force was disbanded. Indeed, the United States turned its back on Afghanistan for the next decade. In 1991 and 1992, I served on President Bush's National Security Council; I don't recall that there was a single principal-level meeting to discuss the situation in Afghanistan during that period. There were, however, numerous meetings to discuss the greatest problem that Washington thought that it still had in Afghanistan: the CIA had sent more Stinger missiles to the mujahedin than they needed to defeat the Soviets and these highly accurate weapons were starting to appear on the international black market, where they could be purchased to shoot down a commercial airliner. The CIA was authorized to buy them back at the U.S. taxpayer expense and did so over the next decade. In the White House Situation Room, frequent meetings monitored the progress of the buy-back program, which was called Operation MIAS (Missing in Action Stingers). Many were bought from the ISI, which bought them from the mujahedin and sold them back to the United States at a profit.[9]

In retrospect it is easy to see that the U.S. neglect of Afghanistan was a major mistake. Because Afghanistan was left to the warlords and the ISI, not only did the Afghan people suffer tremendously but a very toxic environment also was created that would give rise to the Taliban and al Qaeda. But that is hindsight. In the 1990s Washington confronted a host of other urgent crises. The collapse of the Warsaw Pact and East Germany, the Iraqi invasion of Kuwait, the Yugoslav civil wars, and many other crises filled the in-boxes of national security advisers and secretaries of state, all requiring urgent attention. Afghanistan and Pakistan drifted to the bottom of the in-box and stayed there.

However, when the U.S. intelligence community in early 1992 reported growing evidence of ISI support for the Kashmiri and Sikh insurgencies in India, the Bush administration had to consider how to respond. The U.S. government is required by law to make public each year a list of countries that are supporting terrorism. By early 1992, the National Security Council (where I was the Pakistan desk officer) and the State Department, in close consultation with the intelligence community, felt that Pakistan met the criteria for being put on the state sponsor list. It would be a very serious step. By law a state on the terrorism sponsor list cannot receive any assistance whatsoever from the United States, including even indirect assistance. That meant that Washington would have to vote against assistance to Pakistan in global financial institutions like the International Monetary Fund and the World Bank. The sanctions already imposed on Pakistan for violating the Pressler Amendment in 1990 would be toughened considerably.

As a first step, Secretary of State James Baker sent a letter to Prime Minister Nawaz Sharif warning him that Pakistan was on the brink of making the list. Ambassador Nicholas Platt delivered the letter. Husain Haqqani, who was Sharif's special assistant at the time, has written that at first Sharif ignored the letter, then convened his national security team to discuss it in May 1992. Haqqani read the letter to the group. It accused the ISI of providing "material support" to groups that engaged in terrorism and stressed that the information, which was highly reliable, demonstrated that the government of Pakistan, including the prime minister and the chief of army staff, were responsible. Unless the assistance halted and all the ISI training camps were closed, sanctions would follow. The ISI chief, Javid Nasir, declared the letter to be the work of the "Hindu-Zionist lobby" in the United States and denounced Platt as a Jew (he was a Protestant). In response, Nasir simply recommended some minor changes in provision of ISI support to the Kashmiris and Sikhs to better hide ISI's hand. Support would continue, under better cover. In the end, the Bush administration chose to wait another year, until 1993, to see if the threat of sanctions worked.[10]

By the end of the Bush administration, the United States was seriously considering labeling Pakistan a state sponsor of terrorism. An administration that began with a state dinner for the Pakistani prime minister was, four years later, close to declaring Pakistan a pariah nation for breaking international law. U.S. influence in Islamabad was low and getting worse. U.S. influence with the ISI and the Afghan mujahedin was nonexistent. It's unclear what the United States could have done differently. Washington's leverage with Pakistan depended on an aid relationship that was broken. Washington's influence with the mujahedin was a function of U.S. provision of weapons, but by 1992 the arms program was over. In any case, the warlords didn't need the CIA; they had plenty of weapons, and the Saudis provided plenty of money. The warlords and their ISI patrons were unlikely to listen seriously to U.S. envoys who were urging a negotiated settlement between the warlords and the communists. Peter Tomsen, Bush's special envoy to Afghanistan after 1989, tried hard to get a settlement; however, he had little leverage, especially with Pakistan, once the aid relationship was severed.[11]

Pakistan found itself backing its major clients in the mujahedin, especially Gulbuddin Hekmatyar's Pashtun group, against the other mujahedin factions, especially that led by the Tajik leader Ahmad Shah Massoud. The civil war was incredibly complex—and with players switching sides, it became more so—and much violence was directed against civilians. Afghanistan was descending into anarchy; it was not the ally that Pakistan had envisioned to provide strategic depth for Islamabad against India.

Then, following another mysterious death of a national leader, Pakistani politics changed abruptly. General Asif Nawaz, the chief of army staff, suddenly died in January 8, 1993. His wife suggested that he had been poisoned and that the prime minister, Nawaz Sharif, may have been part of a conspiracy to kill him. Asif Nawaz had taken command determined to get the army out of politics. In his first order of the day, he said that it was time for the army to allow the democratic process to work and to return to the business of being a professional military organization. Asif tried to persuade Nawaz Sharif and Benazir Bhutto to reconcile for the good of the nation.[12] Asif also was concerned by the deteriorating security situation in the country's only port, Karachi, where sectarian violence was boiling out of control, and he was increasingly said to be concerned that the prime minister was not up to the job of governing. His mysterious death, which has never been fully explained, would usher in yet another change at the top.[13] Just as Benazir Bhutto had been ousted for corruption, Nawaz Sharif was removed by the president for corruption and for failure to investigate Asif's death adequately. In 1993, new elections were held. Voters returned Benazir to office for a second term as prime minister. To replace the jihadi Nasir, a new ISI chief, General Javed Ashraf Qazi, was appointed; Qazi said that he was determined to reduce the ISI's profile in Pakistani politics and "to make ISI invisible again.[14] The new U.S. president, Bill Clinton, and his team decided not to put Pakistan on the terrorism list and to give Benazir another chance.

In Afghanistan, a new phenomenon emerged that would change the direction of the country and, in turn, deeply affect Pakistan's own course. The Taliban ("students") movement was a result of the years of anarchy that followed the fall of Kabul to the mujahedin. Pakistan did not create the Taliban, but soon after the movement arose, Pakistan, including the

ISI and the Ministry of the Interior, began to give it significant support. Pakistan, under Bhutto, would be the Taliban's champion in the international arena, arguing that the Taliban was the only hope for stability and ultimately peace in the country. Pakistan would be one of only three countries to recognize the Taliban government and to open an embassy in Kabul. It would provide critical oil supplies for the economy and crucial military advice and assistance. When the Taliban's Islamic Emirate of Afghanistan was sanctioned by the United Nations in 1998, Pakistan would stand by the Taliban and continue to give it aid.

At the head of the Taliban is Mullah Mohammed Omar, an unusual man by any standard. He has met with only a handful of non-Muslims in his life. He has no record of any major writings or memoirs. He has been a soldier almost all of his life, and he bears scars from wounds sustained in battle. Since late 2001 he has been in hiding, virtually unseen. Above all, he has led his supporters to two major military successes, first in taking over most of Afghanistan in the 1990s and then in staging a spectacular military comeback after being routed from Afghanistan in 2001 by the U.S.-led coalition and the Northern Alliance. Finally, he developed a remarkable alliance, even friendship, with Osama bin Laden. Throughout, he has worked with Pakistan, strategically if not always easily.

According to his official 2009 Taliban biography, Muhammad Omar was born in 1960 in Kandahar Province into a family of religious scholars. Orphaned at three, he was brought up by an uncle and received religious training. In 1979 he joined the mujahedin and fought for a time in neighboring Orzugan Province. He was wounded three times in the war with the Soviets and lost his right eye on the third occasion. That injury led to a visit to Quetta, in Pakistan, for hospital care. The official biography emphasizes that it was his only visit to Pakistan and that unlike most other mujahedin leaders, he did not reside in Pakistan during the war or send his family there for safety. All stayed in Afghanistan to fight the "Red Soviet Bear," as the official story puts it. The implication is that Mullah Omar was independent and did not succumb to the temptations of the more cultured life across the Durand Line. The official biography ends with the story that Omar even refuses to consume cream or soft bread, preferring more austere alternatives such as soup and stale bread[15]

In fact, Mullah Omar did receive training from the ISI in Pakistan during the war.[16] His rise to power in the 1990s was greatly facilitated by

Pakistan once it concluded that his new party, the Taliban, was the most effective means for advancing Pakistan's ambitions in Afghanistan. The rise of the Taliban has been extensively researched and written about by several authors, most notably Ahmed Rashid, a Pakistani journalist and author. He says that by 1997 the Pakistanis were providing $30 million in aid annually to the Taliban as well as free oil to run the country's war machine.[17] By 1999 one-third of the fighters in the Taliban were either Pakistani fundamentalists or foreign volunteers who arrived by way of Pakistan.[18] Mullah Omar gave Osama bin Laden the authority to run his terrorist empire and to plot attacks abroad from Afghanistan, and al Qaeda became a state within a state. The alliance of the Taliban and al Qaeda would set the stage for 9/11, which in turn set the stage for the U.S. intervention in Afghanistan. The Taliban was quickly toppled from power, and the United States and its NATO allies took on the challenge of building a new Afghanistan. The longest war in U.S. history followed.

The U.S. War and the Soviet War

Rarely does a country fight the same war twice in one generation; to fight it twice from opposite sides is even rarer. Yet in many ways, that is what the United States did in Afghanistan. In the 1980s the CIA engineered the largest covert operation in its history to defeat the Soviet 40th Red Army in Afghanistan, working from a safe haven in Pakistan. After 2001, the United States first overthrew the Taliban Islamic Emirate of Afghanistan and then fought a Taliban-led insurgency in Afghanistan, which again was operating from a safe haven in Pakistan. Many suggest that the outcome will be the same for the United States as it was for the Union of Soviet Socialist Republics—ultimate defeat at the hands of the insurgency. That analysis misses the many fundamental differences between the two wars. But it is also important to note their one major similarity: the role played by Pakistan.

The first and perhaps most critical differences involve goals and objectives. The United States intervened in Afghanistan in 2001 on the side of the Northern Alliance to topple the Taliban Islamic Emirate of Afghanistan only after the emirate had been used as a base for the 9/11 attacks on the United States. The U.S. goal, endorsed by the United Nations and the North Atlantic Treaty Organization, was self-defense against a government that had allowed its territory to be used to launch an act of war against another state. From the beginning the United States has had no ambition to dominate or to subjugate the Afghan people or to stay in Afghanistan once the threats posed by al Qaeda and the Taliban were defeated. President Obama reiterated that position in a speech outlining his new policy for Afghanistan and Pakistan on March 27, 2009.[19]

The Soviet invasion in 1979 was a very different matter. Moscow blundered into Afghanistan with little appreciation of the difficulties that it would face. Its goal was to shore up a communist regime that was on the edge of collapse in the face of a national uprising against it. The Soviet leadership wanted an Afghanistan that would be like other Soviet satellite states—that is, under virtual Soviet imperial rule, with only a façade of independence. The Soviets may also have had ambitions to use Afghanistan as a base for further expansion of their authority south, although the evidence for that is slim. The United Nations, which endorsed the U.S. 2001 action in Afghanistan, condemned the Soviet invasion overwhelmingly in several votes in the General Assembly.

The Soviet invasion and the attempt to impose communism on a rural, religious, and largely illiterate Islamic country with a history of xenophobia produced a predictable result: a national mass uprising. With the exception of small pockets of the urban middle class and a few minority regions—most notably the Uzbek province of Jowzjan, where Abdul Rashid Dostum raised a pro-Soviet militia—virtually the entire country was violently opposed to the new occupation and its atheist ideology. In contrast, polls show that most Afghans have supported the NATO coalition forces that overthrew the Taliban from 2001 on. The Taliban insurgency is restricted to the Pashtun belt in southern and eastern Afghanistan; it has virtually no appeal to the 60 percent of Afghans who are not Pashtuns. For example, because it is an exclusively Tajik area, the famous Panjsher Valley, where the Soviet Union fought its most difficult battles, is today a quiet and calm part of the country with no Taliban presence.[20]

In short, while the Soviets faced a national uprising, the United States faced a minority insurgency that has little support in much of the country. Moscow's task was much more difficult than the one that the NATO coalition forces took on, and the Soviets responded to the uprising with a ferocity and brutality that made the situation even worse. At least 1 million Afghans were killed, another 5 million or so (one in four Afghans) fled the country to Iran and Pakistan, and millions more were displaced within the country. A nation that began the war as one of the poorest in the world was systematically impoverished further and even emptied of its people. Millions of land mines were planted all over the country, with no maps kept of where they had been planted. Nothing even approaching this level of horror is happening today in Afghanistan. The Soviet invasion was condemned by virtually the entire world, except for its client states and India. The campaign to assist the Afghan insurgency, the mujahedin, enjoyed the backing of countries around the world, including China, the United Kingdom, France, Egypt, Saudi Arabia, Iran, and others.

The International Security Assistance Force (ISAF), the NATO force in Afghanistan today, enjoys the support of the United Nations and operates under a UN Security Council mandate. The ISAF, created by the UN in 2001, had troops from over forty countries in Afghanistan at its peak, including the United States, NATO countries, and non-NATO states like Australia, Sweden, and the United Arab Emirates.[21] Moreover, much of the hardest fighting of the war has been done by non-U.S. troops. The British in Helmand Province, the Canadians in Kandahar, and the Dutch and Australians in Oruzgan fought for several years in the heartland of the Taliban. Although the differences between the U.S. and the Soviet experiences are significant, the role played by Pakistan is at least one major similarity. In the 1980s President Zia ul-Haq agreed to support the mujahedin insurgency despite the enormous risks involved in provoking the Soviet Union, then the world's largest military power. The Soviets responded with an intense covert campaign to foment unrest inside Pakistan, especially in the border areas and in the refugee camps. Both the KGB and its Afghan counterpart, the KHAD, conducted terrorist attacks to exert pressure on Zia. Moreover, the Soviets used their military power, especially the air force, to try to intimidate Pakistan. There were several dogfights between Pakistani and Soviet aircraft in which the Pakistanis acquitted themselves well.

Zia insisted that support for the mujahedin from the outside world had to flow exclusively through Pakistani hands, principally through the Pakistani army's Directorate for Inter-Services Intelligence, and the ISI jealously maintained its exclusive access to the mujahedin. Outside players had little choice but to accept Zia's rules. Consequently, Pakistan served as a safe haven for the mujahedin, as their logistical supply line, and as their advocate on the world stage. Ironically, today Pakistan serves as a safe haven and logistical supply line for the Taliban insurgency, and the ISI is again the instrument by which Pakistan maintains its links, this time to the Taliban and other extremist organizations. That should come as little surprise: in the 1990s, the ISI was a critical factor in the creation and development of the Taliban and only reluctantly agreed to distance itself from the Taliban after 9/11, under enormous U.S. pressure. It is now clear that the distancing was far from complete.

The key leadership council of the Taliban sanctuary in Pakistan is the so-called Quetta Shura, named after the capital of Baluchistan, where the senior Taliban leaders, probably including Mullah Omar, reside. Quetta, a city of some 2 million, provides excellent cover for the Taliban leadership, under which it operates and leads the insurgency. For a number of reasons, Pakistan retains links to the Taliban despite the rising incidence of jihadist violence inside Pakistan itself. Most important is the army's calculation that Washington does not have the political will to persevere in Afghanistan. It is widely assumed in Pakistan that U.S. and European determination to fight it out in Afghanistan is eroding, an assumption reinforced by polls that show that support for the conflict is steady declining on both sides of the Atlantic. Supporting the Taliban is thus a useful hedge against the day when NATO gives up the struggle and leaves. Pakistan will then have a relationship with the future Pashtun leaders of southern and eastern Afghanistan and an asset in the struggle for post-NATO Afghanistan. That day is now not far away: President Obama has promised that all U.S. combat troops will leave Afghanistan in 2014. It will soon be known whether the ISI's assessment that the Kabul government will collapse without U.S. troops to back it up is correct or not.

There is one final area in which a comparative study of the Soviet and NATO-led wars in Afghanistan is very illuminating. As already noted, the Soviet Union never put the resources into the Afghan war that were needed to achieve success. For almost the entire campaign, the Red Army stationed about 100,000 troops in the country—far fewer than the number used in Hungary or Czechoslovakia to keep those countries inside the Soviet empire. But the United States and its allies in ISAF and NATO have done even less. For each year from 2002 to 2007, the United States deployed fewer than 25,000 troops to Afghanistan (only 9,000 in 2002–04) and the allies contributed fewer than 5,000. When President Obama took office in 2009, the U.S. force was roughly 32,000 strong and NATO troops numbered about 10,000. In 2009 the president committed to tripling the size of the U.S. force, but with the promise that all combat troops would be removed by 2014. Allied contributions peaked at about 40,000 in 2010. In short, for most of the U.S. war in Afghanistan, the United States deployed far fewer troops than the USSR did for most of its war in the came country.[22] When Washington finally approved a troop surge, it signaled up front that it would be short-lived, thus undermining its impact significantly.

Two senior George W. Bush administration officials involved in managing the war in Afghanistan have written devastating memoirs detailing how few resources it devoted to the war effort in the critical first six years of the struggle. Dov Zakheim, in the Pentagon, was undersecretary of defense for resources, and Ron Neumann was ambassador to Afghanistan during those key years. The title of Zakheim's book tells the story: *A Vulcan's Tale: How the Bush Administration Mismanaged the Reconstruction of Afghanistan*. Neumann's *The Other War* gives the basic reason: the Bush team was preoccupied with Iraq and starved the Afghan war of the necessary resources for too long.[23]

One more comparison deals with the Afghan army and air force. The Soviets made an enormous effort before, during, and after their invasion to try to build an Afghan communist army and air force to defeat the mujahedin. Dostum was their prize pupil. Nonetheless, they failed trying. The Soviets did build an Afghan air force, which at its peak had 400 fixed-wing and 100 rotary-wing aircraft. After a dozen years, the NATO effort falls far, far short of that target, with less than 100 aircraft all told. Only in 2009 did the United States finally get serious about building up Afghanistan's army. It made much better progress then, but the fact remains that for most of the U.S. war, simply too few resources have been allocated to building an Afghan military. The bottom line is that if—an important "if"—the United States and NATO fail in Afghanistan, the burden of blame lies at home. The United States had a better chance of succeeding in the conflict than Moscow had, but it may have failed to do enough, especially early enough, to succeed.

LESSONS OF THE SECRET WAR

THE HEERESGESCHICHTLICHES MUSEUM, a museum of military history in Vienna, contains a remarkable exhibit from one of the most important covert operations in world history: the assassination, on June 28, 1914, of Archduke Franz Ferdinand of Austria, the heir-apparent to the throne of the Austro-Hungarian Empire. In the museum, the Austrians have carefully preserved the car that the archduke and his wife were riding in when they were shot to death, the uniform that the archduke was wearing, and the pistol used by the assassin, Gavrilo Princip, which had been provided by the Serbian intelligence service. The assassination of Franz Ferdinand resulted in World War I, one of the deadliest conflicts in human history. There were many other causes of the Great War, but the murder of the archduke and his wife in Sarajevo was the catalyst.

Covert operations can have consequences never imagined by the planners and operatives who conduct them. One of the key lessons of the CIA's secret war in Afghanistan in the 1980s is that it resulted in outcomes, good and bad, that were never envisioned by the Carter administration or the Near East Division when they began thinking about how to turn Afghanistan into Russia's Vietnam. Nor did the Bosnians and Serbs who plotted to attack the Austrian crown prince in 1914 envision what the attack would bring in its wake. The mastermind of the assassination plot was a Serbian army officer, Dragutin Dimitrijevic, better known by his nom de guerre "Apis," after the ancient Egyptian bull god. He was a founding member of the terrorist group Ujedinjenje ili smrt (Unification or Death), better known as the Black Hand. The group thrived on secrecy and clandestine operations. Its goal was to unite all Serbians into a larger state, even if that meant a state with large minorities of Albanians, Croats, Bosnian Muslims, and Slovenes. Even a hundred years later, many of the details of the plot remain cloaked in mystery.

In August 1913 Apis was appointed chief of intelligence for the Serbian general staff, putting him in charge of all Serbian espionage activities. How much oversight the Serbian government had of his plans is unclear to this day. Equally unclear is what Apis and the Black Hand supposed that the murder of the Austrian heir would accomplish. The crown prince, the leader of the "dovish" camp in the royal family, opposed war with Russia and thus with Serbia, and he had predicted that war would lead to the collapse of the Austro-Hungarian and Russian empires.[1] Some historians have suggested that if Ferdinand had lived, war might have been averted. Perhaps the assassins did not really care about the details; maybe all that they wanted was to cause a crisis in Austria that would open the door to another Balkan war, which they believed would lead to the "liberation" of Bosnia and Herzegovina and the creation of a greater Serbia.[2]

They achieved their goal. At the end of the war, a Serb-dominated state, Yugoslavia, was created from the ashes of the Austro-Hungarian Empire and united the western Balkans for the next 70 years, until it fell apart in the 1990s. The cost was staggering. It is estimated that 37 million people were killed or wounded in World War I. Four great historic empires—the German, Russian, and Turkish empires as well as the Austro-Hungarian Empire—collapsed.[3] Austria paid an especially high price: of the 50 million people who were subjects of the empire in 1914, over 1.25 million became casualties in the first six months of the war alone.[4] Communism and fascism emerged from the war as global ideologies, setting the stage for the even more violent and costly World War II and the subsequent cold war. The Black Hand altered world history, underscoring the fact that covert operations can have consequences and implications far beyond those that they are intended to have.

Of course, the assassination of the Austrian heir and the war in Afghanistan are not identical events. One was an isolated act, the other a sustained campaign. But both had consequences that changed world history. The impacts of the secret war in Afghanistan also extended far beyond the objectives of the leaders who first envisioned it. Jimmy Carter, Zbigniew Brzezinski, and the CIA officers who drafted the first authorization of

arms shipments to the ISI for transshipment to the mujahedin were seeking only to harass and weaken the Soviet occupation forces in Afghanistan. Many were motivated by a simple desire for revenge for the Vietnam War. None envisioned that the mujahedin would actually defeat the
Soviets. No one seriously considered victory to be an option until years
after the covert war had begun; even in 1985, it was a controversial goal
that was shared by only a small minority. So the first lesson of the secret
war is that covert operations can have big impacts far beyond those that
the planners envision when they start. Unintended consequences should
be considered a virtual inevitability. The covert U.S. war offers other lessons, discussed in detail below, pertaining to the policy process, alliance
management, mission clarity, and unintended consequences.

*U.S. foreign policy and covert action are most likely to succeed
when the intelligence and policy communities work well together
but stay in their respective "lanes."*

The decisions to embark on a covert intelligence operation in Afghanistan and Pakistan in 1980 and then to expand it greatly in 1986 provide
useful insights into the connection between policy and intelligence in two
administrations. In neither case did the intelligence service lead the policy
formulation process. In 1980 the White House took the lead in promot-
ing a covert war in Afghanistan. In 1986 pressure from both Pakistan
and Congress led the director of the CIA to push a willing administration
to escalate the war. In both cases, the professional intelligence experts
and managers were somewhat reluctant warriors, at least in the beginning. To put it another way, the spymasters were more conservative and
risk averse than their political masters. While the intelligence service was
a full partner in the policy formulation process, it provided cautionary
advice; it did not push for radical and dangerous programs.

Such risk aversion in the spy world differs from the perception of some
outsiders that the CIA is a rogue institution that takes the law into its own
hands and operates free of oversight by the White House and Congress.
One study by the National Security Archive, based on extensive review of
internal government documents, has concluded that "it was the CIA, ironically, that cautioned against too much covert aid for the rebels [because]
too large a military support operation for the rebels might provoke a

Soviet retaliation against Pakistan. ⑤The CIA was especially risk averse about supplying U.S.-made weapons. The British were much more willing to take risks, including with their own people on the ground. It can be categorically stated that in the Afghan case, the CIA, far from being a rogue organization, obeyed the law and gave cautionary, not crazy, advice.

President Carter and Zbigniew Brzezinski, his national security adviser, were the forces driving the policy process that led to the CIA's war in Afghanistan. They decided to respond aggressively to the Soviet invasion of Afghanistan in the last week of December 1979, reached out to the Pakistanis, and notified Congress of their decision. Stansfield Turner, the director of central intelligence, and his lieutenants in the Near East Division quickly turned that decision into reality in the first days of January 1980. Both the White House and CIA headquarters at Langley wanted to preserve plausible deniability about the U.S. role. So too did Zia ul-Haq. The policy and intelligence communities in two countries, the United States and Pakistan, were in lockstep with regard to how they wanted to fight the secret war. Zia, of course, held the most important cards since all the action would take place in his territory.

President Reagan and his director of central intelligence, William Casey, inherited a mature covert operation in January 1981 and made few changes to it for the first several years of Reagan's first term in office. Again, there was consensus among policymakers and intelligence professionals in both the United States and Pakistan, until 1984 or so, that maintaining plausible deniability required a low-risk approach. The goal was to increase the cost of Soviet occupation, not to drive the Soviets out. The decision in 1985–86 to go for a bigger goal—to defeat the 40th Red Army and drive the Soviets out of Afghanistan—was more complex. The key driver, again, was Zia. Zia was ready to be more aggressive, first by using Blowpipe missiles and conducting cross-border raids into Soviet Central Asia, then by using Stinger missiles. In the U.S. decisionmaking process, Congress was a key driver, especially Charlie Wilson. Once both Zia and Wilson were pressing for escalation, Casey and Reagan were eager to go along. Again, the CIA professionals were somewhat reluctant at first to take steps that would undermine plausible deniability. Casey overruled them and put together a team that shared his goal: total victory in the cold war. The Afghan covert operation was done with the full support of Congress, which was properly notified of each aspect of the operation and given full oversight of the CIA's activities—proof that congressional oversight can assist, not diminish, the likelihood of success in clandestine operations.

The differences in the interplay between the White House and the CIA in the two administrations is striking. Carter was an avid reader of the agency's written materials, especially the "President's Daily Brief." He often asked questions of the CIA briefer who brought the document to the Oval Office each morning; he even wrote notes on it. Once a week, at least early in his tenure, he also had an hour-long special briefing by Turner and experts on a specific subject. Topics included analysis of world events as well as operations activity, intelligence collection systems, and the status of the war in Afghanistan. Carter and Brzezinski were in constant touch with the intelligence community. Turner later wrote that Carter was always totally concentrated on the briefings, oral or written.[6] It was almost unprecedented in CIA history for the agency to have such frequent access to the president and so much feedback. According to a study by the CIA's Center for the Study of Intelligence, the agency had not had such contact with a president since Harry Truman. Other presidents got briefed in various ways "but never in the systematic way that the Agency was able to establish with Carter."[7] Carter later recalled in my interview with him that he found the interaction with the CIA very stimulating.

Reagan was almost the opposite. He did not get regular briefings from the agency after his inauguration. The same CIA study reports that "daily contact was cut off, and intelligence support for the President was provided only indirectly through the National Security Advisor," except for direct interaction with Casey. In eight years Reagan had only one or two briefings by agency personnel, and he rarely made any comments on the written material that he received. So his personal line of communication with Casey provided the president with almost all of his information on intelligence matters, including the secret war in Afghanistan. He was a more remote policymaker, who "valued receiving information from individuals he knew personally and with whom he was comfortable."[8]

During both administrations the policy and intelligence communities interacted effectively in pursuing the secret war in Afghanistan. There were no rogue intelligence operations conducted outside policy or legislative oversight, unlike during the Iran-Contra affair.[9] The intelligence community gave two presidents its best judgment about the situation in

Afghanistan and its best estimate of what to expect next. Not surprisingly, the estimates did not always predict the future perfectly. The community did not expect the Soviets to put troops on the ground in 1979, nor did it anticipate that the Mohammad Najibullah regime would last as long as it did. It did, however, accurately analyze and predict Pakistani behavior during the war and the staying power of the mujahedin.

The policy and intelligence communities were closely connected throughout the war but remained distinctly separate entities. The intelligence experts and professionals offered advice, but they did not try to make policy. The elected policymakers did not try to influence the intelligence estimates, even when they did not agree with them. The system seemed to work best when, as one British intelligence officer put it, "intelligence and policy [are] in separate but adjoining rooms, with communicating doors and thin partition walls, as in cheap hotels."[10]

Alliance management is always more challenging in war than in any other endeavor.

Some have argued, after the fact, that Pakistan was given too large a role in the decisionmaking process. Zia decided who got what equipment and set the pace of operations. Critics like Peter Tomsen, who served as special envoy to the Afghan resistance in the Bush administration after 1989, have argued persuasively that this set the stage for the more extreme factions, like the Hekmatyar and Haqqani groups, to gain the upper hand in the internal civil war that began after the Soviets left and escalated when the Najibullah regime fell.[11] There is no serious disagreement that Pakistan favored its clients in the war and had its own strategic interest in ensuring that they prevailed in the post-Soviet phase. That Pakistani determination to protect its Pashtun clients did not change significantly when Zia and Akhtar died or when Benazir Bhutto took power or even when Nawaz Sharif replaced her.

The real question is whether the United States had any viable policy alternatives to Pakistan or whether U.S. influence could have altered Pakistan's strategy. There the answer is more complex. At one level there was no alternative. As Frank Anderson has rightly noted, there are only three ways to get to Afghanistan: the Soviet Union to the north, Iran to the west, or Pakistan to the east. Pakistan was the only option open to the

United States. Anyone who wanted to help the Afghan freedom movement and fight the Soviets had to work with Zia and Pakistan.[12]

Could Zia or Benazir have been pressured to balance the flow of aid
to ensure a more moderate outcome in the intra-Afghan conflict? The
Reagan administration made no serious effort to persuade Zia to change
his policy of backing the more extreme mujahedin leaders like Haqqani.
Casey deferred to Zia and the ISI on those issues, arguing that they knew
the most effective way to fight the Soviets. British concerns that Ahmad
Shah Massoud was getting too little aid were largely ignored. The Pakistanis came to refer to that period as the golden age in U.S.-Pakistani
cooperation, when "Reagan rules" were used, meaning that the CIA
gave the ISI money and arms and asked no questions about what the ISI
did with them. That is a bit of an exaggeration, but not by much. The
United States needed Pakistan to fight the Soviets and was not inclined
to second-guess Zia.

In 1989 the Bush administration had a different problem: a weak
civilian government led by the 35-year-old Benazir Bhutto that was
largely incapable of controlling the ISI and the army. Bush tried hard to
strengthen Bhutto's hand with symbolic gestures like a state dinner at the
White House, but those gestures meant little to the generals. If anything,
they probably increased their suspicions of her loyalty to the jihad and
to Pakistan. Her ouster in 1990 illustrated how little real control she had
in Afghanistan; to try to pressure her to change ISI policy would have
been a wasted effort. After the Bush administration determined in 1990
that Pakistan was building a nuclear arsenal and cut off military and economic aid—even freezing the delivery of equipment already purchased,
like F-16 fighters—Washington's influence in Islamabad collapsed. With
all aid frozen and no prospect for resumption, Bush simply had no influence with the Nawaz Sharif government, the army, or the ISI.

The other key U.S. ally in the covert war was Saudi Arabia. The Carter,
Reagan, and Bush administrations all devoted considerable diplomatic
effort to managing the Saudi connection carefully. By the mid-1980s the
Saudi ambassador in Washington, Prince Bandar bin Sultan, had become
a regular guest at the White House and a key interlocutor on many issues.
He was also the de facto Saudi intelligence chief in Washington and a
regular visitor to CIA headquarters at Langley; the Saudi ambassador's
residence is to this day only a mile away.[13] With respect to Saudi Arabia,

the goal of U.S. policy in the secret war was to secure Riyadh's financial support for the mujahedin and Pakistan in order to reduce the burden on U.S. finances. Saudi support also rallied the rest of the Islamic world behind the insurgents. The policy worked. It was part of a larger U.S. policy to work closely with Saudi Arabia around the globe to defeat the Soviet threat, contain Iran and militant Shia Islam, and support pro-American regimes from Egypt to Indonesia. It was not designed to oversee Saudi support for Muslim volunteers going to fight in Pakistan. That issue was not on the agenda.

The agenda was full without it. The Saudis were backing Saddam Hussein's Iraq in its eight-year-long war with Iran, and gradually the Reagan administration became more and more deeply involved in supporting Iraq as well as the mujahedin. The administration provided intelligence and diplomatic support, and by 1988 U.S. naval forces were actively engaged in combat with the Iranians. Washington and Tehran were fighting an undeclared naval war while Baghdad and Tehran fought the largest conventional land war since the end of the Korean War in 1953. Riyadh backed Washington and Baghdad, and arms sales to Saudi Arabia went up dramatically during the war. Those issues, not Saudi private assistance to the mujahedin, dominated the dialogue.

Alliance management in warfare is always a challenging proposition. Countries have interests, not friends—especially when they do not have common values. The United States, Pakistan, and Saudi Arabia did not share values in the 1980s. They did, however, have a common interest in defeating the Soviet attempt to occupy Afghanistan, and they succeeded in doing that in 1989. They had significantly different interests in what happened next in Afghanistan. Washington was less and less concerned about Afghanistan, but Pakistan remained next door and its level of concern never changed. As the 1990s progressed, the United States turned its attention from Afghanistan to other issues while Pakistan tried to achieve Zia's goal of establishing a Pakistani protectorate in Afghanistan.

Be absolutely clear about the endgame for a covert action and avoid mission creep.

Carter and Reagan each chose very clear missions for the covert operation in Afghanistan. In Carter's case, it was to weaken the Soviet forces in

Afghanistan and make the occupation as costly as possible without provoking a Soviet invasion of Pakistan. Brzezinski had argued in the immediate wake of the Soviet invasion that Afghanistan offered an opportunity to bog the Russians down in a painful quagmire, a Vietnam-like war, that would strain the Soviet military. Attrition was the goal. Zia agreed. Reagan continued Carter's policy during his first term in office. Then Zia switched to a new goal—victory—and Reagan and Casey followed his lead. Frank Anderson, who managed the war effort during Reagan's second term, has said, "Our plan was simple and time proven: to make life so miserable and costly for the Soviets that they would pack up and leave. Our challenges were cheap and simple compared to those of the Soviets."[14] Victory was achieved in 1989.

Then the United States searched for a new mission. George Bush decided to continue the covert war until the communist regime in Kabul fell. It was an understandable decision, but it led to mission creep and mission confusion. The CIA believed that its job was just to continue providing arms to the ISI to give to the insurgents. The State Department increasingly wanted to use the arms as leverage to produce a moderate mujahedin leadership outside Pakistan's control. Special envoy Tomsen has written persuasively that confusion about the mission helped sabotage the already very slim chances of a smooth and stable transfer of power from the communists to a postwar regime.[15] By 1992 the mission of the covert war was primarily to retrieve the Stinger missiles that had been so influential in achieving victory in 1989. The White House was virtually uninterested in what happened in Afghanistan. Bush was managing the end of the cold war and the dissolution of the USSR—a drastic change in the global order. Afghanistan was no longer a priority. Getting back dangerous surface-to-air missiles before they fell into terrorist hands was.

In retrospect, the result has been rightly judged a mistake. Frank Anderson put it well when he said, "I think we've been strongly and justifiably criticized for not picking up the more complex and costly long-run job of post-conflict development when the Soviets left. The result was an Afghanistan that descended into chaos."[16] But the long-run job was much more of a diplomatic and economic assistance project than a covert operation, and the CIA was the wrong government agency to lead such a project. As Milt Bearden wrote, trying to use the CIA program to affect the political balance among the mujahedin would have been an exercise in "social engineering" and a "recipe for disaster." [17] Whether a more overt program run by the State Department could have done a better job of helping Afghanistan avoid civil war is doubtful, but clearly the CIA was not the right organization to undertake diplomacy and social engineering.

In retrospect, a strong argument can be made that Washington should have accepted victory in 1989 and shut down the covert program in Afghanistan. Washington could have continued to engage the mujahedin through diplomatic channels without continuing arms assistance covertly through the ISI. Taking that approach probably would not have done anything to lengthen the stalemate that occurred after the Soviets left. Pakistan and Saudi Arabia would have continued to provide assistance to the mujahedin, and the Soviet Union would have done the same for the communists. What broke the stalemate in 1992 was the collapse of the USSR, which ended Soviet aid to the communists and prompted Dostum to switch sides. The Pakistanis and Saudis would have been disappointed with Washington for stopping the covert arms flow, but Pakistan was already angered by the invocation of the Pressler Amendment and the cut-off of U.S. aid. Saudi attention after 1990 was focused entirely on the Iraqi invasion of Kuwait and the threat to the kingdom from Saddam Hussein.

That is all clearer in retrospect than it was at the time. It is unfair to judge the Bush team from the vantage point of a quarter-century later. But the lesson is useful. Covert operations should have clear, simple goals. Once those goals are achieved, the mission should be terminated, not given ambiguous new objectives that are not really consistent with the nature of covert operations.

Covert actions always have unintended consequences; monitor the "blowback" closely.

In my first assignment to the White House National Security Council staff in 1991, my boss told me, "You don't know what you don't know." That statement is a useful reminder of the pitfalls of policymaking and intelligence collection and analysis. Unknown or overlooked issues and unintended consequences can prove to be, after the fact, the most important. In the case of the secret war in the 1980s, the development that the United States did not see coming was the wave of Muslim volunteers who came to Pakistan and Afghanistan to help the mujahedin. As noted, it is bad history to argue that the U.S. secret war in Afghanistan created al Qaeda and the global jihad. That argument confuses cause and effect.

The United States did not invite foreign volunteers to join the war, and the CIA did not recruit foreign volunteers. The jihadis came on their own account. Some, like bin Laden, arrived even before the CIA began providing arms to the Afghans and the ISI. Their motive was to help the Afghan people repel a foreign invasion and regain their freedom. Their anger was directed at the Soviets and their Afghan communist allies, not at the United States or the CIA. If any individuals are to blame for starting the global jihad in Afghanistan, Brezhnev and Andropov, not Carter and Reagan, are to blame.

Nor did the Americans have any contact with the foreign volunteers. As discussed earlier, Zia was adamant that the CIA have little or no contact with the mujahedin, and the CIA very deliberately left the burden of dealing with the mujahedin to the ISI. As Milt Bearden has written, "contrary to what people have come to imagine, the CIA never recruited, trained, or otherwise used Arab volunteers. Only Afghan fighters were trained. The Afghans were more than happy to do their own fighting— we saw no reason not to satisfy them on this point.'[18]

The Saudis did have contact with the volunteers. For example, on several occasions Prince Turki met with bin Laden, whom he remembered as a very shy and withdrawn man at the time.[19] Undoubtedly the Pakistanis had even more frequent contact with bin Laden and other foreign volunteers. They would have wanted to know exactly what the foreigners were doing, especially when, like bin Laden, they had access to a lot of money and equipment. Bin Laden's role in building military bases in Afghanistan was done in close coordination with ISI operations.

But if the Americans are not responsible for inviting or working with foreign jihadists in the war years, they are responsible for not keeping a closer watch on what was happening on the ground. The CIA was slow to see that the war was creating a new phenomenon in the Islamic world—that the power of militant Sunni Islam was growing rapidly in the borderlands of Afghanistan and Pakistan. In his memoirs, published in 1996, Robert Gates wrote that the agency did not begin to recognize the importance of the Arab volunteers until 1986.[20] Looking back in 2013, Gates believed that the CIA was very slow to see the rise of the new Islamist phenomenon in the 1980s because its collection and research priorities were still focused on the cold war. The developing jihad in South Asia was not a collection requirement for U.S. spies and diplomats in Islamabad or for analysts back in Washington or at CIA headquarters at Langley.[21] The intelligence community had prepared a special national intelligence estimate (SNIE) in March 1988 assessing the implications of the Soviet withdrawal for Afghanistan, for internal developments in the USSR, for the Soviets' allies and clients, and for Moscow's global position. It did not, however, address the implications of the Soviets' defeat for the nascent global Islamic movement—that slipped under the radar of the SNIE's drafters and the policymakers who read the document.[22] Eighteen months later, another SNIE was published, entitled "Afghanistan: The War in Perspective." Again, the broader implications of the war for the Islamic world were not analyzed.[23]

In retrospect, more attention should have been paid to the writings and speeches of Abdullah Azzam, some of which were being delivered in the United States. His works were readily available. The Jordanian intelligence service was certainly monitoring his activities carefully. The arrival of Ayman al-Zawahiri in Pakistan should have set off some alarm bells because he was involved in the plot to assassinate Anwar Sadat and had served time in Egyptian prisons, where he served as the spokesman for the assassins. But that is all hindsight. No one reading Azzam's works in 1988 could have seen that al Qaeda would attack the United States in 1998. Osama bin Laden himself did not know in 1981 or in 1989 that he was going to engineer the 9/11 attacks, and Zawahiri didn't know either. Certainly more attention should have been focused on the emergence of militant Sunni Islamic narratives during the secret war, but even with the best surveillance of the volunteers and their activities, policymakers would not have been alerted to prepare for the global jihad that developed after 2000.

A better case can be and has been made: that more attention should have been paid to developments in Afghanistan in the mid- to late 1990s, after the communist government had fallen. The Clinton White House did not focus on Afghanistan at all in the early 1990s; it became interested only after the 1998 attacks on U.S. embassies in East Africa. Then it did focus attention and resources. The rise of the Taliban and bin Laden's return to Afghanistan in 1996 were the critical developments that led to 9/11. The interaction between bin Laden and Taliban leader Mullah

Omar is still largely a mystery; so too is the role that the ISI played in bringing the two together.[24]

The lessons learned from the success of the covert operation during the Afghan war can also be dramatically illustrated by looking briefly at the CIA's greatest failure in covert action, the disastrous Bay of Pigs invasion in Cuba. The CIA's own after-action analysis of the operation—in which 1,400 Cuban volunteers who had been trained by the CIA in Guatemala launched a D-Day–like invasion at the Bay of Pigs in April 1961 to overthrow Fidel Castro's government—concluded that the mission failed because communication between the covert operators and the policymakers was confused and misleading. The new administration of John F. Kennedy had an incomplete and mistaken understanding of what the CIA planned to do and then made changes in the CIA's plan that increased the risk of failure. The CIA was then remiss in not making clear to the administration how detrimental those changes were to mission success. The operators and policymakers were not candid enough with each other.

The CIA report concludes that the agency failed to give the mission the "top flight handling which it required." The project relied on weak allies, mostly Guatemala and Panama; it was staffed by too many Americans and not enough Cubans; and "plausible deniability was a pathetic illusion." The mission crept ruinously from a small plan focused on infiltrating arms and men to a full-scale invasion, with no serious review of the implications of the mission creep. Most of all, the failed invasion set in train unintended consequences that led to the Cuban missile crisis a year later—the most dangerous event of the cold war.[25]

Why Did We Win?

The United States provided roughly $3 billion in aid to the Afghan resistance during the covert war.[26] It was a modest investment that had enormous consequences. Success was not inevitable. The Soviets were in a strong position in South Asia in 1980. They were the major arms provider to their ally India, which had won two wars against Pakistan in the previous fifteen years. The Soviets even hosted the 1966 peace conference in Tashkent after the Indo-Pakistani war of 1965. The U.S. local ally, the Shah in Iran, was gone, and Zia's Pakistan was far from a friend. Afghanistan seemed like an easy conquest at first; yet Moscow was defeated after 3,331 days of war. Why was the covert operation so successful? Three reasons seem most critical: Soviet mistakes; strong allies; and the Afghan people.

—*Soviet mistakes.* Soviet mistakes clearly were a major reason. Brezhnev's decision to invade and occupy Afghanistan was a monumental error. It isolated the Soviet Union in the international community as an aggressor and plunged the country into a guerrilla war that it was not prepared to fight effectively. The Soviets did get better at fighting an unconventional war as time went on, and by 1987 CIA officers in Pakistan believed that the Soviets were finally grasping the essentials of modern counterinsurgency operations. But by then, it was too little too late. As one officer has said, "they learned from their mistakes after about six years"—but then came the Stingers[27]

Compounding the mistakes of invasion, occupation, and poor counterinsurgency strategy, the Soviets did not provide the resources needed to succeed. They tried to fight the war on the cheap, and they got predictable results. They never deployed the forces necessary to control the border with Pakistan, thus ceding to the rebels a base of operations at which they could recruit, train, and recuperate—a critical mistake in any guerrilla war. To compensate for the lack of resources, the Russians resorted to using terror tactics to drive the Afghan people out of their country and intimidate those who stayed. "They probably killed close to a million people, which earned them tremendous unpopularity.[28] In the battle for the hearts and minds of the Afghan people, the Soviets played a weak hand very badly. Yet the Soviet Union could have won in Afghanistan. Soviet mistakes alone did not lose the war. Without President Carter's decision to help the mujahedin and his diplomatic efforts with Zia, the Soviets might have won despite all their errors. There is no way to know what would have happened if Carter had stayed out of the war in 1980, but it is reasonably certain that history would have been very different.

In retrospect, it can be seen that the Soviet political and economic system also was in deep trouble in the 1980s. The inherent contradictions in the communist system and its failure to deliver prosperity were a cancer eating away at its prospects for survival. But that too is hindsight. Few saw the weakness of the system in the 1980s. In 1987 the intelligence community, including the CIA, prepared a national intelligence estimate (NIE) entitled "Whither Gorbachev: Soviet Policy and Politics in the

1990s," in which the majority opinion was that most likely Gorbachev would succeed in rejuvenating the existing Soviet system. Systemic reform was considered unlikely (only a one-in-three chance), but rejuvenation would keep the Communist Party in control in the 1990s. No major changes were expected in Soviet foreign policy in the third world.

There was, however, a dissenting opinion. Written by the National Security Agency (NSA), the dissent argued that Gorbachev was not really a reformer at all, that he was interested only in strengthening the party's control of Soviet society. Contrary to the majority opinion, the NSA believed that Gorbachev would have only a modest impact on the future of the Soviet Union and would not produce any significant change. None of the NIE's drafters anticipated the wholesale collapse of the USSR or that in the 1990s it would cease to be a nation.[29] In hindsight, the NIE's mistakes are clear. At the time, almost all experts expected the Soviet Union and the cold war to continue into the twenty-first century. The Soviet invasion of Afghanistan was one of the reasons that their predictions proved wrong.

—*Strong allies.* Strong allies were another reason for the U.S. victory in the covert war. Zia in Pakistan and Fahd in Saudi Arabia were fully committed to the success of the secret war and dedicated the necessary resources to the fight. They were not intimidated by the Soviets or their allies. With a hostile 40th Red Army on his western border and Indira Gandhi on his eastern border, Zia was especially exposed in the early 1980s, but he was careful to avoid disaster. The United States shared few values with either Zia's Pakistan or Fahd's Saudi Arabia. Neither was a democracy, and both had abysmal human rights records. Both emphasized a kind of Islam that most Muslims regarded as extreme. But they did share an interest with the United States in containing and ultimately defeating Soviet aggression in Afghanistan. Much as Roosevelt and Churchill allied with Stalin in World War II to defeat Nazi Germany and imperial Japan, Carter and Reagan worked with the allies that they had in order to defeat the USSR in Afghanistan.

—*The Afghan people.* The Afghan people were the most important factor in the success of the covert war. The vast majority of Afghans rejected the Soviet invasion of their country as a criminal violation of their national sovereignty and territorial integrity. While few had much love for the regime of Hafizullah Amin, the Soviets' decision to murder him as part of the invasion strategy only reinforced the Afghans' hatred for both the Afghan communists and the Soviet occupation force.

The mujahedin fought very bravely against the Soviets, whose army had helped win World War II. The 40th Army, a modern force equipped with all the advanced weapons of the day, could summon enormous resources to fight what was an impoverished and largely illiterate society. The Afghan people, who refused by the millions to accept the Soviet system, suffered enormously as a consequence, but their determination to prevail and defeat the invader never flagged. Soviet soldiers also fought bravely in Afghanistan in the 1980s, but the Afghans fought against what seemed to be impossible odds and won.

The Afghans and their supporters in Washington, London, Beijing, Islamabad, Riyadh, and elsewhere also were patient. They fought a war of attrition with care and deliberation, and as Zia insisted, the pot was not allowed to boil too soon. Time worked against Moscow and for the rebellion. The Afghan people paid for that patience with their blood. Looking back in 2010, Frank Anderson aptly quoted from Rudyard Kipling to describe why the CIA won in Afghanistan in the 1980s: "At that time 'the hillsides teemed with hordes' that flocked to the fight. All we had to do was provide guns, ammunition and a surprisingly small amount of cash to those 'teeming hordes'"[30] The United States helped the hordes of freedom fighters, and they won the war.

The war in Afghanistan in the 1980s was not the first covert war that the United States fought, nor will it be the last. The United States has provided support to underground resistance movements seeking to overthrow foreign invaders and brutal dictatorships in other places at other times. Success depends on many factors, including the right enemy, the right allies, and a determined and patient insurgency. For those who remember them, the lessons of the Afghan war will remain relevant and meaningful for years to come.

NOTES

Introduction and Acknowledgments

ıX -1. Theodore Eliot Jr., "Foreword," in *The Fateful Pebble: Afghanistan's Role in the Fall of the Soviet Empire,* by Anthony Arnold (Norato, Calif.: Presidio Press, 1993), p. viii. Eliot was U.S. ambassador to Afghanistan from 1973 to 1978.

Xı~ 2. Gordon Corera, *The Art of Betrayal: The Secret History of MI6* (London: Pegasus, 2012), p. 296.

X ııı~ 3. Raja Anwar, *The Terrorist Prince: The Life and Death of Murtaza Bhutto* (London: Verso, 1997).

Xııı — 4. Robert M. Gates, interview with author, October 14, 2013.

XıV~5. Rodric Braithwaite, *Afgantsy: The Russians in Afghanistan, 1979–1989* (Oxford University Press, 2011).

XV— 6. For the CIA's view of Mohammad Yousaf, author of *The Bear Trap* and *Silent Soldier,* see Milt Bearden and James Risen, *The Main Enemy: The Inside Story of the CIA's Final Showdown with the KGB* (New York: Ballantine Books, 2003), pp. 284–85.

Chapter 1 ı-35

3 1. For a description of Jowzjan province, see "Jowzhan," Maureen and Mike Mansfield Center, University of Montana (www.umt.edu/mansfield/dclcp/Provinces/jowzjan.aspx).

4 2. Andrea Mitchell, *Talking Back to Presidents, Dictators, and Assorted Scoundrels* (London: Viking, 2005), p. 300.

5 3. Antonio Giustozzi, *Empires in the Mud: War and Warlords in Afghanistan* (New York: Columbia University Press, 2009), pp. 57 and 154 in particular. Giustozzi's book is one of the most complete and insightful biographies of Dostum.

4. Brian Glyn Williams, *The Last Warlord: The Life and Legend of Dostum, the Afghan Warrior Who Led U.S. Special Forces to Topple the Taliban Regime* (Chicago: Chicago Review Press, 2013), pp. 120–33. This biography is based on the author's extensive and exclusive interviews with Dostum. Unsurprisingly, the portrait is very favorable. In this book, Dostam is a very reluctant communist and a firm ally of the United States.

5. Giustozzi, *Empires in the Mud*, p. 57. See also Shaista Wahab and Barry Youngerman, *A Brief History of Afghanistan* (New York: Checkmark Books, 2010), p. 195.

6. Williams, *The Last Warlord*, pp. 138–53.

7. Peter Tomsen, *The Wars of Afghanistan: Messianic Terrorism, Tribal Conflicts, and the Failures of Great Powers* (New York: Public Affairs Books, 2011), p. 461.

8. Giustozzi, *Empires in the Mud*, p. 135.

9. Williams, *The Last Warlord*, pp. 259–68.

10. William Dalrymple, *Return of a King: The Battle for Afghanistan, 1839–42* (New York: Knopf, 2013). See especially pages 197–98 for the impact of the Opium War on the Afghan conflict.

11. Jules Stewart, *On Afghanistan's Plains: The Story of Britain's Afghan Wars* (London: I.B. Taurus, 2011), pp. 157–61. See also Wahab and Youngerman, *A Brief History of Afghanistan*, pp. 106–09.

12. Tomsen, *The Wars of Afghanistan*, p. 72.

13. Cornelius Van H. Engert, "A Report on Afghanistan" (U.S. Department of State, Division of Publications, 1924).

14. Leon B. Poullada and Leila D. J. Puollada, *The Kingdom of Afghanistan and the United States: 1828–1973* (University of Nebraska, 1995), p. 142.

15. Bruce Riedel, *Avoiding Armageddon: America, India, and Pakistan to the Brink and Back* (Brookings, 2013), p. 55. The book provides an analysis of the development of U.S.-Pakistani relations.

16. Tomsen, *The Wars of Afghanistan*, p. 91.

17. Douglas MacEachin, "Predicting the Soviet Invasion of Afghanistan: The Intelligence Community's Record" (Central Intelligence Agency Center for the Study of Intelligence, April 15, 2007), p. 2.

18. Tomsen, *The Wars of Afghanistan*, p. 91.

19. Wahab and Youngerman, *A Brief History of Afghanistan*, pp. 125–27.

20. Riedel, *Avoiding Armageddon*, p. 56.

21. Kenneth Conboy and James Morrison, *The CIA's Secret War in Tibet* (University of Kansas Press, 2002), pp. 55–56, 60–79.

22. Wahab and Youngerman, *A Brief History of Afghanistan*, p. 127.

23. Tomsen, *The Wars of Afghanistan*, p. 96.

24. Ibid., p. 99.

25. Christina Lamb, *The Sewing Circles of Herat: A Personal Voyage through Afghanistan* (London: HarperCollins, 2002), p. 118.

26. Tariq Ali, *The Duel: Pakistan on the Flight Path of American Power* (New York: Scribner, 2008), pp. 118–19.

27. MacEachin, "Predicting the Soviet Invasion of Afghanistan," p. 4.

28. On the shah's longtime relations with Helms, see Helm's wife's memoirs, Cynthia Helms, *An Intriguing Life: A Memoir of War, Washington, and Marriage to an American Spymaster* (Lanham, Md.: Rowman and Littlefield, 2013), p. 139.

29. Wahab and Youngerman, *A Brief History of Afghanistan*, p. 138.

30. Ibid, p. 138.

31. Director of Cent████████████ "The Soviet Invasion of Afghanistan: Implications for Wa███████████y Intelligence Memorandum, NI IIM 80-10017jx, October ████████ sanitized and released by CIA Historical Review Program.

32. MacEachin, "Predicting the Soviet Invasion of Afghanistan," p. 5.

33. The numbers are from Director of Central Intelligence, "The Soviet Invasion of Afghanistan," pp. 13–16.

34. Ibid., p. 13.

35. Tomsen, *The Wars of Afghanistan*, p. 159.

Chapter 2

1. Director of Central Intelligence, "The Soviet Invasion of Afghanistan: Implications for Warning," Interagency Intelligence Memorandum NI IIM 80-10017jx, October 1980, p. 15. Sanitized and released by the CIA Historical Review Program.

2. Douglas MacEachin, "Predicting the Soviet Invasion of Afghanistan: The Intelligence Community's Record" (Central Intelligence Agency Center for the Study of Intelligence, April 15, 2007).

3. Ibid., p. 11.

4. Jimmy Carter, *White House Diary* (New York: Farrar Straus and Giroux, 2010), p. 382.

5. Director of Central Intelligence, "The Soviet Invasion of Afghanistan," p. 38.

6. Vasily Mitrokhin, "The KGB In Afghanistan," Working Paper 40, Cold War International History Project (Washington: Woodrow Wilson Center, updated July 2009), p. 98.

7. Director of Central Intelligence, "The Soviet Invasion of Afghanistan," p. 39.

8. MacEachin, "Predicting the Soviet Invasion of Afghanistan," p. 15. The literature on Soviet decisionmaking drawn from the Soviet archives is considerable and growing. Much of the raw material is held at the National Security Archive at George Washington University in Washington. An oral history project was held in Oslo, Norway, in 1995 to get more Russian input to add to the documents. Douglas MacEachin's CIA study draws on the Oslo project as well. Two

excellent books on the subject are Gregory Feifer, *The Great Gamble: The Soviet War in Afghanistan* (New York: HarperCollins, 2009), and Rodric Braithwaite, *Afgantsy: The Russians in Afghanistan 1979–1989* (Oxford University Press, 2011). Braithwaite was British ambassador to Moscow in 1988–1992.

9. Braithwaite, *Afgantsy*, p, 73.

10. Mitrokhin, "The KGB in Afghanistan," p.81.

11. Braithwaite, *Afgantsy*, p. 77.

12. Odd Arne Westad, "The Road to Kabul: Soviet Policy on Afghanistan, 1978–1979," in *The Fall of Détente: Soviet American Relations in the Carter Years*, edited by Odd Arne Westad (Oslo: Scandinavian University Press, 1997), pp. 134–35.

13. MacEachin, "Predicting the Soviet Invasion of Afghanistan ," p. 17.

14. Braithwaite, *Afgantsy*, p. 84.

15. Mitrokhin, "The KGB In Afghanistan ," pp. 110–11.

16. Ibid., p. 141.

17. Ibid., pp. 135–37.

18. Artemy M. Kalinovsky, *A Long Goodbye: The Soviet Withdrawal from Afghanistan* (Harvard University Press, 2011), p. 134.

19. Braithwaite, *Afgantsy*, p. 136.

20. Ibid., pp. 122, 342–45.

21. Ibid., p. 124.

22. Ibid., pp. 84 and 125.

23. Directorate of Intelligence, "The Costs of the Soviet Involvement in Afghanistan" (Central Intelligence Agency, February 1987), pp. iii–7; declassified at National Security Archive, George Washington University. The Congressional Research Service estimates the cost of the Vietnam War, adjusted for inflation in 2011, as $738 billion. See Stephan Daggett, *Costs of Major U.S. Wars* (Washington: Congressional Research Service, 2010), p. 2.

24. Directorate of Intelligence, "Costs of Soviet Involvement," p. 11.

25. Mohammad Yousaf and Mark Adkin, *The Bear Trap: Afghanistan's Untold Story* (London: Leo Cooper, 1992), p. 46.

26. Robert D. Kaplan, *Soldiers of God: With Islamic Warriors in Afghanistan and Pakistan* (New York: Vintage Books, 2001), pp. 184–88, 223.

27. Feifer, *The Great Gamble*, pp.173–74.

28. Braithwaite, *Afgantsy*, p. 232.

29. Robert M. Gates, interview with author, October 14, 2013.

30. David Isby, *Russia's War in Afghanistan* (London: Osprey, 1986), pp. 12–13.

31. Kalinovsky, *A Long Goodbye*, p. 97.

32. Ibid., p. 130.

33. There is no single, comprehensive review of the campaign in Afghanistan. Because the war was fought in a series of disjointed battlefields across the country and because the mujahedin were not a cohesive army, much of the reporting on

the campaign is disjointed. This analysis draws on a number of studies including Isby, *Russia's War in Afghanistan,* and Braithwaite, *Afgantsy.*

34. V. E. Korol, "The Price of Victory: Myths and Reality," *Journal of Slavic Studies,* vol. 9, no. 2 (June 1996).

35. Russian casualties in Afghanistan were much smaller. The official figure is 13,833 dead and 35,000 wounded. Unofficial estimates range as high as 40,000 to 50,000 dead. See Anthony Arnold, *The Fateful Pebble: Afghanistan's Role in the Fall of the Soviet Empire* (Novato, Calif.: Presidio Press, 1993), pp. 190–91.

36. Braithwaite, *Afgantsy,* p. 124,

37. Isby, *Russia's War in Afgh* 9.

38. Feifer, *The Great Gamble* 172.

39. Braithwaite, *Afgantsy,* pp

40. Ibid., pp. 140–42.

41. Kalinovsky, *A Long Goo* 0.

42. Raja Anwar, *The Terrorist Prince: The Life and Death of Murtaza Bhutto* (London: Verso, 1997), pp. 90–91.

43. Ibid., p. 98.

44. Mitrokhin, "The KGB In Afghanistan ," p. 136.

45. Anwar, *The Terrorist Prince,* pp. 112–113.

46. Ibid., p. 116.

47. Ibid., p. 135.

48. Ibid., pp. 70, 75–77, 138, 193–99.

49. Shuja Nawaz, *Crossed Swords: Pakistan, Its Army, and the Wars Within* (Oxford University, 2008), pp. 482–85.

50. Fatima Bhutto, *Songs of Blood and Sword: A Daughter's Memoir* (London: Jonathan Cape, 2010).

51. Benazir Bhutto, *Daughter of the East: An Autobiography* (London: Hamish Hamilton, 1988), pp. 147–53.

52. David Glantz and Jonathan House, *When Titans Clashed: How the Red Army Stopped Hitler* (Kansas University Press, 1995), p. 300. See also Max Hastings, *Retribution: The Battle for Japan, 1944–45* (New York: Knopf, 2008), pp. 482–503.

Chapter 3

1. Robert M. Gates, interview with author, October 14, 2013.

2. Janet M. Lang and others, *Becoming Enemies: U.S.-Iran Relations and the Iran-Iraq War, 1979–1988* (Plymouth, U.K.: Rowman & Littlefield, 2012).

3. Shaista Wahab and Barry Youngerman, *A Brief History of Afghanistan* (New York: Checkmark Books, 2010), pp. 177–81.

4. Mohammad Yousaf and Mark Adkin, *The Bear Trap: Afghanistan's Untold Story* (London: Leo Cooper, 1992), pp. 75–76.

5. Peter B. DeNeufville, "Ahmad Shah Massoud and the Genesis of the Nationalist Anti-Communist Movement in Northeastern Afghanistan, 1969–1979," Ph.D. dissertation, Mediterranean Studies Programme, King's College, University of London, May 2006, pp. 72–73.

6. Gilles Dorronsoro, *Revolution Unending: Afghanistan, 1979 to the Present* (Columbia University Press, 2005), p.78.

7. Ibid., p. 76.

8. DeNeufville, "Ahmad Shah Massoud and the Genesis of the Nationalist Anti-Communist Movement," pp. 76–106.

9. Vanda Felbab-Brown, *Aspiration and Ambivalence: Strategies and Realities of Counterinsurgency and State Building in Afghanistan* (Brookings, 2013), p. 126.

10. DeNeufville, "Ahmad Shah Massoud and the Genesis of the Nationalist Anti-Communist Movement," pp. 4–16.

11. Steve Coll, *Ghost Wars: The Secret History of the CIA, Afghanistan, and Bin Laden, from the Soviet Invasion to September 10, 2001* (New York: Penguin, 2004), p. 117.

12. Gordon Corera, *The Art of Betrayal: The Secret History of MI6* (London: Pegasus Books, 2012), pp. 293–305. Several former MI6 officers have privately confirmed Corera's account to the author.

13. Gary Schroen, *First In: An Insider's Account of How the CIA Spearheaded the War on Terror in Afghanistan* (New York: Ballantine Books, 2006), p. 89.

14. Paul Cruickshank, "Suicide Bomber's Widow Soldiers On—Wife of Assassin Professes Undying Affection for bin Laden," CNN, August 15, 2006.

15. Marcela Grad, *Massoud: An Intimate Portrait of the Legendary Afghan Leader* (Webster University Press, 2009), p. 194.

16. Vahid Brown and Don Rassler, *Fountainhead of Jihad: The Haqqani Nexus, 1973–2012* (London: Hurst, 2013). See page 1 for Admiral Mullen's statement.

17. Ibid., pp. 28–42.

18. Ibid., pp. 44–47.

19. Quoted in Brown and Rassler, *Fountainhead of Jihad*, p. 52.

20. Lester Grau and Ali Ahmad Jalali, "The Campaign of the Caves: The Battles for Zhawar in the Soviet-Afghan War," *Journal of Slavic Military Studies*, vol.14, no. 3 (December 2007), p. 70.

21. Yousaf and Adkin, *The Bear Trap*, pp. 159–64, and Brown and Rassler, *Fountainhead of Jihad*, pp. 66–69.

22. Quoted in Brown and Rassler, *Fountainhead of Jihad*, p. 68.

23. Gregory Feifer, *The Great Gamble: The Soviet War in Afghanistan* (New York: HarperCollins, 2009), p. 225.

24. Grau and Jalali, "The Campaign of the Caves," pp. 72–75.

25. Yousaf and Adkin, *The Bear Trap*, pp. 164–77.

26. Brown and Rassler, *Fountainhead of Jihad*, p. 72.

27. Grau and Jalali, "The Campaign of the Caves," pp.76–85.

28. Feifer, *The Great Gamble*, pp. 231–38.

29. Brown and Rassler, *Fountainhead of Jihad*, p. 69.

30. Ibid., pp. 72–74.

31. Michael Scheur, *Osama bin Laden* (Oxford University Press, 2011), pp. 59–61.

32. Brown and Rassler, *Fountainhead of Jihad*.

Chapter 4

1. Jack O'Connell, *King's Couns of War, Espionage, and Diplomacy in the Middle East* (New York: Norton, 1), p. 104; and Jack O'Connell, interview with the author, October 12, 2001.

2. His Royal Highness Prince Hassan bin Talal, interview with the author, April 11, 2010.

3. Shuja Nawaz, *Crossed Swords: Pakistan, Its Army, and the Wars Within* (Oxford University Press, 2008), p. 337.

4. See J. F. R. Jacobs, *An Odyssey in War and Peace: An Autobiography* (New Delhi: Roli Books, 2011) for the account of the war by the second-in-command, Lieutenant General Jacob Richards, who is Jewish. The commander was Field Marshal Sam Manekshaw.

5. Raja Anwar, *The Terrorist Prince: The Life and Death of Murtaza Bhutto* (London: Verso, 1997), p. 11.

6. Stanley Wolpert, *Zulfi Bhutto of Pakistan: His Life and Times* (Oxford University Press, 1993), p. 262.

7. Mohammad Yousaf and Mark Adkin, *The Bear Trap: Afghanistan's Untold Story* (London: Leo Cooper, 1992), p. 11. Akhtar would be Zia's essential partner and right hand in the Afghan war, and the two would die together in a suspicious airplane crash in 1987.

8. Anwar, *The Terrorist Prince*, p. 13.

9. Seyyed Vali Reza Nasr, *The Vanguard of the Islamic Revolution* (University of California Press, 1994), p. 189.

10. Nawaz, *Crossed Swords*, p. 384.

11. C. Uday Bhaskar, "Hamid Karzai Clarification and Grey Sheen over AF-Pak," *Economic Times*, October 26, 2011.

12. Steve Coll, *Ghost Wars: The Secret History of the CIA, Afghanistan, and Bin Laden, from the Soviet Invasion to September 10, 2001* (New York: Penguin Books, 2004), p. 180.

13. Ayesha Siddiqa, *Military Inc.: Inside Pakistan's Military Economy* (London: Pluto Press, 2007), p. 186.

14. The definitive account of the ISI's war from a Pakistani perspective is Yousaf and Adkin, *The Bear Trap*. Yousaf was the ISI Afghan Bureau chief from 1983 to 1987. The book is dedicated to General Akhtar Rahman, about whom Yousaf also wrote a biography (see note 16).

15. Milt Bearden and James Risen, *The Main Enemy: The Inside Story of the CIA's Final Showdown with the KGB* (New York: Ballantine Books, 2003), p. 230.

16. Mohammad Yousaf, *Silent Soldier: The Man Behind the Afghan Jehad General Akhtar Abdur Rahman Shaheed* (Lahore: Jang Publishers, 1991), pp. 27–29. This book is dedicated to all who fought, suffered, and died and those who are still fighting, suffering, and dying for the Afghan jihad.

17. Daveed Gartenstein-Ross, "Religious Militancy in Pakistan's Military and Inter-Services Intelligence Agency," in Daveed Gartenstein-Ross and others, *The Afghanistan-Pakistan Theater: Militant Islam, Security, and Stability* (Washington: FDD Press, 2010), p. 33.

18. Yousaf, *Silent Soldier,* pp. 16, 70.

19. Fouad Ajami, "With Us or against Us," *New York Times,* January 7, 2007, p. 14.

20. Yousaf and Adkin, *The Bear Trap,* p. 25, and Yousaf, *Silent Soldier,* p. 39.

21. Katherine Frank, *Indira: The Life of Indira Nehru Gandhi* (London: HarperCollins, 2002), p. 441.

22. Nawaz, *Crossed Swords,* pp. 372–373. Prince Turki confirmed this account in an interview with the author.

23. Ibid., p. 386.

24. Ibid., p. 387.

25. Yousaf and Adkin, *The Bear Trap,* p. 20.

26. Ibid., p. 29.

27. Ibid., pp. 98–101.

28. Ibid., pp. 8, 116.

29. Ibid., pp. 113–15. See also Nicholas Thompson, "Losing Afghanistan: A New Account of the Soviet Union's Long, Hard Battle," *New York Times,* March 15, 2009.

30. Yousaf and Adkin, *The Bear Trap,* pp. 81, 95–96.

31. Robert Gates, *Duty: Memoirs of a Secretary at War* (New York: Knopf, 2014), p. 335.

32. Yousaf and Adkin, *The Bear Trap,* pp. 83–91, and Yousaf, *Silent Soldier,* p. 77.

33. Yousaf and Adkin, *The Bear Trap,* p. 93.

34. Ibid., pp. 146–54.

35. Ibid., pp. 189–98.

36. Ibid., p. 198.

37. Artemy M. Kalinovsky, *A Long Goodbye: The Soviet Withdrawal from Afghanistan* (Harvard University Press, 2011), p. 234.

38. Yousaf and Adkin, *The Bear Trap,* p. 205.

39. Yousaf, *Silent Soldier,* p. 23.

40. Paul Kennedy, *The Rise and Fall of the Great Powers: Economic Change and Military Conflict from 1500 to 2000* (New York: Random House, 1987), p. 513. Richard N. Haass, "The Use and Mainly Misuse of History," *Orbis,* vol. 32, no. 3 (Summer 1988), p. 419.

41. Nawaz, *Crossed Swords,* pp. 374–75. In the end, Zia died in mysterious circumstances, most likely assassinated.

42. Quoted in ibid., p. 378.

43. Arif Jamal, *Shadow War: The Untold Story of the Jihad in Kashmir* (New York: Melville House, 2009), pp. 107–11.

44. Jamal, *Shadow War,* p. 115.

45. Kuldip Nayar, *Beyond the Lines* (New Delhi: Roli Books, 2012), p. 291.

46. K. Sundarji, *Blind Men of Hindoo* 5 *Pak Nuclear War* (New Delhi: UBS Publishers, 1993).

47. Bearden and Risen, *The Main E*

48. The best chronicle of the Brass by P. R. Chari, Pervaiz Iqbal Cheema, and Stephen P. Cohen, *Four Cr a Peace Process: American Engagement in South Asia* (Brookings, 2007).

49. Yousaf and Adkin, *The Bear Trap,* p. 220.

50. Separate interviews of two Indian former intelligence officers by the author, 2012.

51. Feroz Hassan Khan, *Eating Grass: The Making of the Pakistani Bomb* (Stanford University Press, 2012), p. 185.

52. Yousaf and Adkin, *The Bear Trap,* pp. 180–81.

53. Ibid., p. 182.

54. Ibid., p. 187.

55. Nawaz, *Crossed Swords,* p. 398.

56. Mohammad Yousaf makes this case in Yousaf and Adkin, *The Bear Trap.*

57. Barbara Crossette, "Who Killed Zia?" *World Policy Journal,* vol. 22, no. 3 (Fall 2005), pp. 94–102.

58. Benazir Bhutto, *Daughter of the East: An Autobiography* (London: Hamish Hamilton, 1988), pp. 317–22.

59. Government of Pakistan, *Report of the Abbottabad Commission* (Islamabad, 2013), p. 324. The classified report was leaked by al Jazeera in July 2013.

60. Phillip Corwin, *Doomed in Afghanistan: A UN Officer's Memoir of the Fall of Kabul and Najibullah's Failed Escape, 1992* (Rutgers University Press, 2003), p. 8.

Chapter 5

1. Peter Tomsen, *The Wars in Afghanistan: Messianic Terrorism, Tribal Conflicts, and the Failures of Great Powers* (New York: Public Affairs, 2011), p. 205.

2. Mohammad Yousaf and Mark Adkin, *The Bear Trap: Afghanistan's Untold Story* (London: Leo Cooper, 1992), p. 106.

3. Tomsen, *The Wars in Afghanistan,* p. 248. Tomsen's source was the CIA officer Milton Bearden.

4. Natana J. Delong-Bas, *Wahhabi Islam: From Revival and Reform to Global Jihad* (Cairo: American University Press, 2005).

5. Jean Pierre Filiu, *Apocalypse In Islam* (University of California Press, 2011).

6. Yaroslav Trofimov, *The Siege of Mecca* (New York: Doubleday, 2007) pp. 4, 275. See also Karen Elliot House, *On Saudi Arabia: Its People, Past, Religion, Fault Lines, and Future* (New York: Knopf, 2012), pp. 222–23.

7. Thomas Hegghammer and Stephane Lacroix, *The Meccan Rebellion: The Story of Juhayman al Utaybi Revisited* (Bristol, U.K.: Amal Press, 2011), p. 20.

8. Harold Macmillan, *At the End of the Day, 1961–1963* (London: Harper and Row, 1973), p. 276.

9. Jesse Ferris, "Soviet Support for Egypt's Intervention in Yemen, 1962–1963," *Journal of Cold War Studies*, vol. 10, no. 4 (Fall 2008), pp. 5–36.

10. Saeed M. Badeeb, *The Soviet-Egyptian Conflict over North Yemen, 1962–1970* (Boulder, Colo.: Westview Press, 1986), pp. 66–69.

11. Ibid., p. 70.

12. Joseph A. Kechichian, *Faysal: Saudi Arabia's King for all Seasons* (Tallahassee: University Press of Florida, 2008), pp. 71–73.

13. Duff Hart Davis, *The War that Never Was: The True Story of the Men Who Fought Britain's Most Secret Battles* (London: Random House, 2011), p. 96.

14. Ibid., pp. 135–40. Nahum Admoni, the Mossad officer who led Operation Leopard, confirmed that account with the author.

15. Ibid., pp. 210–26.

16. Badeeb, *The Soviet-Egyptian Conflict over North Yemen*, especially chapter 4.

17. Muhammad Yousaf, *Silent Soldier: The Man behind the Afghan Jehad, General Akhtar Abdur Rahman Shaheed* (Lahore: Jang Publishers, 1991), p. 87.

18. Michael Scheuer, *Osama bin Laden* (Oxford University Press, 2011), p. 49. Scheuer was a senior CIA analyst during the Afghan war and the chief of the CIA's bin Laden unit from 1996 to 1999.

19. Ibid., pp. 22–29.

20. Ibid., p. 49.

21. Ibid., p. 51.

22. Ibid., pp. 62–64.

23. Ibid., p. 65.

24. Author's interview with Efraim Halevy, former head of the Mossad, the Israeli secret intelligence service, November 20, 2008.

25. The best biography of Azzam is by Thomas Hegghammer, "Abdallah Azzam," in *Al Qaeda in Its Own Words*, edited by Gilles Kepel and Jean-Pierre Milelli (Harvard University Press, 2009), pp. 81–102.

26. Shaul Mishal, *West Bank, East Bank: The Palestinians in Jordan, 1949–1967* (Yale University Press, 1978).

27. Zaki Chehab, *Inside Hamas: The Untold Story of Militants, Martyrs, and Spies* (London: Tauris, 2007), p. 193.

28. Lawrence Wright, *The Looming Tower: Al Qaeda and the Road to 9/11* (New York: Knopf, 2006), p. 102.

29. Matthew Levitt, *Hamas: Politics, Charity, and Terrorism in the Service of Jihad* (Yale University Press, 2006), p. 150.

30. Hegghammer, "Abdallah Azzam," in *Al Qaeda in Its Own Words*, edited by Kepel and Milelli, p. 108.

31. Ahmed Rashid, *Taliban* (Yale University Press, 2001), p. 132.

32. John Wilson, "Lashkar e Tayyeba," Security Research Unit Brief 12 (University of Bradford, 2007); and ... Tellis, "Bad Company: Lashkar e-Tayyiba and the Growing Am... amist Militancy in Pakistan," Testimony before the House Comm... reign Affairs, March 11, 2010 (http://carnegieendowment.org/2010/03/1... d-company-lashkar-e-tayyiba-and-growing-ambition-of-islamist-militancy-in-pakistan/44h4).

33. Chehab, *Inside Hamas*, p. 193.

34. Asaf Maliach, "Bin Ladin, Palestine, and al Qaida's Operational Strategy," *Middle Eastern Studies*, vol. 44, no. 3 (May 2008), p. 355.

35. Paul McGeough, *Kill Khalid: The Failed Mossad Assassination of Khaled Mishal and the Rise of Hamas* (London: New Press, 20090, p. 405.

36. Benazir Bhutto, *Reconciliation: Islam, Democracy, and the West* (New York: HarperCollins, 2008), p. 56.

37. Roger Hardy, *The Muslim Revolt* (Columbia University Press, 2010), pp. 156–59.

38. Michael W. S. Ryan, *Decoding al Qaeda's Strategy: The Deep Battle against America* (Columbia University Press, 2013), p. 201.

39. Milt Bearden and James Risen, *The Main Enemy: The Inside Story of the CIA's Final Showdown with the KGB* (New York: Ballantine Books, 2003), p. 357.

40. Rashid, *Taliban*, p. 130.

41. Brynjar Lia, *Architect of Global Jihad: The Life of Al Qaida Strategist Abu Mus'ab al-Suri* (London: Hurst, 2007).

42. Robert Malley, *The Call from Algeria: Third Worldism, Revolution, and the Turn to Islam* (University of California Press, 1996), p. 246.

43. Robert M. Gates, *From the Shadows: The Ultimate Insider's Story of Five Presidents and How They Won the Cold War* (New York: Simon and Schuster, 1996), p. 349.

44. Robert M. Gates, interview with the author, October 14, 2013.

Chapter 6

1. Stansfield Turner, *Secrecy and Democracy: The CIA in Transition* (Boston: Houghton Mifflin, 1985).

2. Kai Bird, *The Good Spy: The Life and Death of Robert Ames* (New York: Crown, 2014), p. 32.

3. John Helgerson, *Getting to Know the President: CIA Briefings of Presidential Candidates, 1952–1992* (Washington: Center for the Study of Intelligence, Central Intelligence Agency, 1996), pp. 105–16.

4. Adam Gopnik, "Closer than That," *New Yorker,* November 4, 2013, p. 106.

5. Robert Gates, *From the Shadows: The Ultimate Insider's Story of Five Presidents and How They Won the Cold War* (New York: Simon and Schuster, 1996), pp. 145–46.

6. Jimmy Carter, *White House Diary* (New York: Farrar, Straus, and Giroux, 2010), p. 470. Carter kept a very detailed diary during his years in the White House. In 2010 he published excerpts from it, but much more was left unpublished. The president generously gave me access to excerpts from the unpublished diary during a visit to Georgia in September 2013 as well as an extensive interview with him. In the notes below, the excerpts from the unpublished diary entries are referred to by the date that President Carter made the entries.

7. Dennis Kux, *The United States and Pakistan, 1947–2000: Disenchanted Allies* (Johns Hopkins University Press, 2001), pp. 232–33.

8. Ibid., pp. 237–38.

9. Husain Haqqani, *Magnificent Delusions: Pakistan, the United States, and an Epic History of Misunderstanding* (New York: Public Affairs, 2013), pp. 231–32.

10. Central Intelligence Agency, National Foreign Assessment Center Office of Political Analysis, "A Review of the Evidence of Chinese Involvement in Pakistan's Nuclear Weapons Program," December 7, 1979. Approved for release on October 5, 2012, and available at National Security Archive, George Washington University.

11. Carter diary, December 29, 1978.

12. Carter diary, January 1, 1979.

13. Carter diary, January 9, 1979, and January 28, 1979.

14. Zbigniew Brzezinski, *Power and Principle: Memoirs of the National Security Adviser, 1977–1981* (New York: Farrar, Straus, and Giroux, 1983), p. 427.

15. Carter diary, April 4, 1979, and May 23, 1979. The diary also shows that Carter and Vice President Mondale discussed a possible CIA covert role in Afghanistan on May 7, 1979.

16. Gates, *From the Shadows,* p. 143. Also Haqqani, *Magnificent Delusions,* p. 242.

17. Haqqani, *Magnificent Delusions,* p. 235.

18. Kux, *Disenchanted Allies,* pp. 242–44.

19. Carter diary, November 21, 1979.

20. Haqqani, *Magnificent Delusions,* p 243.

21. David Welch, interview, November 3, 2012. David was a junior political officer in the embassy.

22. Carter diary, November 21, 1979.

23. Gates, *From the Shadows,* p. 134.

24. Interview with President Carter, the Carter Center, Atlanta, September 11, 2013.

25. Hamilton Jordan, *Crisis: The Last Year of the Carter Presidency* (New York: Putnam, 1982), pp. 98–99.

26. Memo from Brzezinski to Ca[...] [...]tions on Soviet Intervention in Afghanistan," December 26, 1979, N[...] [...]rity Archive, George Washington University. See also Haqqani, *Ma[...] [...]lusions*, p. 245.

27. Carter diary, December 28, 19[...], and January 4, 1980.

28. Kux, *Disenchanted Allies* p. 252.

29. Gates, *From the Shadows*, p. 146.

30. Charles G. Cogan, "Partners in Time: The CIA and Afghanistan since 1979," *World Policy Journal*, vol. 10, no. 2 (Summer 1993), p. 79.

31. Carter diary, December 28, 1979.

32. Carter diary, January 4, 1980.

33. Owen Bowcott, "UK Discussed Plans to Help Mujahideen Weeks after Soviet Invasion," *The Guardian*, December 29, 2010.

34. Carter diary, January 12, 1980.

35. Carter diary, February 4, 1980.

36. Brzezinski, *Power and Principle*, pp. 448–49; author's interview with Brzezinski, October 16, 2013.

37. Author's interview with Brzezinski, October 16, 2013.

38. Carter diary, February 6, 1980.

39. Carter diary, February 12, 1980, and February 14, 1980.

40. S. Frederick Starr, *Xinjiang: China's Muslim Borderland* (New York: M.E. Sharpe, 2004); author's interview with Brzezinski, October 16, 2013.

41. Tim Wells, *444 Days: The Hostages Remember* (San Diego, Calif.: Harcourt Brace Jovanovich, 1985), pp. 327, 357.

42. "Interview with Dr. Charles Cogan, August 2009," and "Soldiers of God: Cold War Interviews," National Security Archive, George Washington University, p. 2.

43. Brzezinski, *Power and Principle*, p. 451.

44. Gates, *From the Shadows*, pp. 130–31.

45. Janet Lang and others, *Becoming Enemies: U.S.-Iran Relations and the Iran Iraq War, 1979–1988* (Plymouth, U.K.: Rowman and Littlefield, 2012), pp. 70–72.

46. Carter, *White House Diary*, p. 469.

47. Haqqani, *Magnificent Delusions*, p. 255.

48. Carter diary, September 4, 1980.

49. Carter, *White House Diary*, p. 471; Carter diary, October 3, 1980.

50. Gates, *From the Shadows*, p. 149.

Chapter 7

1. Bob Woodward, *Veil: The Secret Wars of the CIA, 1981–1987* (New York: Simon and Schuster, 1987), pp. 24–29.

2. Ibid., p. 28. Brzezinski confirmed to the author in our interview on October 16, 2013, that the failure to predict the Soviet invasion in 1979 cost Turner credibility with the White House.

3. Woodward, *Veil*, pp. 36–38. See also Joseph E. Persico, *Casey: The Lives and Secrets of William J. Casey, from the OSS to the CIA* (New York: Viking, 1990). Persico had access to some of Casey's private papers for his biography.

4. William J. Casey, *Where and How the War Was Fought: An Armchair Tour of the American Revolution* (New York: William Morrow, 1976).

5. Hamilton Jordan, *Crisis: The Last Year of the Carter Presidency* (New York: Putnam, 1982), p. 101.

6. William J. Casey, memorandum for the president, "Progress at the CIA," May 6, 1981; declassified by the CIA April 2003.

7. Frank Anderson, "Cold War Interviews," National Security Archive, George Washington University, August 1997.

8. Charles G. Cogan, "Partners in Time: The CIA and Afghanistan since 1979," *World Policy Journal*, vol. 10, no. 2 (Summer 1993), p. 79. Cogan describes the meeting as taking place in April 1981 but Gates and other sources point to 1982.

9. Persico, *Casey*, p. 309.

10. Ibid., pp. 312–13.

11. Robert M. Gates, *From the Shadows: The Ultimate Insider's Story of Five Presidents and How They Won the Cold War* (New York: Simon and Schuster, 1996), p. 252.

12. Ibid., pp. 251–53, 320–21.

13. Anderson, "Cold War Interviews."

14. Dennis Kux, *The United States and Pakistan, 1947–2000: Disenchanted Allies* (Johns Hopkins University Press, 2001), p. 257.

15. The estimate was partially declassified for release in June 2004. It can be found in Anuj Dhar, *CIA's Eye on South Asia* (New Delhi: Manas Press, 2009), pp. 374–84.

16. Ibid., pp. 375–82.

17. Ibid., pp. 382–84.

18. Kux, *The United States and Pakistan, 1947–2000*, pp. 267–68.

19. Ibid., p. 272.

20. Milt Bearden and James Risen, *The Main Enemy: The Inside Story of the CIA's Final Showdown with the KGB* (New York: Ballantine Books, 2003), pp. 201–06. Se also Milt Bearden, *The Black Tulip: A Novel of War in Afghanistan* (New York: Random House, 1998).

21. Gates, *From the Shadows*, p. 350.

22. George Crile, *Charlie Wilson's War* (New York: Grove Press, 2003), p. 31. Wilson asked the Israelis to build weapons for the mujahedin, including a surface-to-air missile, but they were never used in Afghanistan.

23. Gates, *From the Shadows*, p. 349.

24. Ibid., p. 347.

25. Anderson, "Cold War Interviews."

26. Gates, *From the Shadows*, p. 320.

27. Ibid., p. 321.

28. Zia was less worried about the Israelis. At one point Charlie Wilson proposed to one of his many girlfriends and planned to marry her in a spectacular ceremony in the Khyber Pass. When he asked Zia if he would provide a military escort and an official delegation, Zia agreed. Charlie also said that he would want to invite his Jewish friends, American and Israeli, and again Zia agreed. Unfortunately, the relationship broke up before the wedding got off the ground.

29. Bearden and Risen, *The Main Enemy*, p. 61.

30. Ibid., p. 209.

31. Anderson, "Cold War Interviews."

32. Bearden and Risen, *The Main Enemy*, pp. 270–71.

33. Robert M. Gates, interview with author, October 14, 2013.

34. Rodric Braithwaite, *Afgantsy: The Russians in Afghanistan, 1979–1989* (Oxford University Press, 2011), pp. 272–76.

35. Artemy M. Kalinovsky, *A Long Goodbye: The Soviet Withdrawal from Afghanistan* (Harvard University Press, 2011), p. 185.

36. Charles Cogan, "Cold War Interviews," National Security Archive, George Washington University, August 1997.

37. Kux, *The United States and Pakistan, 1947–2000*, p. 289. See also Gabrielle Rifkind and Giandomenico Picco, *The Fog of Peace: The Human Face of Conflict Resolution* (New York: IB Tauris, 2014), pp. 26–28.

38. Kalinovsky, *A Long Goodbye*, p. 243.

39. Braithwaite, *Afgantsy*, pp. 294–96.

40. The SNIE is available at the National Security Archive at George Washington University or on the archive website (www2.gwu.edu/~nsarchiv/). "Special National Intelligence Estimate: USSR: Withdrawal from Afghanistan, March 1988." The Bearden and Anderson views are from Roy Gutman, *How We Missed the Story: Osama Bin Laden, the Taliban, and the Hijacking of Afghanistan* (Washington: United States Institute for Peace, 2008), p. 12.

41. Braithwaite, *Afgantsy*, pp. 204–205, 143.

42. Bearden and Risen, *The Main Enemy*, p. 261.

43. Ibid., p. 350.

Chapter 8

1. Benazir Bhutto, *Reconciliation, Islam, Democracy, and the West* (New York: HarperCollins, 2008), pp. 195–201.

2. Benazir Bhutto, *Daughter of the East: An Autobiography* (London: Hamish and Hamilton, 1988), p. 400.

3. Arnaud de Borchgrave, "Army Back on Top," *Washington Times*, March 30, 2010.

4. "Report of the United Nations Commission of Inquiry into the Facts and Circumstances of the Assassination of Former Pakistani Prime Minister Mohtarma Benazir Bhutto," April 2010, paragraphs 38 and 218.

5. Arif Jamal, *Shadow War: The Untold Story of Jihad in Kashmir* (New York: Melville House, 2009), p. 136.

6. P. R. Chari, Pervaiz Iqbal Cheema, and Stephen P. Cohen, *Four Crises and a Peace Process: American Engagement in South Asia* (Brookings, 2007), p. 86.

7. Husain Haqqani, *Pakistan: Between Mosque and Military* (Washington: Carnegie Endowment for International Peace, 2005), p. 220.

8. "Dr. Abdul Qadeer Khan Discusses Nuclear Program in TV Talk Show," Karachi Aaj Television, August 31, 2009, translated by Open Source Center.

9. Robin Wright and John Broder, "U.S. Bidding to Regain Stingers Sent to Afghans," *Los Angeles Times,* July 23, 1993.

10. Husain Haqqani, *Magnificent Delusions: Pakistan, the United States, and an Epic History of Misunderstanding* (New York: Public Affairs, 2013), pp. 271–75.

11. Peter Tomsen, *The Wars of Afghanistan: Messianic Terrorism, Tribal Conflicts, and the Failures of Great Powers* (New York: Public Affairs, 2011). See also Charles Cogan's review of the Tomsen book, "The Wars of Afghanistan," *Foreign Policy,* September 15, 2011.

12. Haqqani, *Pakistan: Between Mosque and Military,* p. 228.

13. The most thorough investigation has been done by Asif's brother Shuja Nawaz in *Crossed Swords: Pakistan, Its Army, and the Wars Within* (Oxford University Press, 2008), in appendix 3, "Investigation into the Death of General Asif Nawaz," pp. 599–605. He states that there was no direct evidence linking Prime Minister Sharif to the death, but the mystery remains.

14. Haqqani, *Pakistan: Between Mosque and Military,* p. 229.

15. *Mullah Mohammad Omar Mujahid* (Quetta: Azzam Publications, 2010).

16. In his memoirs, Pervez Musharraf confirms that Omar was trained in Pakistan and recovered from his eye wound in a Pakistani hospital, but he puts that in Peshawar rather than Quetta. Pervez Musharraf, *In the Line of Fire: A Memoir* (New York: Free Press, 2006), p. 210.

17. Ahmed Rashid, *Taliban: Militant Islam, Oil, and Fundamentalism in Central Asia* (Yale University Press, 2001), p. 183.

18. Gilles Dorronsoro, *Revolution Unending: Afghanistan, 1979 to the Present* (Columbia University Press, 2005), p. 236.

19. "Remarks by the President on a New Strategy for Afghanistan and Pakistan," March 27, 2009, White House Office of the Press Secretary.

20. Vanda Felbab-Brown, *Aspiration and Ambivalence: Strategies and Realities of Counterinsurgency and State Building in Afghanistan* (Brookings, 2013), pp. 42–51. See also Michael O'Hanlon and Hassina Sherjan, *Toughing It Out in Afghanistan* (Brookings, 2010).

21. At peak deployment, in 2010, the United States had 100,000 troops in Afghanistan and th   n ISAF had another 40,000.

22. All U.S.   troop numbers are derived from the "Brookings Institution Afgha   a periodically updated account of all available statistics on the wa   ble on the Brookings Institution website. These numbers were taken   index on November 28, 2013.

23. Dov Zakheim,   *Vulcan's Tale: How the Bush Administration Mismanaged the Reconstruction of Afghanistan* (Brookings, 2011); and Ronald Neumann, *The Other War: Winning and Losing in Afghanistan* (Washington: Potomac Books, 2009).

Chapter 9

1. Max Hasting, *Catastrophe 1914: Europe Goes to War* (New York: Knopf, 2013), p. xxix.

2. The plot to assassinate Archduke Franz Ferdinand and his wife Sophie Chotek has been studied by historians for a century now. The best recent examination is Christopher Clark, *The Sleepwalkers: How Europe Went to War in 1914* (New York: HarperCollins, 2013), pp. 11–47. See also Margaret MacMillan, "The Rhyme of History: Lessons of the Great War," Brookings Essay, December 14, 2013 (www.brookings.edu/research/essays/2013/rhyme-of-history); and David Fromkin, *Europe's Last Summer: Who Started the Great War in 1914?* (New York: Random House, 2005).

3. Niall Ferguson, *1914: Why the World Went to War* (London: Penguin, 2005), p. 9.

4. Hastings, *Catastrophe 1914*, p. xviii.

5. Steve Galster, "Afghanistan: The Making of U.S. Policy, 1973–1990," September 11th Sourcebooks, National Security Archive, George Washington University, October 9, 2001, p. 12 (www2.gwu.edu/~nsarchiv/NSAEBB/NSAEBB57/essay.html).

6. Stansfield Turner, *Secrecy and Democracy: The CIA in Transition* (Boston: Houghton Mifflin, 1985), pp. 129–35.

7. John Helgerson, *Getting to Know the President: CIA Briefings of Presidential Candidates* (Center for the Study of Intelligence, Central Intelligence Agency, 1996), p. 127.

8. Ibid., p. 141.

9. See Malcolm Byrne, *Private Blank Check: The Iran-Contra Affair* (University of Kansas, 2014).

10. Percy Cradock, *Know Your Enemy: How the Joint Intelligence Committee Saw the World* (London: John Murray, 2002), p. 296.

11. Peter Tomsen, *The Wars of Afghanistan: Messianic Terrorism, Tribal Conflicts, and the Failures of Great Powers* (New York: Public Affairs, 2011), pp. 265–89.

12. Frank Anderson, interview with author, July 12, 2013.

13. William Simpson, *The Prince: The Secret Story of the World's Most Intriguing Royal, Prince Bandar bin Sultan* (New York: HarperCollins, 2006) is a useful, if biased, biography. The two forewords are by Nelson Mandela and Margaret Thatcher.

14. Frank Anderson, quoted in "America in Afghanistan," *Middle East Policy*," vol. 17, no. 1 (Spring 2010), p. 10.

15. Tomsen, *The Wars of Afghanistan*, p. 112.

16. Anderson, quoted in "America in Afghanistan," p. 10.

17. Milt Bearden and James Risen, *The Main Enemy: The Inside Story of the CIA's Final Showdown with the KGB* (New York: Ballantine Books, 2003), p. 236.

18. Ibid., p. 237.

19. Prince Turki, interview with author, October 9, 2010.

20. Robert Gates, *From the Shadows: The Ultimate Insider's Story of Five Presidents and How They Won the Cold War* (New York: Simon and Schuster, 1996), p. 349.

21. Robert Gates, interview with author, October 14, 2013.

22. SNIE 11/37-88, "USSR: Withdrawal from Afghanistan," Director of Central Intelligence, March 1988, available at the National Security Archive, George Washington University, and on the archive website.

23. SNIE 37-89, "Afghanistan: The War in Perspective," Director of Central Intelligence, November 1989, available at the National Security Archive, George Washington University, and on the archive website.

24. See, for example, Roy Gutman, *How We Missed the Story: Osama bin Laden, the Taliban, and the Hijacking of Afghanistan* (Washington: United States Institute for Peace, 2008). I have tried to answer these questions in another book, *Deadly Embrace: Pakistan, America, and the Future of the Global Jihad* (Brookings, 2012).

25. The CIA after-action report was written in late 1961 by the agency's inspector general, Lyman Kirkpatrick, who was my thesis adviser at Brown University in 1975. It was declassified in 1998 and published in Peter Kornbluh, *Bay of Pigs Declassified: The Secret CIA Report on the Invasion of Cuba* (New York: New Press, 1998); see especially pp. 41, 53, 55, and 57. The CIA branch running the operation had 588 employees on the day that the invasion occurred, including 160 in Miami, in stark contrast to the less than 50 ever employed on the Afghan mission at one time. The 1,400 Cuban volunteers faced a communist army and militia of more than 230,000 armed men. Also useful for understanding the debacle is James G. Blight and Peter Kornbluh, *Politics of Illusion: The Bay of Pigs Invasion Reexamined* (London: Rienner, 1998), and Peter Wyden, *Bay of Pigs: The Untold Story* (New York: Simon and Schuster, 1979).

26. Galster, "Afghanistan," p. 13.

27. Marc Sageman, quoted in "America in Afghanistan," p. 15.

28. Sageman, p. 15.

29. Director of Central Intelligence, "Whither Gorbachev: Soviet Policy and Politics in the 1990s," National Intelligence Estimate NIE 11-18-87, November 1987, pp. 3–11, released by the Center for the Study of Intelligence, Central Intelligence Agency.

30. Anderson, quoted in "America in Afghanistan," p. 10.

INDEX